Lou Taylor
to my buddy
Marvin [illegible]
12/25/99

Mr. Turkey

A biography of Bil Mar Foods co-founder

Marvin DeWitt

By

Michael Lozon

"Life is a constant struggle for perfection.

Each day, you get as close as you can to that ideal."

Marvin DeWitt

CREDITS

DESIGN *Carol Apsey*

EDITING *Paul VanKolken*

PHOTOGRAPHY *Cory Olsen, cover and pages 54, 167, 171, 227, 230, and 242*

OTHER PHOTOS AND ILLUSTRATIONS *Advance Newspapers, Builder & Contractor, DeVries Studio of Photography, Gary DeWitt, Jack DeWitt, Keith DeWitt, Marvin DeWitt, Grand Rapids Press, Holland Historical Trust Collection of the Joint Archives of Holland, Holland Sentinel, Hope College, Dr. Carl Hoyt, Michigan Farmer, Muskegon Chronicle, and Poultry & Egg Marketing.*

PRINTING *Integra Printing*

PHOTO AND TEXT COPIES *CPI Photo, Lakewood Photo & Video, Litho Tech Printing Inc., and The Frame & Mat Shop.*

CONTENTS

PROLOGUE

The history of Marvin DeWitt and Bil Mar Foods Inc. cannot be told without paying homage to the turkey. Without the turkey, there would be no Bil Mar.

The bird, known scientifically as Meleagris gallopava, has been the mainstay product for Bil Mar since its founding by Marvin and his brother Bill in 1938, on the family farm north of Zeeland, in southwestern Michigan.

But the turkey's history begins long before Bil Mar's founding. Fossils have been dated to show turkeys roaming North America 10 million years ago.

The continent's largest native game bird, turkeys were first domesticated in Mexico by the Aztec Indians who used them for sacrifice and food. In 1530, Spanish conquerors introduced the Mexican species to Europe where domestication continued. All varieties bred throughout the world are descendants of the North American wild turkey, presumably from the Mexican stock. Early American colonists from Europe brought the Bronze and Black domesticated varieties back to this country. In the early 1800s, in Rhode Island, domestic stocks were crossed with the wild turkey, thus establishing the forerunner of the present-day commercial bird.

The bird's name has several possible origins. One source claims the American Indian name for the bird was firkee, which was translated by English-speaking settlers as turkey. Another source believes the bird was named by explorer Christopher Columbus, whose sailing trips were supported by Spain. He believed the New World was connected to India and that turkeys were really peacocks [actually, the turkey is a variety of pheasant]. With that connection in mind, he named them tuka, which is peacock in the Tamil language of India. Merchants who sold turkeys in Spain changed the Tamil tuka to the Hebrew tukki, which has evolved into the English turkey. Yet another tale has the name derived from the guinea fowl, which was imported to Europe from Africa through Turkey. The Turkish name for guinea fowl was turkey-cock. And there are others who believe the name came from the alarm call of the bird, a soft "turk," "turk," "turk."

Folklore says the turkey, which roamed wild in America's Northeast woods, was one of the staples at a Thanksgiving dinner celebrated by early settlers sometime between Sept. 21 and Nov. 9, 1621, in Plymouth, Mass. The meal was attended by 91 Indians from the Wampanoag tribe and 56 Protestant settlers, now known as the Pilgrims, who had fled religious persecution in England and The Netherlands. The menu for the three-day feast, patterned after English Harvest Festivals, was duly recorded in a journal kept by Plymouth Colony Gov. William Bradford. But there is no mention of turkey along with entries for ducks, geese, lobsters, clams, bass, venison, corn, green vegetables, and dried fruit.

Thanksgiving Day was not formally recognized until 1863, following the Civil War battle of Gettysburg, when President Abraham Lincoln declared the fourth Thursday in November as a national holiday.

Serving turkey as the traditional main course for the holiday was not firmly established until the end of World War II, when the National Turkey Federation aggressively promoted the supposed Pilgrim tradition. With the war's end in 1945, the government canceled contracts with turkey growers who had been producing birds to feed American troops overseas. The Federation created the Eat-More-Turkey advertising campaign to address the surplus of turkeys being grown to fulfill that fall's canceled war contract. The marketing effort at making the stuffed bird an image of American abundance was successful. The bird ends up on the plates of 91 percent of Americans each Thanksgiving.

Today's domesticated turkey bears no resemblance to its wild ancestor or even the early commercial breeds. The modern turkey has been bred to produce more meat – larger breasts, thicker thighs, and heftier drumsticks. Because of the larger size and shape, it is physically impossible for today's tom turkey to mate naturally with a hen. As a result, commercial breeding relies on artificial insemination. The modern turkey is also white in appearance, as compared to the wild turkey, the bronze turkey and other breeds that have colored feathers. The color has been bred out of the feather to make the processed skin more appealing to consumers. When the feather is plucked from the colored birds, a small amount of fluid pigment may run from the quill, leak under the skin, and leave a spotty look. A white feather is void of pigment and, when plucked, leaves the skin clear and attractive.

Until the 1960s, the turkey industry was seasonal, bound by a consumer mind-set to purchase turkey during the five-week Thanksgiving and Christmas holiday period. The change in the bird's holiday-only image began when the industry, including Bil Mar, introduced a method of further processing – cutting the birds into boneless parts and cooking the meat to manufacture an assortment of mostly white-meat turkey products. With further processing, Bil Mar evolved from being a seasonal business to a year-round operation by originally supplying products mainly to food-service customers such as hotels, restaurants, schools, prisons and hospitals. In the mid-1970s, Bil Mar established a retail division to market processed dark-meat items to supermarkets under the Mr. Turkey brand. The further-processed trend really took off in the 1980s, coinciding with the start of the low-fat craze among consumers.

Recent statistics bear testimony to the changing tastes of consumers when it comes to the venerable turkey – a low-calorie, low-fat protein source. Since 1970, turkey consumption among Americans has doubled to more than 18 pounds per person each year. Of the more than 300 million turkeys raised each year, only 45 million end up on the Thanksgiving dinner table as whole birds. The majority of turkeys are used to manufacture further-processed products, like those made by Bil Mar.

Bil Mar is one of the industry leaders in boning and roasting turkey parts, along with Louis Rich and ConAgra. Bil Mar operates one of the most technologically advanced processing facilities, built after a 1984 fire that destroyed the original plant. Now owned by Sara Lee Corp., the company can claim a number of other distinctions during its 61-year history:

- First to freeze turkeys, both conventionally and with a quick-freeze method using brine water to keep whole turkeys from turning red.
- First to integrate processing by operating a hatchery and on-site feed mill.
- First to market dark-meat turkey rolls.
- First to market a two-pound turkey roast.
- First to market a three-and-a-half pound dark roast.
- First to market ground turkey.
- First to use vacuum-sealed packaging for poultry.
- First to use vacuum-sealed cook-in bag technology for roasting on a large scale. The method gives the meat a better slicing quality and helps retain moisture.
- First to use a water-based system of continuous cooking and cooling. The continuous conveyor system uses water to cook and then chill the vacuum-packaged product, making it ready for boxing and shipping when it comes out of the oven.
- First to market a salt-free turkey breast.
- First major turkey processor to package retail products free of monosodium glutamate.
- One of the broadest product lines in the processed-turkey industry.
- Made the longest hot dog in the world, at 1,996 feet, to kick off Sara Lee's sponsorship of the 1996 summer Olympics in Atlanta, Ga. The previous record was also established by Bil Mar in 1984 when the company made a 1,757-feet long version to celebrate the success of the turkey dog. The giant hot dog was introduced at the dedication of Huizenga Park in Zeeland.

Bil Mar employees unwind one of the world's largest hot dogs in the summer of 1984.

INTRODUCTION

Like a human tornado, Marvin DeWitt had been whirling in and out of the burning Bil Mar Foods plant for hours.

Marvin, Bil Mar's co-founder and chairman of the board, was in constant motion and jumping to wherever he thought his help was needed.

When he wasn't carrying something out of the smoke-filled building, he was guiding the salvage efforts of employees and family members that cool September morning in 1984.

He also worked with more than 200 hundred firefighters from 15 area departments, directing them around a 26-year-old plant he had helped build from scratch.

Marvin, always more comfortable in the plant than behind an executive's desk, was dressed in his trademark khaki work clothes and knee-length rubber boots. The clothes were soaked and his boots were full of water. Yet Marvin, known for his tough demeanor, gave no hint he might be chilled by the early morning temperatures.

Burly with a voice to match, the 65-year-old maintained his breakneck pace from the fire's eruption at 2:15 a.m. until he realized no amount of effort was going to save the plant.

That reality was inescapable in the early morning light. In huge portions of the burned-out building, all that remained standing were steel girders twisted by the intense heat.

Devastated was a business that had been founded 46 years earlier by Marvin and his brother Bill at the tail-end of the Great Depression. The Bil Mar title combined the first three letters in each of their given names. Dirt-poor farmers, they started in the late 1930s with a small flock of turkeys and seemed destined to remain growers in the whole-turkey business.

However, Marvin, a life-long risk taker with a take-charge personality, pushed the brothers into manufacturing individual turkey products such as boneless breasts, hot dogs, luncheon meats, ham, and sausage.

The gamble paid off big. Bil Mar grew to become one of the nation's largest producers of processed turkey products and posted $170 million in annual sales just before the fire wrote another chapter in the company's history.

The blaze forced 1,100 employees out of a job. And as the smoke rose from the ashes, many of them wondered aloud about the company's future.

The same thought crossed Pastor Mike Van Buren's mind as the fire raged out of control. But the minister at Ottawa Reformed Church was more concerned about the emotional effect the devastation might have on Marvin, his friend and fellow church member.

He had been watching Marvin closely from the time the sun rose on the fiery inferno, looking for his reaction to the chaos swirling around him. There was none, even late in the morning as firemen doused the last of the flames that had ravaged a plant covering more than six acres.

At that point, Marvin turned his attention away from the destruction and toward the cause of the fire in the center of the plant. Always inquisitive, he wanted to see for himself the source of the blaze – a fryer used to brown breaded meat. Marvin asked Van Buren to join him. As they walked among the charred remains, the two men could feel the reflected heat on their faces from the scorched processing equipment and steel beams. The water from the fire hoses was ankle deep in places as they sloshed toward the fryer, dodging the rubble that had been Bil Mar Foods.

When they reached the burned-out fryer room, Marvin assessed the damage for awhile before reaching up to a rack of charred drumsticks. He grabbed one and asked Van Buren "How about dinner?" Marvin then laughed and shrugged his shoulders as he threw the drumstick behind him. They walked away and Marvin never looked back.

Van Buren felt a sense of relief at his friend's joking reaction to the disaster. Taking things in stride was characteristic of Marvin DeWitt. In that simple gesture with the drumstick, he was acknowledging the toll the fire had taken. He was also showing a readiness to move on as he had after every other setback in his life.

Before the day was out, he made it clear that the business would rise from the ashes. He felt an obligation to his customers, employees, and family.

Marvin's determination to survive can be traced, in part, to his hardscrabble upbringing during the Depression. He also inherited the conservative, hardworking ways of his Dutch ancestors – farmers on both sides of his family.

Marvin's parents with his two older sisters,
Georgianna and Angeline, near the homestead barn.

CHAPTER ONE

Bloodline in the Soil

If bloodlines mean anything, Marvin DeWitt was destined to be a farmer.

His great-grandfather Gerrit S. DeWitt was a farmer's helper in The Netherlands before he emigrated to America in 1848 on a sailing ship that took 41 days to cross the Atlantic Ocean. The penniless 17-year-old, writing in the ship's log that a "desire for adventure" was his reason for emigrating, arrived in the Michigan settlement of Holland, a year after the Rev. Albertus Van Raalte founded the Dutch colony.

Gerrit discovered adventure his first night in the wilderness colony, sleeping underneath the shelter of boards he set up along the Black River. The next morning, he traveled by ox team, with other Dutch newcomers, to the plain known as East Holland. There he met some settlers, who gave him information about jobs in the region.

His job search took him to the Kalamazoo area, where he worked for a number of farmers and boarded in their homes. He even worked a short time for the Michigan Central Railroad, earning 75 cents a day. Once a year, he visited friends in Holland. On one of those trips, he traded a horse for 40 acres of land in Fillmore Township, southeast of Holland. The property, near where I-196 is today, later became his homestead.

He met his wife Mary Meijaard while staying at a boarding house in Kalamazoo. She had come to America in 1847 with a group of settlers, including the Rev. Cornelius Vander Meulen, who was the Zeeland colony's first pastor. Gerrit and Mary were married in Zeeland but lived on the farm of a lawyer near Kalamazoo for two years before striking out on their own and establishing their homestead in 1856 – eight years after Gerrit arrived in America.

"Only those who have experienced it know what it means to make a beginning in a thick woods, where a tree has not yet been chopped – hard work and poverty," said Gerrit in a diary. "We chopped down trees and made them fall as much as possible in heaps. In between those heaps, we planted our first corn and potatoes."

Marvin's parents, with his sister Georgianna, in front of their Borculo farmhouse.

On their homestead, Gerrit and his wife raised nine children. The family's last name, spelled DeWitte in The Netherlands, means the White One or Blond One. The church was a central part of life for the DeWitts, a tradition carried on by future family members, including Marvin and his offspring.

The Gerrit DeWitt family originally attended services given by a Methodist preacher in a school house near the homestead. The family made a profession of faith to the Reformed Church in America after meeting the Rev. Van Raalte. The RCA is a Protestant denomination established in 1628 by Dutch settlers in New York. Four of Gerrit's nine children, including Marvin's grandfather George were baptized at Ninth Street Church in Holland, which is now known as the Pillar Church. The DeWitts attended the downtown Holland church until Ebenezer Reformed Church was built on the Ottawa and Allegan county line, close to their homestead.

3-year-old Marvin on the family homestead.

Marvin's grandfather also spent his life as a farmer in Fillmore Township and raised a family of four with his wife Anna Boeve.

George's three sons, including Marvin's father Gerrit, became farmers after he bought them a parcel of land at their chosen site. Gerrit's two brothers stayed in Allegan County's Fillmore Township, while he picked an 80-acre parcel northeast of Holland on 96th Avenue in Ottawa County's Olive Township – the site of today's Bil Mar Foods plant.

Gerrit and his wife Susan Van Den Berge, whose family operated a dairy farm in the East 16th Street area of Holland, started their married life on the 80-acre site. In 1919, Marvin was the youngest of six children born on the DeWitt homestead, including Georgianna, Angeline, William, Marie and Sena.

But boyhood on the homestead was short-lived for Marvin. In 1923, when Marvin was 4-years-old, his father rented the homestead property and then moved the family into Zeeland, where he could be closer to some factory jobs. Gerrit's decision was guided by his ill health, not a desire to leave the farm. For a number of years, he had experienced periodic stomach flare-ups, which sometimes made the farm work too strenuous.

Marvin's family rented homes in Zeeland before buying one on Lincoln Street. The move into town did nothing to suppress Marvin's restless spirit whose intensity sometimes propelled him into trouble – like the time he ran into the side of a car and broke his arm while hurrying to play with some friends.

"The main thing I remember about Marvin when he was younger is that he was always getting into something and forever being scolded," said Marie Steketee, one of his sisters. "He was full of ideas, and always wanted to do more and know more. That curiosity trait was always there."

Moving into the city also did not curb his inborn fascination with farming. His first attempt at earning some spending money was an early sign that his ambition might take him places in agriculture.

One spring, the 8-year-old went to a hatchery near his home and picked up some culls, disfigured baby chicks that were normally destroyed. He fed them oatmeal, dispensed water from an eye dropper, and warmed them with the heat from a light bulb. The chicks were kept in the family's barn, along with a cow and chickens. Back then it was common for city residents to milk a cow and raise chickens as a way to stretch their food dollar. He raised the culls for the family dinner table. During the process, he realized there was money to be made in raising poultry if someone was willing to make a small investment. From some of his odd jobs, he saved enough money to purchase a box of healthy chicks. He raised the 60 laying hens and sold the eggs for a profit.

He kept some of the money he earned from the egg-laying venture. The rest went into the family's reserve fund to help pay for the children's clothes or other bills. All the DeWitt children were expected to provide for the family's welfare in some way. They learned early on that work was necessary to survive. There was no social welfare system to provide a handout.

"We were taught the value of hard work and to treat people right," said Marvin's brother Bill. "Those were the basic values handed down to us from our parents and through our religion."

Bill worked at a number of jobs before and after quitting school at the ninth-grade level. He did chores on an uncle's farm in Fillmore Township. He cleaned up at Frank's confectionery store in Zeeland. He made handles for wire brushes at a local lumber company. And he drove a team of mules for a construction crew building roads in the Holland and Zeeland areas. One of those projects, in 1929, laid the first pavement for 96th Avenue from Zeeland to Borculo, the closest settlement to the DeWitt homestead. The Blendon Township town was founded in 1867 by Jackus Klamderman, who named it after his native village of Borkulo in The Netherlands.

One of Marvin's first jobs was picking strawberries. He also worked on neighboring farms. One of them was the Kalmink produce farm, where he helped plant and harvest cabbage, celery, onions, radishes, spinach, and cucumbers. He accompanied the Kalmink family when they sold the produce at the wholesale farm market on Leonard Street in Grand Rapids.

He also sold ice cream bars for a man who operated a peanut/ice cream wagon during summertime band concerts in Zeeland's VanderLuyster Square. The wagon, complete with an attention-getting steam whistle, was a converted Model T Ford. For his efforts, Marvin was rewarded with an ice cream bar. He also sold door-to-door merchandise – magazine subscriptions at first, and then baked goods on a Zeeland-area route operated by Sam Ploegstra, one of his father's cousins who lived near Grand Rapids.

The cousin would pick up Marvin at 4 a.m. on Saturdays to begin the motor route. Occasionally, the relative would let the 11-year-old boy approach potential customers. Marvin was nervous but it turned out to be a good learning experience.

"It took a lot of stops to eventually make a sale," he said. "But it taught me how to deal with people and how to make change in my head. I believe that all of those early working experiences had something to do with my success later in life. They helped me to become more self-assured."

Marvin was not able to achieve the same ego boost in the classroom, where his performance was lackluster. Always full of energy, he felt confined in a structured classroom setting. He excelled at only one subject, math, but admits his favorite time in school was recess when he could be more active. Sitting in a classroom, governed by repetition and recitation, did not fit his definition of accomplishment.

Schoolmates describe him as being daring, loud, and boisterous. One of them, Angie Van Hoven, remembers feeling relieved after she didn't run into him on the way to school while walking past his house on Lincoln Street.

Marvin, with tail in hand, 'horses' around with a friend.

"My friends and I always felt afraid of him because he acted like a bully. It was not that he ever did anything to us or that I saw him do anything to anyone else. It was just the impression he gave because he was loud and pushy," said Van Hoven, who became a registered nurse and part-owner of Woodhaven Nursing Home in Zeeland. "Now that I look back, I think it was just his way of compensating for not being a good student. I didn't see much future for him, given his lack of formal education and the way he behaved in school."

The traits that put off Van Hoven also did not endear Marvin to his teachers, who sought to control his behavior by putting him in the front row during classes.

Making matters worse for teachers, his best friend in grade school, Russ Munro, was also a prankster. Marvin was held back in second grade, and he still wonders if that was a ploy by teachers to separate the two mischievous friends.

"What Russ wouldn't think of to cause trouble in school, I would," Marvin said with a twinkle in his eye.

Despite Marvin's irritating behavior at school, he was smart enough to know that alienating teachers was not in his long-term best interest. That is why he would go out of his way to stay on their good side when possible. He could not please them academically, so he offered to do projects for them – cutting down a tree to decorate the school for Christmas or building a trellis used for an exhibit at the annual agricultural fair in Holland.

When he wasn't in school or doing odd jobs, he played hard like other kids of the day. He did affordable things such as roller-skating, softball, and sledding and skiing down hills. The skis were made out of barrel staves.

Marvin and Munro made snow houses and tunnels in the winter, and shacks in the city dump during the summer. During Halloween, they also pulled their share of tricks. Halloween back then was a week-long celebration. Each night, the kids had some special mischief up their sleeves. One of the nights was dedicated to tin cans, one was cabbage night, and another was pumpkin night – all guaranteed to make noise or a mess.

The boys also put on humorous skits for neighborhood children on an impromptu stage in the upstairs of the barn behind Marvin's house. They charged a penny for the entertainment. Because the two of them were together so much, they picked up the nickname of Mutt and Jeff, two popular cartoon characters of that era.

But Marvin's carefree days in the city with Munro were numbered after the start of the Great Depression in 1929. Like so many others of his generation who came of age during the Depression, the economic upheaval was a catastrophic moment in history that would leave an everlasting imprint on his life.

Marvin works at a relative's farm in the Upper Peninsula.

CHAPTER TWO

DEFINED BY THE DEPRESSION

Marvin was 10-years-old when the stock exchanges on New York's Wall Street crashed in October of 1929. The collapse put the United States and the rest of the world into an economic tailspin that would last through most of the 1930s until America's entry into World War II.

As a youngster, Marvin had no clue as to what led up to the hard times – the easy credit that fueled widespread stock speculation, the industrial overproduction that out paced consumer purchasing power, and the protectionist trade policies that denied foreign markets an opportunity to buy products made in the United States.

He was well aware of the consequences – bank closings, business failures, falling agricultural prices, long unemployment lines, and the financial turmoil in his own home.

His father could not keep a steady job. Unable to pay their mortgage, the family lost the house in town like hundreds of thousands of people across the country. His father also lost $3,000 he had invested in the stock market. To make that investment, he had taken out a second mortgage on the family homestead in Olive Township.

America had experienced economic downturns before but none as devastating. Prior depressions had occurred during a time when the country was primarily agricultural and most people could grow what they needed in hard times. The America of 1929 was more urbanized and more industrialized.

By 1931, the dire consequences of the Depression persuaded Marvin's family that their best chance for survival was back on the 80-acre homestead on 96th Avenue. However, the move back to the farm was delayed for two years until the family could earn enough money to buy supplies, equipment, and livestock.

To raise the funds in the faltering economy, Marvin's family followed his brother Bill's path to Michigan's Upper Peninsula, where some DeWitt relatives had established successful farming operations. They included Grandpa DeWitt's brother William and a family cousin by marriage, Henry Hesselink.

At the age of 16, Bill traveled north in 1930 to work on Uncle William's farm for room and board. He hitchhiked most of the way with a cousin. During the winter, he harvested trees with a cross-cut saw and an ax. The timber was hauled out of the woods with a team of horses.

In the summer of 1931, Marvin and his parents drove north in a Model T Ford to help Bill on a farm he was renting and on the farms of relatives in the Rudyard area, between St. Ignace and Sault Ste. Marie. Travel between Michigan's two peninsulas was by ferry across the straits of Mackinac. Given the rickety condition of cars and roads, those were the days when motorists considered themselves very lucky if they didn't break down or experience a flat tire. Minor repairs were fixed by the side of the road.

In the fall of 1931, after a summer of farm labor in the Upper Peninsula, Marvin and his parents went back to Zeeland where his father was able to pick up some odd jobs to keep food on the table. The following summer, in 1932, they returned to Rudyard after losing the house in Zeeland to foreclosure. They were forced to stay up north until they raised the money for the move back to the homestead property.

They worked on the Hesselink dairy farm, where Bill was already employed.

Marvin's father received $2 a day for his work. Marvin worked for milk, eggs, and his meals. The work was backbreaking because the farm had not yet been mechanized with tractors. Hay was cut and windrowed with a large rake in the field. Then it was loaded by hand onto a horse-drawn wagon.

As fall approached, Marvin had to transfer to school in Rudyard – a prospect that sparked an idea on how to end his academic career a year earlier than scheduled. He was set to enter the 7th grade. Yet when teachers asked him about his grade level, Marvin proudly announced he was an eighth grader. The ruse worked for a couple of weeks, until his records from the Zeeland Public School District caught up with him.

By the spring of 1933, the family had earned enough money to buy most of what they needed to farm again on the homestead. Even Marvin pitched in with $8, an amount that did not reflect the steep emotional price the 13-year-old paid for the family's return to Borculo. To raise the money, he reluctantly sold his first pet, a faithful terrier.

"That dog followed me everywhere and was a constant companion. If I sat on the davenport, he would sit on the davenport. He would stand on a table to watch me come home from school. I sure didn't want to sell him," he said about the loss of the prized pet.

The trip back home almost ended in disaster for Marvin, his parents, Bill, and his future wife, Martha, whose family were farmers in the Rudyard area. Bill was driving down a steep grade when a truck suddenly stopped in front of them for a railroad track. Unable to stop the vehicle, Bill swerved to miss the truck and sideswiped an oncoming car that also veered to avoid a head-on collision. No one was hurt and there was surprisingly little damage to either vehicle. All of the DeWitt's luggage was knocked off the car's running board and their clothes were scattered along the roadway.

The family had earned $600 while working in Rudyard, but Hesselink was only able to pay them half the total upfront. He gave the family a promissory note for $300 and Marvin's grandfather George covered the owed amount so they could buy horses, a cow, a plow, and a wagon. The first income the DeWitts earned after returning home came from the half-acre of pickles they grew and sold to the Heinz plant in Holland. The family also grew sugar beets that were sold to the Holland Sugar Co.

Unlike the DeWitts, most Americans during the Depression did not have the option of returning to the family farm. Marvin's family was able to produce their own eggs, milk, meat and produce. Having a homestead, however, did not put the family on easy street. After paying for equipment and livestock, they were nearly broke. And they still needed to pay their bills, including the farm's outstanding mortgage.

Moving from Zeeland back into the country also meant giving up some homey comforts, like central heating and an indoor toilet. In the farm house, there was a combination wood/coal heat stove in the kitchen and a fuel oil stove in the living room. The rest of the home was not heated. The farm was not hooked up to electricity until 1936. Instead of flipping a light switch, family members found their way in the dark with kerosene lamps and lanterns. There was no indoor plumbing, other than a cold-water pipe that ran into the kitchen from an elevated tank in the barn. The tank was filled by windmill power with water from a well. Going to the bathroom meant a walk outside to the outhouse or using an indoor pot in the middle of the night. For toilet paper, they used the pages from catalogs, courtesy of Sears and Montgomery Ward.

They cooked their meals, and heated water for washing themselves and their clothes, on a kerosene cook stove equipped with wicks. Using a small wash tub and a cloth, family members mostly took stand-up sponge baths and only infrequently in colder weather. Clothes washing was such a chore that they were urged to wear their clothes more than one day, sometimes until they were stiff from dirt and sweat. Until mechanization came along, women first washed with scrubboards and tubs, and later progressed to hand-cranked ringer washers. Just-washed clothes were hung on an outside line to dry in the summer and on a line inside during the winter.

Most of the family's clothes were handmade. Their meals were simple – a lot of fried potatoes and eggs. School lunches, carried in empty syrup pails, consisted mainly of lard and sugar on bread. Much of the food was canned to get through the winter, even meat. With its uniform slices, the occasional loaf of store-bought bread offered a real treat.

"Someone who thinks they are poor today knows nothing about being poor. When your family had to struggle to pay their property taxes, you didn't complain about not having a toy or a bike. No one went out to eat after church, like they do today. It was really a hand-to-mouth existence," Marvin said. "We were brought up with the attitude of 'waste not, want not.' Nowadays, people are too quick to throw things away, including food. "

Marvin's brother Bill and their father worked full-time on the farm. Bill's fiancée Martha had a job doing housework, typical of so many young women during the Depression, including Marvin's sisters. Marvin finished his academic career in 8th grade at the one-room Ovens School, about two miles from the homestead.

With his school days behind him, he worked on the family farm and for neighboring farmers during the middle years of the Depression.

As Marvin became older, he worked at some full-time jobs further away from the family farm. He was employed at Speet Dairy in Holland, owned by the family one of his sisters married into. His job, for $2 a day, was to wash bottles and carry milk cans to the delivery trucks.

One of the toughest winter experiences of his life occurred when he was working at the dairy in 1936 at the age of 17. At week's end, a vicious winter storm shut down everything and plugged up the north-south roads. There were places out in the country where the snowdrifts rose nearly above the telephone poles.

As was his routine, he left the dairy Saturday afternoon for the nine-mile walk home to help his father with weekend chores. The walk usually took a little more than two hours. But the howling storm forced him to stop after only two miles and stay overnight in Zeeland at the home of his sister Georgianna.

He left the next morning in bone-chilling cold to complete the remaining seven-mile journey home. The weather was so nasty that the churches were even closed. Once beyond the city limits, Marvin realized he was not dressed warmly enough, so he walked even faster north along 96th Avenue. He stopped at three farms along the way to warm up. One of the those stops was at Townline Poultry Farm, owned by the Geerlings family.

"I clearly remember him walking in that storm from Zeeland to his house and stopping by our hatchery to warm up," said Henry Geerlings. "It didn't surprise me that he was out in that kind of weather. He was husky, strong, and rugged. Nothing seemed to stand in his way."

Wanting a higher-paying job, Marvin relied on persistence to secure a position at the Heinz plant in Holland. To get a job during the Depression, it helped to know someone. Otherwise, each morning you stood with a group of other men outside a plant gate hoping to be picked randomly by a company supervisor. One morning, the plant superintendent at Heinz bypassed Marvin in selecting some employees. Not willing to just walk away, he chased after the superintendent and pleaded for work. Impressed with young Marvin's boldness, the plant boss hired him on the spot. His daily routine consisted of early-morning farm chores at home, Heinz work all day, and late-afternoon chores. With the money Marvin saved, he was able to buy his first car from a relative – a 1924 Chevrolet.

"It didn't take me long to figure out that no one was going to give me anything. If I wanted something, I would have to go after it," Marvin said. "There is no question that my upbringing during the Depression had a lot to do with my eventual success. We had next to nothing, just like so many others during that time."

Despite the hard times of the Depression, he found opportunity for recreation and just plain fooling around. He started hanging out with the Morren boys, Jerry and Ray, when he was 14. The Morrens, who lived a half mile from the DeWitts, were his closest neighbors. They spent many summer nights playing softball, first on church teams and later on a Zeeland league. The city team squared off with rivals from other towns, like Hudsonville and Drenthe.

Marvin, playing the catcher's position, brought to the game of softball the same level of enthusiasm he applied to the rest of his life.

"Marvin wasn't much of a batter. He was a good catcher and a tough competitor though. When someone came into the plate from third base, Marvin would stand there and hold his ground," said Jerry Morren, a retired chicken farmer. "And he could rattle members of the other team when they came up to bat. His mouth was going the whole time they were at the plate. More than once, an angry hitter would turn around and tell him to shut up. Marvin never did. Everyone knew they weren't going to push him around."

Marvin (back row, second from left) was the catcher on this softball team.

Sometimes Marvin's zeal for playing softball interfered with his obligation to do farm chores. On one occasion, he tried to save time before taking off to a ball game by only partially milking the family's cow. Bill alerted their father about the indiscretion and he proceeded to literally kick Marvin out of the barn for his laxness.

Softball may have been the only organized sport the boys played. Yet they found other activities to keep them busy throughout the year. They played hockey on the frozen farm fields, using a tree branch for a stick and a tin can for a puck.

The boys devised a risky pastime after they bought their first cars. In the winter, they attached a rope to the back of a car and skied behind the moving vehicle – on the snow-covered road and in the ditch. To avoid injury while moving through the ditch, they would have to quickly whip the rope over the top of the roadside mailboxes.

More than any of the fellows in his group, Marvin seemed to take great delight in risk taking. His friends soon learned they had to be careful about daring him. He never backed away from a challenge.

When he was younger, horses were still used for most of the field work. Someone dared him to ride one of the big gray field horses and he was on the animal's broad back in the blink of an eye. The horse, not accustomed to riders, spooked and jumped a fence. The horse fell and rolled over on him. His friends figured he was killed or, at the very least, severely injured. Both the horse and Marvin walked away without a scratch.

"Marvin was a risk taker and never gave up. For those reasons, I thought he would succeed at whatever he tried," said Menser "Mintz" VandenHeuvel, one of the teenaged friends Marvin met on the ball field and now the retired owner of a flying service in Battle Creek. "He would put out a double effort to accomplish something he set out to do. If he couldn't get something done one way, he would try something else. He was just not the type of person to let life pass him by."

The activities of Marvin and his friends were not confined to the ball field and the farm. A good part of their social life, like other country kids geographically isolated from the city, was centered around the church.

At the urging of his friends, Marvin left Borculo Christian Reformed Church to join Ottawa Reformed Church on Stanton Street. The change brought him back to his religious roots.

His ancestors had strong ties to the Reformed faith. They attended Ninth Street Church, now known as the Pillar Church, in downtown Holland and then Ebenezer Reformed Church in Fillmore Township.

Then Marvin's father converted to the Christian Reformed denomination at the time of his marriage. And the family attended Third Christian Reformed Church while living in Zeeland and Borculo Christian Reformed after moving back into the country. Marvin's brother, Bill, stuck by the family's denomination and became a life-long member of Rusk Christian Reformed Church.

For Marvin, belonging to Ottawa Reformed Church meant twice-on-Sunday church services, Sunday school, and mid-week catechism.

The church also ministered its young people through a Christian Endeavor group.

Each Reformed church in the area had a similar young people's group, whose members became acquainted on hayrides, sleigh rides, and picnics. Even at these outings, Marvin did not repress his bold behavior.

At a lakeside picnic, he bet another fellow that he could eat more hamburgers. It was no contest. Marvin won easily by chowing down 12 burgers, all of them on buns.

During another church outing, a group of teenaged girls and boys was walking in the woods west of Ottawa Reformed Church when they came across a plank spanning a creek 10 feet below. Scared of heights, one of the girls was hesitant to cross. Without saying a word, Marvin picked the girl up and carried her over the divide.

"Whether Marvin was behind the catcher's plate or at a Christian Endeavor activity, you knew he was there," VandenHeuvel said. "I don't mean to say that he was obnoxious. It is just that he always had an opinion and he would share it. He was outspoken and also had an answer for everything."

It was his assertive, outgoing behavior that attracted the attention of Jerene Bekius, a member of the Christian Endeavor group at Ottawa Reformed Church and a farm girl from Robinson Township. Beneath his brash exterior, she uncovered someone who was generous and principled to the point of extreme.

Like Marvin, Jerene only went through eighth grade at a one-room country school. Most young women of the day were neither expected nor encouraged to continue their education. They were generally expected to become homemakers. Jerene excelled in her studies and enjoyed the academic routine. However, she gave in to the tradition of the time – quitting school to work. Her first job involved housework for a family in Grand Haven. She lived at the home of her employer, coming back to her family's farm on Thursday and Sunday afternoons.

Marvin grew very fond of Jerene and her family. He spent time there playing cards, piecing puzzles together, and singing to the accompaniment of the family's guitar and piano. He liked the beehive of activity generated by eight Bekius children and all of their visitors. Visiting with family and friends, especially for lunch, was another popular and inexpensive way of socializing in those days.

Marvin, who admits to being a person who lives to eat rather than one who eats to live, enjoyed the family's big meals, including the rich cakes and pies that topped them off. He felt comfortable and accepted there.

At the age of 17, though, he almost wore out his welcome. On New Year's Eve of 1936, he showed up at the house drunk – for the first and last time in his life.

Before arriving at the house, Marvin and some of his friends spent the evening driving around and sampling some bottles of flavored cooking wine, which tasted more like a soft drink than an alcoholic beverage. While most of the group sipped the beverage, Marvin guzzled away like someone stranded in the desert without water. By the time the group of tipsy young men reached Jerene's house, Marvin was intoxicated. He knocked over the family's Christmas tree before Jerene could scoot him out of the house, unbeknownst to her sleeping parents. He proceeded to fall off her porch into the spirea bushes.

His future brother-in-law, Dale Bekius, was not surprised by the behavior of his sister's boyfriend.

"Marvin went all the way in everything did," Bekius said. "He never did anything half way, even the one time he drank in his life."

Marvin knew he couldn't go home in such an unfit condition and decided to walk off the intoxication. He soon found that impossible. A thawing rain turned 10 inches of snow into piles of slippery slush. When his friends urged him to climb inside VandenHeuvel's car, Marvin insisted he wasn't drunk and tried to prove the claim by counting the barbs on a wire fence. His pals were able to coax him into the car only after he fell head first into a snowbank. Before they could get him home, he became extremely ill and vomited in the car.

The friends hauled Marvin's limp body up to his porch, knocked on the door, and took off running for the car to avoid explaining his impairment to anyone in the DeWitt family. By the time his father and sister Sena came to the door to find him in a slump, all they could see were the taillights of the car speeding down the road.

Never having seen anyone drunk before, his sister thought he might be fatally ill. In total misery, Marvin was also contemplating his departure from this world. Their father, recognizing the reason for Marvin's condition, knew his suffering son would live to see another day. He was right. Marvin woke up the next morning with a headache, knotted stomach, and orders from his father to milk the cows as if nothing had happened the night before. To add insult to injury, VandenHeuvel drove his car over to Marvin's house so he could clean the dried-up mess off the upholstery. Marvin was not to suffer in silence. Between fits of laughter, his father and brother Bill supervised the clean-up from the front porch of the homestead house.

Marvin's ill-fated encounter with alcohol was a lesson he vowed never to forget.

"I learned a valuable lesson that night. I am a foodoholic and I was afraid the same thing might happen to me with alcohol," he said. "I steered clear of alcohol the rest of my life. I have been a lot of places where alcohol was offered, and I have been around a lot of people who liked to wine and dine. I never took any. Instead, I ordered a glass of milk."

Marvin went into the new year of 1937 with the sober realization that he needed a higher-paying job than his Heinz position and brother Bill assisted him in that objective. With the help of a cousin, Bill moved up the wage ladder in 1935 when he secured a job at Grand Haven Brass. The job allowed him to marry in 1936. Bill was able to get Marvin a part-time job at the brass plant the following year.

At that point, their relatives and friends believed the family farm would forever be a sideline and the brothers would spend their lives working in a factory, like Grand Haven Brass.

But working for someone else would not be a part of Marvin's future. A born entrepreneur, he was more comfortable leading than following.

Marvin tends turkeys on the range.

CHAPTER THREE

TURKEY ENTREPRENEUR

The two brothers never thought about getting into the turkey business full-time when they bought their first birds in early 1938, a year after Marvin started working at Grand Haven Brass. They looked at the purchase as a way to earn some extra money, similar to a lot of other farmers in the area.

In the Holland Evening Sentinel, Bill, then 24, spotted a sale ad for baby turkeys – known as poults – and the brothers bought 14 hens and three toms for $60. Bill had the money to pay for his half. Marvin, then 18 and only working part-time at Grand Haven Brass, was short of cash. He had to borrow his share from their sister Sena, who was making $4 a week doing housework.

Despite the ongoing Depression, the brothers couldn't have picked a better time to raise turkeys. They were on the ground floor of a relatively new enterprise that would boom three years later with

America's entry into World War II. The war produced severe shortages of beef and pork products, making turkey a valuable commodity.

Their father was not happy when he learned about the expansion of the farm operation into turkey raising. Gerrit heard about the news upon his return to the farm from a trip to the University of Michigan Hospital in Ann Arbor, where he was diagnosed with stomach cancer.

Gerrit, who had grown exceedingly cautious after the loss of the family's home in Zeeland, would have preferred that his sons not get involved in any new ventures. He told their sister Marie that the boys "would lose their shirts" if they invested too much in the turkey business.

Their father's apprehension mirrored the anxiety of the times. Most headlines in early 1938 dealt with the sagging national economy and the impending war in Europe and the Far East, which was being kindled by the aggression of Germany and Japan toward its neighbors. The Depression showed no signs of easing. One story reported the sharpest winter decline in employment and a prediction that the relief rolls would jump again. America's participation in the war also looked like a possibility. One story said the political conditions in Europe and in the Far East were more threatening than at anytime since 1918, when World War I ended.

Ignoring the doom-and-gloom headlines, the DeWitt brothers went ahead with their plan to add another cash crop to the family farm operation.

But as the turkey flock began to produce eggs, the brothers ran into an unexpected problem. The hatcheries in the area weren't interested in dealing with such a small number of eggs. The dilemma faced by the brothers was ironic, given that the Holland/Zeeland area was home to about 40 hatcheries and known as the Midwest hatchery capital. A sign on the outskirts of Zeeland once boasted that 15 million chicks were produced annually and shipped by mail to all parts of the country. Even Zeeland High School's nickname for its sports teams, the Chix, reflected the intense hatchery activity.

The largest hatchery in town was DeWitt's Zeeland Hatchery, owned by three brothers, Dick, Jack, and Ben DeWitt, who were no relation to Marvin and Bill. The three brothers later operated DeWitt's Zeeland Poultry Processing Co., DeWitt's Modern Feeds, and Automatic Poultry Feeder Co. The trio decided in the late 1940s to concentrate on one core business, the automatic feeders for poultry and other livestock, and that company later became Big Dutchman Inc. Over the years, Bil Mar bought much of its equipment from Big Dutchman for the expanding turkey-growing operation.

Marvin and his brother finally persuaded the DeWitt brothers to hatch their first eggs, only after Bill went back a third time. They sold their first eggs to the hatchery and, in turn, bought back some of the day-old poults – 60 breeder hens and a few toms to increase their flock. By the fall of 1939, Marvin and Bill had produced 200 turkeys for marketing during the Thanksgiving and Christmas holidays. Their first customer was Bill McKay, who owned a butcher shop on West 16th Street in Holland near where the Schooner Restaurant II is now located. They sold the turkeys live for 16 cents a pound.

Marvin and his wife, Jerene, after they were first married.

Besides the first sale of turkeys, 1939 was also memorable for Marvin when he married fellow church member Jerene Bekius at the home of her parents, Dan and Jennie. Marvin and Jerene, like so many rural people of their day, ended up marrying neighbors and members of their church because they had a smaller circle of friends than their city counterparts. For a honeymoon, they spent a couple of days in the Rudyard area visiting Marvin's Upper Peninsula relatives. Cash short, they moved into the upstairs of the DeWitt family's farmhouse after returning from their wedding trip. Bill and Martha had the same living arrangement for about six months after they were married, until they found a farm to rent on nearby Fillmore Street for $5 a month.

By the time Marvin was married, the two brothers had settled into a rigorous work schedule that included the family homestead, Bill's farm, and Grand Haven Brass. The work day for Marvin and Bill started long before they ever punched the clock at the brass factory. The brothers did their farm chores before the drive to Grand Haven. And they did farm chores after they returned home. At that point the two DeWitt farms were raising cows, hogs, chickens, and turkeys, and growing wheat, oats, and hay. They sold milk, chicken eggs, turkeys and hogs. The chores were not confined to the farms. One of the frequent tasks was to pick up 50 gallons of free "soup" from Heinz to use as a cost-saving feed supplement for the cattle. The liquid, left over from making vinegar out of grain, was transported in a 50-gallon drum the DeWitts rigged to a truck.

Early brooder coops for raising young turkeys.

Their work routine was temporarily upset when Marvin, a year after he married, abruptly quit his job at Grand Haven Brass over a wage dispute. He had toiled at the foundry for three years, doing some of the dirtiest and toughest jobs. One of his tasks was to unload molding sand from railway cars. He also unloaded trucks filled with old brass fittings, which were dumped into a two-wheeled cart that held up to 1,000 pounds. He would wheel that cart to the blast furnaces, where the brass was melted.

The job was supposed to pay 52 cents an hour, yet the company was only giving him 45 cents. Marvin admitted that quitting was a foolish thing to do. But he felt cheated. He received seven weeks worth of unemployment compensation, totaling $49, after he left the brass company. Marvin and Jerene used the money to pay down a furniture bill they incurred after getting married.

Marvin worked on the family farm full-time for a couple of months until he found a job at Hart & Cooley in Holland, putting furnace registers together for 60 cents an hour. The job didn't last long, however. After his father died of cancer in the summer of 1941, at age 59, Marvin had to quit and devote his full attention to the family farm. By then, Marvin and Jerene's family was growing and they needed more room. They had one son, Gary, and a second child was on the way. On Dec. 7, 1941, the day the Japanese bombed the United States naval base at Pearl Harbor, Hawaii, the young family moved to the larger downstairs in the family farmhouse, while Marvin's mother went upstairs. Not long after, they divided the downstairs to make room for a bathroom and installed indoor plumbing. The toilet system was crude yet effective. The outgoing toilet pipe was hooked to a water tank sunk in a hole near the house.

The first brooder house.

While running the farm full-time, Marvin realized how much he enjoyed working for himself. From that realization, he decided to significantly expand the turkey-raising operation. In 1941, he secured a $1,500 loan from First Michigan Bank & Trust Co. in Zeeland to put up a 47 x 110-foot brooder house to raise baby turkeys. The controlled conditions of a barn devoted to poult raising helped assure their maximum survival as opposed to rearing the young birds in small brooder coops or in space set aside in existing farm buildings. Both brothers and their wives co-signed for the first loan, an act that would be repeated many times during the company's history.

"When it comes to the success of the business, we have to give a lot of credit to our wives," Bill said. "They always stood by us. When we came home with a piece of paper for them to sign, they never asked any questions."

The loan came at a perfect time. America, drawn into World War II with the Pearl Harbor attack, turned its attention and resources toward the war effort. Turkey became a popular commodity because the smaller animals required much less grain for growth than cows or pigs. The DeWitts also didn't suffer the same rationing restrictions as other Americans because agriculture was considered a priority industry. And the agricultural status allowed the brothers to receive deferments from having to serve in the military.

First business sign in front of the homestead property.

While the war raged on, the DeWitt turkey business prospered to the point where the brothers printed some business cards and put a name to the operation – Bill and Marve's Turkey Farm. They would liked to have called the business by their last name but thought it might be confused with operations owned by the three DeWitt brothers in Zeeland. During the four war years, Bill and Marvin increased their production from the original 17 turkeys to more than 6,000. The expansion allowed Bill to quit his job at Grand Haven Brass in 1943, the same year the brothers bought their first tractor – a Moline that rolled on metal wheels instead of tires because of the wartime rubber shortage.

Each time Marvin announced plans for another increase in turkey production, his mother bristled with opposition. She supported their efforts. However, she was afraid they were going to dig themselves into a deep financial hole from which there would be no escape. She tried to act as a brake on her youngest son's big ambitions. Family members said Marvin and his mother – alike, in that they were not afraid to strongly express an opinion – frequently argued over the expenditure of money for the turkey business. Other family members, like Jerene's father, also questioned the wisdom behind some of his investments.

Marvin forged on anyway, like he did as a youngster when taking a dare. By the mid-1940s, the DeWitt brothers were minimally processing the birds and selling them New York-dressed, which meant they only removed the blood and feathers. They delivered the dressed turkeys to stores, restaurants, and hotels throughout the state. They also delivered live birds to processors in the Detroit, Chicago, and New York areas.

Customer delivery was the last step in a 30-to-34-week-long growing period for toms and 18-to-20 weeks for hens. The growing process started with a six-to-eight week brooding period when the young turkeys were the most vulnerable.

During the brooder period, the young poults grew quickly under warming lights. Brooder rings confined them to sources of heat, feed, and water until they were accustomed to the new environment. Hindered by poor vision, poults were slow in learning to eat and drink. If food was scattered over the ground, they would find it only by chance. The DeWitts would put colored marbles in their feed and water to catch their attention.

Marvin takes Gary and Marilyn for tractor ride.

After the birds established their eating and drinking habits in about 10 days, Marvin and Bill de-beaked them to prevent cannibalism – the habit of one bird pecking another to the point of injury or death. The de-beaking of toms and hens was done with an electrically heated blade that cauterized as it cut about half of the beak. Toms were also de-snooded to prevent pecking of the fleshy growth that hangs down over the beak. Hens had four toes removed to prevent scratching. As an added precaution, the brothers made sure to provide enough floor, water, and feed space in the brooder house to prevent aggressive behavior.

The brooder house was also equipped with roosts, where the birds could perch off the floor to rest or sleep. The roosting areas prevented injuries and suffocation caused when the poults – acting on instinct to what they perceive as danger – attempted to run away and ended up piling on top of each other when startled at night by noises, rodents running across the floor, or even a power outage. The DeWitts had to maintain a good rodent-control program. Rats and mice were disease carriers and feed stealers. The larger rats can also kill young poults.

The brothers also had to be vigilant for the outbreak of fires in the brooder houses packed with young turkeys. The buildings were extremely vulnerable to fire caused by brooder stoves with an open gas flame. The flame produced hot carbon that could spark a fire by falling into the litter, the absorbent material used to cover the floor. The stoves have since been improved to reduce flash fires.

Marvin feeds young turkeys in battery coop.

The DeWitts modified the brooder process with the construction of a battery-coop building. Instead of being started in a brooder house, the poults were put in battery coops stacked on top of each other. The coops saved space and made it easier to heat, feed, and water the poults before they were put into the brooder house.

After the poults matured, in about six to eight weeks, Marvin and Bill moved them outdoors from the brooder house to fenced-in range land to finish the growing process. The brothers were able to reduce feed costs by putting them outside where the turkeys could forage to supplement their diet. Portable A-frame shelters had to be established for the birds, along with outdoor watering and feeding equipment. The shelters provided roosting space and protection from weather extremes.

The earliest ranges were on the DeWitt homestead alongside 96th Avenue – a location that sometimes caused problems when traffic passed by. Curious by nature, the turkeys would gather at the fence to watch the traffic. After a while, the birds in the back would climb on those upfront to get a closer look. The weight of the birds knocked the fencing over and the brothers had to move them further from the road.

The raising of the birds was timed so that their slaughter would start after Labor Day in September and end just before Christmas, when demand for the birds peaked. The birds were strung up by their feet on a clothesline and had their jugular veins severed. After the blood drained, the carcasses were put in a cast-iron pot, filled with boiling water, to loosen the feathers. Then came the tedious job of pulling the feathers by hand.

Wagon brings water to turkeys on the range.

Family members and neighbors first pitched in. By the early 1940s, the business employed its first full-time employees – Egbert Kuyers and Dale Bekius, one of Jerene's brothers. Bekius remembers the slaughtering pace as grueling, once working from midnight Sunday until Tuesday at 6 p.m. Even Marvin's wife Jerene and his older sisters and mother pitched in when things became hectic. Marvin's mother had no qualms about getting into the processing mess, including sitting around a large table picking feathers. She had always preferred farm chores to housework. Marvin's sister Sena worked part-time for the company from 1943 until 1964, and then was employed full-time until her retirement in 1977.

After the first brooder house was built, the DeWitts used one end of that building for slaughtering and feather pulling. Each season the dressing process became more efficient with the introduction of mechanization. For slaughtering, the brothers devised a funnel-like device in which the turkey's head protruded through the lower end. The gadget helped restrain the bird while cutting the jugular vein, and it prevented some of the struggling that led to bruising and broken bones. Hand pulling of feathers gave way to the use of a drum-like machine with rubber fingers that was rolled around the turkey to remove the thin, outer layer of skin. The tiny immature pin feathers still had to be removed by hand.

Pulling feathers by hand.

Marvin and Bill started with the Broad-Breasted Bronze variety of turkey. In the mid-60s, they switched to Broad-Breasted Whites. That type, unlike other breeds, didn't produce the ink spots from the pin feathers, which detracted from the dressed appearance. After the dressing process, the birds were put into ice water to reduce the chance for spoilage.

The first boom years for the turkey business ended with the close of the war in 1945, prompting a number of small producers to bail out. Yet neither the market fluctuation nor disease and weather problems that same year would deter the ever-persistent Marvin from his vision of further expanding the business far beyond the expectations of the more-cautious Bill. Marvin also wasn't discouraged by the size of his paycheck. In 1946, he was taking home $25 a week, while the company's full-time employees were drawing $36 a week. Marvin's weekly wage was about $6 more than what he had been making at Hart & Cooley, his last job away from the farm.

Considering the number of hours he worked, the turkey-farming wage and the factory wage were probably comparable.

Even so, Marvin had no intention of giving up something in which he had invested seven years of his life. He likes to joke that maybe he wasn't smart enough to get out of the business like so many others did after the war. The truth was just the opposite. He was perceptive enough to realize there were opportunities in the turkey business for someone who was willing to work hard and take risks. Both DeWitt brothers had been raised by their parents to be hard workers and neither one gave up easily.

According to Bill, "We were a success because we weren't afraid of hard work. In the early days, we worked day and night, and pretty much did everything ourselves. We also worked as a team. We signed both of our names for all of the loans. We were in it for the two of us. We both made our contribution to the success of the business by taking care of our own part of the business. I liked the farming part. Marvin was the promoter and the idea man. That doesn't mean all of his ideas worked. But he had enough good ones to keep us going and growing."

Bill (left) and Marvin DeWitt in the early days of the business.

Marvin's grand ideas were ridiculed by skeptical neighbors, who not only questioned the intellectual ability of the brothers to run a business. They also predicted their ultimate failure.

Some of the tongue wagging was pure jealousy. Some of the negative speculation probably was rooted in the conservative and cautious character of area residents.

"People around here would never thought of borrowing money over and over to expand the business like Marvin did," said Dale Bekius, Bil Mar's first full-time employee.

Marvin's spunk paid off though. By 1947, two years after WW II, the business was raising 15,000 turkeys a year. However, even that wasn't enough for the restless Marvin, who was always looking for ways to improve and expand the business.

He wanted to control every facet of turkey production, from beginning to end, just like Henry Ford did with his automobile company. And for the DeWitts, that meant an additional chore – hatching the turkey eggs.

Marvin dips eggs in disinfectant.

CHAPTER FOUR

HATCHING MORE EXPANSION

Marvin's decision to go into the hatchery part of the turkey business in 1947 did not get the whole-hearted support of his brother Bill, who questioned the need for the expansion.

The difference in opinion clearly defined the unique personalities of the two brothers and the direction in which the company would grow. Bill was on the quiet side, easygoing and cautious in his manner. He was also reluctant to show emotion or express his opinion – like his father and most other members of the early DeWitt clan. His great-grandfather Gerrit DeWitt was described in a family history as "being of calm nature, slow in his movement and his speech."

Marvin was more like his mother's side of the family, the Vandenburgs – take-charge, outspoken, and highly motivated. Marvin had all the personality traits associated with the classic entrepreneur –

independent, impatient, impulsive, aggressive, singleminded and adventuresome.

When it came to operating the business, Marvin is variously described by close business associates as the instigator, sparkplug, opportunist, and visionary. He carried the bulk of the work load in terms of promoting the business and making it prosper. He was always thinking about the business and coming up with new ideas on how to make improvements. He enjoyed finagling and manipulating his way in and out of a deal. A born risk-taker, he was not afraid to carry a heavy debt load.

"An entrepreneur who fails in a business does so for two reasons – they were either too dumb to see the risks or too dumb to see the opportunities. A wise man can see both, and Marvin was a wise man," said Phil Vanden Berge, former senior vice president of finance at Bil Mar and the highest-ranking non-family member before the 1987 merger with Sara Lee.

Bill was nearly always in the background. Going out of his way to avoid publicity, he was truly the silent partner. That doesn't mean he never voiced an opinion or expressed anger if something didn't work out. Though, for the most part, he offered few ideas for the growth of the business and went along with most of Marvin's.

Marvin looked at the world in absolute, black-and-white terms. Bill's view of the world was less exact and he could see shades of gray.

Observations by former Bil Mar employees and family members confirm the personality distinctions between the two brothers and the effect those differences had on the eventual success of the business.

"Their personalities were like night and day. Bill came across as more friendly and less volatile. Marvin was not afraid to show his temper and was always expressing his opinion," said Marge Boersen, Bil Mar's computer operations manager until she retired in 1996 after 25 years of service. "Bill was more interested in the agricultural side of the business. Marvin was interested in getting the products made and sold. They both took care of different parts of the operation. However, Marvin gets more credit for the success of the business, and for good reason. He was more aggressive in pushing the company into trying new products and processes. He found markets for products. He was out there hustling. He was a hands-on executive, who got involved in every facet of the business and became its leader. He watched over everything and had an interest in what everyone was doing. The business never would have become that successful if Marvin hadn't been open to new ideas. Bill certainly wouldn't have pushed anything. It just wasn't his nature."

The differing personalities of the brothers actually suited their partnership well. Had both brothers been like Marvin, they probably would have disagreed to the point where the business would never had grown, or their combined risk taking might have buried them in debt and ultimate failure. Had both brothers been like Bill, they would have remained turkey farmers and Bil Mar Foods would not exist.

"Dad and Uncle Bill are like oil and water. Uncle Bill is a farmer at heart. As the years went on, he knew less and less about what was going on inside the plant," said Keith DeWitt, Marvin's youngest son. "But they should both be given credit for the success of the business. Uncle Bill worked very hard and, like Dad, signed his name on all of the loans."

Despite their differing approaches to life, the two brothers did share some personality traits that helped steady the business. As Christian businessmen, they lived by the Golden Rule: do unto others as you would want them to do unto you. As a result, they built the business on a reputation for hard work, honesty, fairness, and dependability.

They defined their work ethic not only by the number of hours they labored but also by giving their best effort. Once they decided on a course of action, they were not quick to change their minds. Marvin, especially, had a stubborn streak that wouldn't allow him to admit failure after he started something. He would find a way to make it work.

The brothers were fiscally conservative. They plowed all their early profits back into the business. They neither borrowed nor spent more than was necessary.

And they relied on the least number of employees and pieces of equipment to get the job done. Marvin stockpiled old equipment, hoping to salvage parts someday. Until the business was well established, he never bought something new when he could purchase used and still get the job done. When Marvin came up with an idea for an original piece of equipment, he would turn to his maintenance supervisor, Frank DeWind, for assembly.

Some of the contraptions invented by Marvin – like the converted cement truck pulling four turkey-manure spreaders – looked goofy yet they worked. The odd-looking fertilizing machine saved time by traveling down the road faster than an ordinary tractor and by reducing the trips from the farm to the corn fields.

Marvin said having talented and loyal employees, like DeWind, was necessary for Bil Mar's early operation. There was no place in the budget for the preventative maintenance so popular among businesses today.

"Today, company's replace machinery parts after a certain amount of time, whether they need changing or not. They call that preventative maintenance," Marvin said. "We didn't have that luxury back then. We made due with what we had by cobbling up things to make them work. And then we ran it until something wore out. We couldn't afford to do it any other way. What people forget is that a new part can cause problems too. If you have an old part that is working right, then why not leave it alone and get the longest life out of it. I still tend to do that today."

His conservative streak in money matters did not dampen the inborn entrepreneurial spirit driving him fearlessly down the road to success. While one turkey grower was mulling over a decision, he would have made 10 in the meantime. Maybe only five of those choices turned out to be right. That still put him ahead of most everyone else in the turkey business.

"One of dad's biggest strengths was his willingness to take chances, especially when it came to going deeper in debt to get bigger. That attitude led to innovations like further processing and the convenience foods part of the business," said Marvin's son Merle. "He was not a book-smart person. He would follow his gut instincts, which usually turned out to be right."

His willingness to take risks was bolstered by a self-assured attitude that dismissed failure as just another adversity to conquer, according to his daughter Nancy Haveman.

"Dad is able to take a stand, to follow through, and to do something. He is not wishy-washy and always has an opinion. He also was not one to give up in the face of adversity," she said. "There was no question in his mind that he was going to grow and succeed. There was always a drive to try a new product or process."

One of those processes involved the operation of a hatchery, against Bill's better judgment. While Bill may have questioned the wisdom of hatching turkey eggs, he didn't stand in his brother's way.

"I think Bill knew I was pretty well determined to do what I was going to do. I have always been aggressive about anything I was involved in," Marvin said about his decision to forge ahead with the hatchery idea. "I was lucky that my brother trusted my judgment on so many things. I couldn't have asked for a better partner. We only had a few minor disagreements."

Bill agreed.

"Overall, our partnership worked pretty smoothly. I only remember having little disagreements. We were too busy working to argue."

Marvin liked the idea of hatching his own birds. He could eliminate a middle man between the breeding and brooding process. Because a hatchery operation would produce far more birds than Bil Mar needed, the company could also earn some extra operating money by selling poults to other turkey farmers – some of whom were processing like the DeWitts.

"The big difference between Marvin and other turkey growers is that he decided to go the whole gamut – from breeding turkeys to hatching eggs to raising turkeys to processing turkeys," said Ed Lamse, Bil Mar's insurance agent for many years. "With farming, timing is everything, and Marvin was a master of timing. He wanted to control all of the factors that went into the business so he could assure quality from the beginning to the end of the process. Marvin was like the Henry Ford of the turkey business."

The DeWitts opened their hatchery in 1947 by constructing a building that stands today as the Bil Mar Country Store, a retail outlet in the shadow of the sprawling processing plant. With the expansion of the business, the brothers had to change the company name to Bill & Marve's Turkey Farm & Hatchery. The longer company title inspired Marvin to come up with the Bil Mar brand name by combining the first three letters in each of their given names.

By opening the hatchery, the DeWitt brothers controlled every aspect of their turkey production. They also had a lot more work on their hands, including the sale and delivery of poults. In addition, the DeWitts sold breeder stock.

Company's first business card.

"One of my big mistakes in business was trying to do everything myself. One example was the hatchery business. I saw others doing it, and I figured I would have a go at it," Marvin said. "It proved to be one of those things in life where the grass is greener on the other side of the fence. It never fell into place like I thought it was going to and there was a tremendous amount of work involved. It was always a tough, uphill battle."

At first, the DeWitts allowed the turkeys to breed naturally for egg production, putting canvas saddles on the hens to keep their skin from being cut by the spurs of the males. They switched to artificial insemination in the 1950s to improve the fertilization and hatching rates.

The artificial process requires semen to be collected from the toms and then administered to the hens. No easy task, the collection process requires two people. One holds the tom with the tail end toward the other person, who grips the rear of the copulatory organ with his thumb and forefinger. The semen is then squeezed out with a short sliding downward movement into a holding tube. Jack DeWitt, Marvin's second-oldest son, was the most proficient at that process.

The job of inseminating the hens usually rested with Bill. He also got a helping hand from Marvin's oldest son, Gary. To inseminate, the opening of the hen's oviduct is exposed and a semen-filled glass tube is inserted. Jacob "Jake" Voetberg, who retired from Bil Mar in 1989 after 36 years as farm manager, always kidded Bill about having the "holiest" job on the farm.

Marvin focused a lot of his attention on the hatchery and its temperamental incubators. The temperature and humidity in the incubators had to be carefully monitored for uniformity to assure the survival of the birds. To keep tabs on the incubators when not in the hatchery, he ran a wire from the machines to the original DeWitt farmhouse where a bell would sound if there was a malfunction. In 1949, Marvin ran the same wire into a new home he built nearby for his family. Bill also lent a hand in the hatching process, which took 28 days from the time an egg was placed in the incubator.

incubators hatch turkey eggs.

The DeWitt incubators were similar to those used in other large commercial hatchery operations. The fans of the incubator forced warm air, averaging 99.5 degrees, through the machine and around the eggs. For the first 26 days, the eggs lay in setting incubators. During that period, the trays were tilted about four times a day as a way of turning the eggs to prevent the embryo from sticking to the shell membrane – similar to how a hen would move on the nest to distribute heat evenly to all the eggs. Proper humidity of 85 percent was especially important at this stage when the eggs will lose weight through evaporation at a rather definite rate. At the end of the setting period, the eggs were checked with a candling light to determine which ones were fertile and ready to be placed in the hatching incubators. The two-day hatching period, when the turkeys pecked their way out of the eggs, was the most crucial. For that reason, Marvin would sleep two nights on a cot in the hatchery to make sure nothing went wrong. The first hatch, on April, 15, 1947, totaled 3,360 poults. At its peak, in the early 1970s, the hatchery produced about 20,000 poults a week.

Marvin and Bill kept a certain number of poults for their processing business, and sold the rest to other turkey growers throughout the Midwest and on the East Coast. The poults were shipped, according to sex, in padded boxes stapled together at the farm. Holes were punched in the boxes for air. The number of holes was determined by the temperature outside – more for warmer weather, fewer during cooler periods.

Bill and Marvin inspect poults before shipment.

The brothers received some assistance in the hatchery operation from their sons and daughters after they turned old enough to handle routine chores at the ages of 7 and 8. The kids gathered eggs from the nests, placed them in the incubator trays, candled them, took the poults out of the hatching trays, and cleaned the trays. In addition, they assembled poult delivery boxes, put baby turkeys in the containers, and stuffed envelopes with advertising directed at potential customers.

The hatchery business kept Marvin's phone line humming. There was a business phone in the hatchery and a family phone in the house, both sharing the same number and ringing simultaneously. When Marvin wasn't in the hatchery, his wife or oldest daughter Marilyn would answer the phone in the house.

So they could get Marvin's attention for a business call while he was in the farmyard, he attached a car horn to the roof of the hatchery. Whoever answered the phone in the house would push a buzzer to sound the horn, letting him know to pick up the phone in the hatchery. In the early days of the company, Marvin and his family had to share their residential phone line with 15 other families. Much to the relief of the DeWitts and the other families on the party line, a separate line was soon installed for the hatchery phone.

Marvin also took care of the office work for the growing business. Early on, he would write a business letter and ask a neighbor to check the spelling, punctuation, and grammar. With the opening of the hatchery, the volume of business correspondence increased and he hired the company's first secretary, Lois Vollink [now Weaver], a Borculo resident who was fresh out of high school. Her parents operated Vollink Brothers Grocery Store in Borculo. One day a week, she would show up at the hatchery and he would hand her a stack of handwritten letters to type, along with orders and price lists. She corrected his writing mistakes, without altering his folksy style.

Lois (Weaver) Vollink, Bil Mar's first secretary.

"As a young woman, with no secretarial experience, I sometimes felt pressured working for Marvin DeWitt, even though he was a good person to work for. He was a jovial sort with a good sense of humor. He seemed to have a positive attitude about everything, refusing to let setbacks get him down," she said. "But I had to get a lot done in a relatively short time, and he had a reputation for being a hard worker and expecting his employees to have the same level of energy. He always seemed to be in a hurry to get something done or to be somewhere. He had that fast pace built into his gait and mannerisms."

One of Weaver's jobs was to help produce Bil Mar's annual poult brochure, which Marvin created. The 1953 brochure touted a Record On Performance (ROP) breeding program, in which Bil Mar carefully monitored the mating patterns of its toms and hens from year to year to assure the highest quality egg production.

"Yes, friends, we are sure our Broad-Breasted Bronze poults will excel any poults you have ever raised before in livability, early maturity, finish, meat quality and size. Extra pounds make the difference between profit and loss. Don't be pennywise and pound foolish. Low-priced, ordinary poults should never be your choice if you want to get the most return on your investment and labor. May we be your poult supplier this year? Thank-you for your kind attention."

Marvin kept close track of customer orders and wasted no time sending a second inquiry to those who didn't respond to the original brochure.

"We surely wish we could have the pleasure of delivering your 1953 poult requirements to start you correctly for those extra pounds of meat profit at market time. Buy your poults this year from the only ROP turkey-breeding farm in Michigan. This fact alone assures you of better-bred poults to start with. A race horse stable owner wouldn't go to an auction sale of buggy horses to replenish his racing stock. He would go to a breeder of thoroughbreds known for racing qualities. So too, turkeys should be bought, with the same precaution, from a breeder known for broader-breasted turkeys."

Marvin's attention to detail, from breeding to delivery, paid off in a wealth of satisfied customers. The DeWitts received a number of letters praising the hatchery operation, like the two in 1958 from Snyder's Turkey Farm in Pennsylvania. "We received 101 white hen poults and they arrived in perfect shape," said the first letter. A couple weeks later, a second letter marveled at the health of the poults: "It is the first time we have had a perfect record on any flock."

When Marvin wasn't taking orders for poults, he was taking turns with Bill delivering them. The delivery to customers, as far away as Philadelphia, forced them to put in some mind-numbing hours – working all day on the farm and then driving all night to their faraway destinations. To help him stay awake, Marvin, who detests the smoking habit, would puff on a few filtered cigarettes without inhaling. Bill's son, Bill Jr., and Marvin's sons, Gary and Jack, also took turns making long-distance runs, when they reached driving age.

Company's first marketing brochure.

The DeWitts operated the hatchery for almost 25 years, until 1971, when it no longer suited their business interests. By then, they invested the majority of their time and capital in the further processing of turkeys – cutting up the birds and cooking the boneless parts to make a variety of food products, such as a combination white-and dark-meat turkey roll, roasted split breast, roasted thigh set, and whole-roasted breast. And for further processing, they were only interested in the larger tom turkeys. With the end of the hatchery era, Bil Mar bought poults from such suppliers as Janssen's Farms Hatcheries Inc. in Zeeland.

First on-site feed mill (foreground) attached to brooder house.

The hatchery operation did not return big profits for Marvin and Bill. However, the profit margin was enough to provide them with extra operating money. And hatching rewarded the company with other dividends, such as advancing the brothers' reputation throughout the poultry industry as being trustworthy businessmen. Time and again during the company's history, relationships forged during the hatchery years proved invaluable in the growth of Bil Mar as a food-processing business.

"We can second-guess ourselves forever whether it was the best decision to get into the hatchery business. It was not as big a money maker as I thought it was going to be and it was a lot of hard work," Marvin said. "Yet it was all part of the business and its growth. It did give us a certain amount of money that we otherwise wouldn't have had until the fall of the year when we started selling turkeys. And all of the contacts we made paid off later because we treated them right. They were in the same business, and some of them helped us to sell things later on when we got into further processing in the early 1960s."

The time-consuming involvement in the hatchery business did not divert Marvin from his mission of improving and expanding the processing operation as the 1950s began.

They added a small feed mill to the brooder house to mix soybean meal, bone meal, and animal fat with corn and oats grown on the farm. The on-site mill saved money by reducing their reliance on the services of local feed mills. They were also able to wean themselves off the premixed feeds, from such companies as Arcady Feeds in Chicago.

The addition of the feed mill was followed by the 1954 construction of the largest barn for turkey breeder and brooder operations in the Midwest.

The DeWitts also began to offer customers oven-ready birds – fresh and frozen – by removing the innards instead of just the blood and feathers. The frozen birds were packed in airtight Cryovac bags to extend their shelf life and expand the marketing period beyond the holidays.

Quonset building doubles as brooder house and freezer.

Freezing gave Marvin another idea for picking up a few dollars – selling the birds to area employers who, in turn, gave them as holiday gifts to their employees, clients and friends. For many years, he personally delivered the frozen turkeys to corporate customers in southwest Michigan.

In the early days of freezing, the DeWitts stored the birds in a small freezer in the hatchery. As business for the frozen birds increased, they were forced to rent frozen storage space. The farm just did not have enough voltage to power a large freezer unit. Then Marvin worked with the power company to boost electricity from the feed mill in Borculo to his property so he could freeze the birds on-site in a semi circle-shaped barn known as a quonset building.

The barn, built in 1951, was actually a multi-purpose building equipped with refrigeration pipes. In the winter, the DeWitts bred some of the turkeys in the quonset. In the spring, they used the building as the brooder house to start raising the birds. At processing time, in the fall, the refrigeration was turned on in the quonset. Temporary freezer units were constructed each year in the building by installing partitioned walls and insulating them on their tops and sides with sawdust waste from the Chris-Craft boat plant in Holland.

Marvin speeded up the freezing process in 1955 by dipping the bagged, table-ready turkeys in super-cold liquid brine. The quick-freezing process eliminated the discoloration that came with conventional freezing in a refrigerated unit. Marvin had spotted a brine freezer in operation during a visit to a poultry plant in Indiana. He came home and built his own 30 foot long fiberglass dipping tank.

The quonset barn was used for cold storage until its 1966 relocation on the property to make room for the company's first permanent freezer unit. The quonset was then used for storing equipment parts until its demolition in 1983 to make way for further plant expansion.

By 1957, the DeWitts were no longer selling live turkeys or the minimally processed New York-dressed variety. They concentrated, instead, on oven-ready fresh and frozen birds for customers such as restaurants in Michigan, Illinois, and Ohio; grocery chains like A & P and Kroger; hotels like the Pantlind in Grand Rapids [now Amway Grand]; and distributors like City Poultry and McInerny-Miller in Detroit, and Gordon Food Service in Grand Rapids.

At each new step in the business, the DeWitts had to hire more full-time and part-time help, and increasingly rely on the assistance of their older sons, Gary, Jack, and Bill Jr. Unable to raise all the birds they needed, the DeWitts also began contracting in the early 1960s with outside growers in the area, like Henry Smith in Middleville.

Still there didn't seem to be enough hours in the day to get everything done during a typical year. There was work to do in the fields where feed crops were grown. There were breeding and hatching chores. The young turkeys in the brooder building and the older birds on the range were in need of care. There was the hectic slaughtering and processing period in the fall. And there were poults and dressed turkeys that needed to be delivered.

On top of everything, Marvin had to step up his marketing efforts to keep the business on a growth track. When it came to advertising the business, he never missed an opportunity. For many years, the two brothers engaged in horse-pulling competitions, a hobby that took them to county fairs around the state. Marvin had the business name prominently displayed on the harnesses.

His most successful marketing technique was not so eye-catching. He essentially built the business one client at a time, by making delivery promises with a solid handshake and then keeping them. His goal was to make money doing business – but not at the expense of his integrity. Marvin was as interested in making a friend as he was lining up another customer, an attribute he sometimes finds lacking in today's business world.

Hatchery and DeWitt farmhouse.

"Things have changed when it comes to business dealings today. I am not saying there isn't any friendship between the buyer and seller. Though I think relationships are a lot more formal than they were in the earlier days of our business. In my day, I think there was more loyalty between the buyer and seller. I think there were a lot more deals handled with a handshake then," Marvin said wistfully. "Business people rely more on contracts today. Just because you have a contract doesn't mean you can't break it. Whether its a handshake or a contract, you are only as good as your word. That is all that matters.

"I don't think I ever made an enemy in my business dealings with customers. I may have rubbed people the wrong way with my impulsive personality. Yet they knew I would always treat them fairly and honestly. I learned early on that you don't build relationships in a day. You treat people right and you don't take advantage of them. No one could ever say that Marvin DeWitt was out to get them. Whatever we agreed upon, that is the way it went. That is why so many of our customers became friends."

One of those individuals was Joe Cotton, a commodities broker who Marvin met at a National Turkey Federation convention in Dallas, Texas. Cotton, based in Boston, Mass., was always impressed with Marvin's personal treatment in dealing with customers. Cotton received the same treatment with his first order from Bil Mar, a truckload of frozen turkeys boxed for holiday giving at factories in the Boston area. Marvin and his wife Jerene drove the delivery truck from Borculo to Boston, arriving at 2 a.m. After a few hours sleep at Cotton's house, Marvin delivered the orders to Cotton's customers.

"I always thought of Marvin as one of the pioneers in the industry, a real leader. He was known for his honesty, respectability, and willingness to go out of his way for a customer. With Marvin, what you saw is what you got. There was no hidden agenda," said Cotton, who represented Bil Mar from 1961 to 1990.

Banking on the DeWitts' reputation, customers lent them money to finish raising turkeys when they ran short of cash. When the customers bought the turkeys, they would deduct the loan amount from their bill.

One time, with City Poultry in Detroit, Marvin noticed that a $10,000 advance on the turkeys had not been deducted from the bill. He quickly called the company to let them know of the error, a gesture that impresses the company owner to this day.

"When I first met Marvin DeWitt, we were a pretty big company and Bil Mar was relatively small. I was primarily impressed by his integrity and solid values," said Harold Haas, who was a partner in City Poultry. "After he pointed out that $10,000 error, I never thought twice about lending him money. In all the years of trading merchandise with him, we never had an argument or exchanged a mean word. I knew I could trust Marvin. You could always depend on him to pay up on a loan or come through for you with an order. In the food business, everything hinged on integrity. You made a lot of deals and most of them with a handshake."

As if all their business activities weren't enough to keep the DeWitts busy, Marvin decided in the early 1950s that the brothers should make more contacts in the turkey business by attending industry trade shows, conventions, and meetings.

Among the industry groups they affiliated with were the Michigan Turkey Growers Association, Michigan Turkey Improvement Association, Michigan Allied Poultry Industries, and the National Turkey Federation.

The brothers were so cash-strapped that they had to share a one-bed motel room at their first convention. Both over 200 pounds, the combined weight of the husky brothers caused the bed to keep sinking in the middle. They spent part of the night shoving objects under the bed to support the mattress.

True to his out-going personality, Marvin soon became well-known in turkey circles. He was not afraid to ask tough questions or state his opinions.

"He was a person you would remember. He was always at the meetings and he was never quiet," said Dr. Carl Hoyt, a district marketing agent for Michigan State University's Cooperative Extension Service, who first met Marvin at a poultry meeting in Lansing. "He didn't wait until the break to ask questions and he asked good questions. He was not afraid to voice his opinion on something. You knew he was someone moving ahead in the turkey business, even back then."

Building the business consumed most of Bill's and Marvin's waking hours, which could sometimes stretch into the early morning. Marvin remembers a wake-up call one morning at 4. Bill had been out plowing a field all night when his tractor slipped into a ditch and rolled onto its side. Marvin was asked to join a salvage crew from Borculo in retrieving the tractor. After the tractor was back in the field, Bill hopped backed on and finished the plowing.

Bill loads eggs onto truck.

"That is the way it was in the early days when we were building the business by ourselves," said Marvin about the work ethic of the brothers. "When the iron is hot, you have to strike. When something needed to be done, you did it no matter how long it took. We didn't have the time or the inclination to take a sabbatical and attend classes on how to run a turkey business. We learned by doing things. To succeed, we had to get our minds and our bodies involved in the business. We never thought about getting rich. We just worried about getting the bills paid and taking care of our families."

The arduous work schedule in those early days kept them away from home much of the time. There is a joke among Bill's children that their father left for work one day and by the time he returned his hair had turned gray. It was an obvious exaggeration, referring to their father's hair turning prematurely gray. There was an element of truth to the story, however.

Driven by a perfectionist streak, Marvin was determined to oversee every facet of the business – breeding, hatching, raising, processing, marketing, sales, delivery, and administration. In the earlier days, Bill also shouldered some of those responsibilities. After 1950, he spent most of his time working in the fields and raising turkeys. The niche suited him perfectly. Bill was content to be a farmer – from his sweat-stained work hat to the turkey manure on the bottom of his farm boots. He did not harbor a vision of running a large turkey-processing business. He left the vision part of the busi-

Bil Mar in the mid-1950s.

ness, and most everything else, up to Marvin.

Marvin's wife once wished out loud for her husband to be an ordinary farmer so they could have more time to spend together as a family. Her wish never came even partially true.

He was able to turn his attention homeward mainly for eating and sleeping.

That changed when the company began to hire more employees, and the teen-aged sons of Bill and Marvin started taking on more responsibility. Even then, the business spilled over into Marvin's home life.

"I have no regret for not spending more time with my family. What's done is done. If I had to do it all over again, I would have hired some of those chores out," he said about his busy work routine. "I can't believe how hard we worked to build that business. There are times when I am glad it is all behind me."

DeWitt kids dress up: (top to bottom) Gary, Marilyn, Jack, Don, Nancy, Merle and Keith.

CHAPTER FIVE

FAITH AND FAMILY

Home life for Marvin's family in the 1950s was geared to mesh with the business.

With so much work to accomplish, meals were expected to be ready when Marvin and his two older sons, Gary and Jack, came through the door.

Discussion at the kitchen table usually centered around turkeys – not news of the day, sports, or the children's schoolwork. With Marvin rushing to be somewhere, little time was spent at the meal table.

"We were involved in family, church, and school activities. But our home life was geared to support the men in our lives and their work," said Marilyn Norman, Marvin's oldest daughter, who helped her mother run the household. "Time was precious and everything had to run like clockwork."

Marilyn was 8-years-old in 1949 when the family moved from the downstairs of the homestead house to a three-bedroom ranch house where all seven of the DeWitt children grew up. Marvin helped contractors build the new family house by doing most of the rough-in work. His mother continued to live upstairs at the homestead house, while the downstairs was occupied by married hired hands.

Much of Marilyn's day was spent helping her mother prepare breakfast, dinner and supper and cleaning up the resulting mess. She would just barely finish the breakfast dishes when Gary, Jack, their cousin Bill Jr., and some of the hired hands would pop back into the kitchen for a mid-morning break about 10 a.m.

One of the favorite family breakfasts was bread dipped in bacon fat and covered with Karo syrup. The same syrup topped another family favorite – Balkenbrij. The dish consisted of pork, usually from a hog's head, which was cooked, ground up and mixed with buckwheat flour, spooned into a loaf pan for cooling in the refrigerator, and then sliced, fried and covered with Karo.

DeWitt clan at meal time.

Given the nature of the business, the family ate more than their fair share of turkey in a variety of dishes – from soup to sandwiches. Marvin's insistence at making sure his customers were satisfied meant the family ate the company's rejected birds, not the Grade A turkeys shipped off the farm. Even the cracked and double-yoked turkey eggs ended up on the DeWitt table.

He was also rigid when it came to the size of helpings his offspring put on their plates. They were taught early on not to waste anything by taking only what they could eat.

"If you took it, you had to eat it," said Jack DeWitt. "It trained you not to waste, to share with others, and be polite. It was also another way of teaching you to follow through and do things well. Dad always stressed that if you were going to do a job, you should always make every effort to do your best. He also emphasized that if you start a job, you finish a job. A meal was no different."

Nancy and Keith square off at Christmas party.

Marvin's wife Jerene usually ate her meal after everyone finished theirs, especially when the family grew to seven children. The brood, with a 15-year spread between the oldest and youngest, included Gary, Marilyn, Jack, Don, Nancy, Merle, and Keith. During the meal, Jerene was just too busy making sure that everyone's needs were met. And that included friends of the children after they got older, or visitors, like the feed salesmen Marvin would bring home unannounced. Eating after the kitchen cleared out also gave her a chance to reflect in silence before tackling the next household chore.

She established a routine by designating chores for particular days – Monday for washing clothes and Tuesday for ironing. Time also had to be made for making and mending clothes, gardening, canning and cleaning. The family didn't own a clothes dryer when the children were younger. So the clothes were hung outside to dry in nice weather and put up in the utility room at other times. Jerene juggled the care of the children with her chores by doing two things at once – like darning socks and helping the kids with their homework or catechism lessons.

Merle, Keith, and Nancy on Christmas morning.

The routine of house work and her ability to accomplish all of the tasks, without supervision, always impressed Marvin.

"Dad was complimentary when it came to women doing housework before the days of so many household conveniences," Marilyn said. "He said women in the home had the hardest job to do. They did most of it themselves and without anyone giving them direction."

It was not all tedium around the house. Jerene did take time to listen to some of her favorite radio programs, like "Arthur Godfrey and His Friends" and "Heaven and Home Hour." She always stopped her chores to watch the soap opera, "Edge of Night," after the family purchased a television set in 1952. She also belonged to a group of neighbor women who met once a month, at each other's homes, to share lunch and sing hymns. She napped each afternoon to recharge her strength, which was sapped by a chronic condition of anemia, a deficiency in the blood's oxygen-carrying capacity.

There were also some breaks in the household routine with visits by grocery and bakery peddlers, and door-to-door salesmen of home products, such as Stanley and Raleigh. The grocery peddler, from Vollink Brothers Grocery Store in Borculo, stopped one day a week. The Colonial man visited three days a week with baked goods.

Marvin's wife was his personality opposite. Less excitable, she kept her opinions to herself. She trusted her husband to do the right thing by her, the family, and the business. She never raised her voice, and showed no trace of anger or frustration with what was going on around her. She did speak up on behalf of the children, however. More than once during harsh winter weather, she asked her husband to drive the children two miles to the one-room Ovens School.

Mrs. DeWitt with (from left) Jack, Marilyn, and Gary.

She truly enjoyed raising her family and being in charge of the household. She was always more comfortable at home than in any other setting and drew greatest satisfaction from taking care of others. She had the ability to keep the peace in the midst of turmoil, like distracting an upset child.

The kids grew up seeing her as the family's anchor – someone they could always count on to be at home.

Marilyn, so used to having her mother around, was shocked to come home from school one day and not find her there. Marvin's mother was watching the younger kids while his wife was helping pack turkeys for the Thanksgiving rush.

Gary with family dog.

The boys also looked to their mother for support and guidance.

"Mom had her own mission, looking after the kids and, in later years, the grandkids," Jack said. "Because of her, home was a caring, loving, sustaining place where the family was held together. She gave balance to the family. She was the one we turned to when we needed help with our schoolwork or catechism."

The children weren't the only ones to witness the stabilizing effect she had on the family. The Rev. Mike VanBuren, former pastor at Ottawa Reformed Church, described Jerene as an inviting woman who never gave the impression that you were intruding on her time.

"Jerene has really been the stabilizing influence in that family, especially with Marvin," Rev. Van Buren said. "She is the only person who could have any measure of control over him – through faith, through love, and through kindness."

Minnie DeWitt, married to Marvin's son Don, shared a similar perspective.

"Don's mom is very kind, patient, loving and caring. If I can be half the grandmother she has been, I will be a good grandmother."

Marvin also recognized his wife as a constant in the family and expressed appreciation for her role.

"My wife was always there, supporting all of my efforts. I could always count on her to stand by me, even accompanying me to turkey conventions. Like Bill's wife, she never questioned any of our decisions when it came time to sign her name on a loan application. For that, I was a very lucky man," he said. "I have nothing but praise for the way she handled things at home. I taught the kids the world of work. Mom was in charge of teaching the kids in the house with their schoolwork and their catechism. It was a real advantage having a wife stay home to take care of the children and keep an eye on the household."

Marilyn and Gary in farmyard.

The DeWitt children drew strength from more than just a stable home life. Both Marvin and his wife kept faith in the forefront, which offered the children a spiritual dimension to their lives.

Marvin was brought up to believe that a person would be rewarded if they put their trust in God and lived up to His commandments to the best of their ability. For that reason, he defines his success in the context of faith. He believes that his prosperity is a blessing from God.

Marvin, however, did not preach to his offspring when it came to his religious beliefs. He preferred to set an example by incorporating his principles into the fabric of everyday life.

"We were brought up with a set of values, including integrity and honesty. We were taught to give and to share. We were taught to be frugal and to spend within your means," Gary said. "There was no one who didn't know where we stood and what our values were. My parents taught those values by example in their daily lives."

Marilyn also remembers her moral upbringing based, in large

part, on the example set by her parents.

"My dad was a big believer that religion was caught, not taught. He didn't preach honesty and fairness," Marilyn said. "Dad didn't have to. He was a good role model, like mom. He practiced honesty and fairness in his personal and business dealings. He also didn't drink, smoke or swear."

Marvin didn't evangelize away from home either. He had no interest in converting others to his way of thinking and showed great tolerance for other religions. Through the business, he made friends with people of differing faiths, including a number of Jews. He attended their weddings, bar mitzvahs, and temple ceremonies.

"They had their beliefs and I had mine. I didn't try to convert them," he said. "I will defend my religion against anybody. Yet I am not the type of Christian who argues over every verse in the Bible. There is room for interpretation in the Bible."

The DeWitt family church.

Participation in religious activities was integral to life in the DeWitt household. Every meal, Marvin led off with a prayer. His wife finished the meal with a Bible reading. The family attended regular church services on Wednesday nights and twice on Sunday. Marvin believed that if a congregation hired a preacher to give two sermons, the members should be there for both.

On Saturday, the children attended catechism classes. Adults and children attended their own Sunday school session. The children also were involved in the Christian Endeavor group at the church and attended Vacation Bible School in the summer. Their father, with his flexible work schedule, drove the Bible School bus.

By Marvin's example, the children were taught early on to give a fair share of their earnings to the church. The money for tithing, considered untouchable even for a family emergency, would go into a sugar bowl in the cupboard over the stove.

"That was holy money and you didn't mess with it," said Don, the middle son. "It was split up among the kids and handed down the pew just before the collection. Everyone in the family had to put something in the collection plate."

In the DeWitt household, Sunday was considered a sacred day – a time for rest and worship. Only necessary chores, such as checking the well-being of the turkeys in the hatchery or on the range, were scheduled. On some Sunday nights, the family visited new church families at their homes to make them feel welcome. They also stopped by the home of Jerene's parents after church.

Gary gives Jack and Marilyn a sled ride.

There was a ban on Sunday recreation that extended to visitors. Don Pike, a business acquaintance of Marvin's from Ohio, was visiting the DeWitts one weekend after the death of his wife. He enjoyed riding horses and asked Nancy if she wanted to join him on Sunday. Nancy declined, saying her father did not allow such activity on the Sabbath.

"I told her that it wouldn't be any problem. I was one of her father's best customers," Pike recalled. " In the end, we didn't go horseback riding that afternoon. It didn't matter how good a customer or friend I had been. I was reminded again that the man not only had principles, he stood by them."

Marvin's interest in his offspring's adherence to religious traditions did not carry over to their school work.

Neither Marvin, his brother Bill, nor their sisters had finished high school. Marvin didn't think his boys needed a lot of education. They had a ready-made career in the turkey business, which could be learned by experience. He expected his boys to follow him into the family business and he would have been sorely disappointed if they had not. There was some anxiety on his part that the boys might become interested in another career if they followed a higher-education path. As for his daughters, Marvin accepted the conventional wisdom of the 1940s and 1950s, which offered no great expectations for women to succeed outside the home.

Of Marvin's seven children, only two graduated from college – Gary and Marilyn. Gary attended Central Michigan University at the urging of his fiancée, Joyce, who he met at Zeeland High School, and her parents. However, Gary was never too far removed from the family business during his college years. He worked at Bil Mar on many weekends and during the summers. He came back to the business after graduation from CMU, where Joyce received a teaching degree. While working at Bil Mar, he furthered his career education by attending Michigan State University's Kellogg Young Farmers Study Program and later a program for executives of family businesses at the Wharton School of Business at the University of Pennsylvania in Philadelphia. Marilyn, a Hope College graduate, pursued a teaching career in elementary education at the suggestion of a high school teacher. Marilyn, who now works part-time as an assistant chaplain at Holland Community Hospital, received her master's degree in religious education from Western Theological Seminary.

"My parents really didn't believe that further education was worth anything, especially for a woman. That was also the belief in the rest of the community at the time. They saw women as just getting married and raising children," Marilyn said. "Dad questioned me a number of times about what I thought my education was going to do for me and what I thought it was worth. That was Dad's way of getting you to think hard about your decisions and whether they had long-term value."

The DeWitt home near the plant.

The rest of the children, except Don, graduated from high school. Don quit in his senior year to work full-time at

Bil Mar when he lost his academic eligibility to play football. Jack had entertained thoughts about following in Marilyn's footsteps and becoming a teacher. But the lure of a ready-made job at Bil Mar, and the money to be made, was too strong to resist. Besides Gary and Marilyn, only Nancy sought further education after high school, receiving a degree in cosmetology.

Although Marvin had little interest in his children's academic success, he did exert considerable influence on their behavior.

*DeWitt kids among the turkeys:
(from left) Don, Marilyn, Jack, Nancy, and Gary.*

CHAPTER SIX

King of His Castle

With a booming voice and a stern gaze, Marvin did not have to resort to physical punishment for his children. His potential for wrath was enough to keep them in check. Marvin, remembering his mischievous childhood, didn't give his children much opportunity to misbehave. He ran a very orderly and disciplined household.

Even when the youngest kids were playing, they wanted to stay on the good side of their father. Merle, Nancy, and Keith used the code word "bear" to alert each other when he was nearby. They thought the code word suited their Dad's sometimes gruff personality.

"Dad very seldom hit one of us. He didn't have to hit. All he had to do was raise his voice or give you a look that would melt you down," Don said. "You never knew when he would poke his head out from someplace, so you had better not be horsing around. We would breathe a sigh of relief when he would go away on a convention for a few days. It took the pressure off us."

Marvin's method of discipline was simple. He set rules and expected his children to follow them. In hindsight, his children are glad he did.

"I think Dad gave us the best upbringing you could have," Merle said. "He could be tough at times. He put some demands and limits on us. He also taught us about taking responsibility."

Whatever the kids were doing, Marvin had no trouble keeping track of them. He knew a lot of people in the community and would keep tabs on the children through those contacts. As an eighth grader, Marilyn found out about his surveillance abilities when she skipped out of an afternoon orientation session at Zeeland High School. Marilyn and her girlfriends spent the afternoon in downtown Zeeland, instead of becoming acquainted with the school they would attend the next year. She was amazed that her father knew all about her afternoon escapade.

"Dad found out about it and let me know he didn't think what I had done was right. To him, it was like skipping school and he figured I should be there," she said. "Even though Dad didn't push us about grades or school work, he did want us to follow the rules."

He was particularly hard on his children when it came to restricting them from drinking and smoking. Marvin's father chewed tobacco and his brother Bill smoked cigarettes. No one on either side of his family drank heavily. Marvin, who neither smoke nor drank, considered them vile habits that could lead to self-destruction.

"When it comes to drinking and smoking, I was way ahead of the health community in condemning those habits as being bad. I already knew the consequences. I didn't have to have someone tell me that," he said.

He was determined, almost to the point of obsession, that those habits would not ensnare his children. None of the children drink to excess and only Don smokes, but never in front of his father. When he was younger, Don avoided smoking in front of his dad because he feared reprisal. Now he does so out of respect.

When Don was a teen-ager, Marvin took his car away for two weeks after finding cigarettes in it. He also thrashed Don one hot summer afternoon when he found out about his teen-age son trying to sneak a drink of beer. Don had talked one of the employees at the company's feed mill into buying him a couple bottles of beer, thinking it would be a good way to quench his thirst. Another employee told his dad about the sneaky transaction.

Don was driving a feed truck down a country road, with the beer in the front seat, when he spotted his father's car gaining behind him. His dad flagged him over and quizzed him about the beer. Although Don was about the same size as his dad and playing on the high school football team, Marvin picked the boy up and threw him to the ground. After his father drove off, Don shook the road dust from his clothes and decided to drink the beer out of spite. He took one swallow, then dumped the rest. He figured that drinking must be a terrible thing if the behavior drove his father to rage.

Seldom was Marvin's reaction so severe to the occasional waywardness of his children. It didn't have to be. Usually, just worrying about what their father might do and knowing their parents were disappointed in their behavior could be tougher than physical punishment – like the time Jack got caught shoplifting with three of his friends at a store in Grand Rapids. Marvin was notified by the store about the indiscretion and drove to Grand Rapids to address the matter. He settled it by chastising them in front of the store manager and letting Jack know that he wouldn't be allowed to use his car for awhile.

"Why would you do such a stupid thing. You could afford to buy a thousand pair of gloves," said Marvin, lashing out at Jack, who at the time had more than $5,000 in his bank account.

The boys apologized to store personnel and paid for the things they took. Marvin made three of them drive back in his car, while the other boy brought his car back alone. He had a reason for separating the boys.

"If I had let them all drive back together in the other car, they probably would have been smarting off. With me, they weren't laughing or joking. I had them all pretty scared that night," he said. "One thing I never did was to harangue anyone after the initial criticism. I took care of it at the time and then forgot about it. I didn't bring it up again."

However, his way of publicly criticizing could sometimes be embarrassing for the family. That was the case when he walked out on a bearded preacher's sermon at Ottawa Reformed Church. Like smokers and drinkers, bearded men were high on his list of pet peeves. His disdain for that personal fashion statement was rooted in the lax morality of the 1960s when rebellious teenagers began wearing their hair longer and growing beards, partly in protest against the Vietnam War. Marvin saw the trend as a disrespect for authority. There was also a practical side to his dislike of beards – the facial covering made it harder for him to read the true expression on someone's face, even a minister.

An unshaven student minister came to the church to assist for a short time as part of his training. Marvin immediately approached the young man and asked him if his parents approved of the beard. The minister indicated they didn't and Marvin joined in the disapproval. A few weeks later, the student gave a sermon when a group of young people in the church, including Marvin's daughter Nancy, made their profession of faith. When the minister began to speak, Marvin walked out of the church in protest. Members of his family did not agree with the public rejection of the preacher. Yet they respected him for his strong feelings.

He said the censure was a good example of his belief that a person should not bother complaining unless they are willing to confront the person who has the power to change a situation.

"There are some people who say I complain too much, but I don't complain any more than anyone else. It's just that I don't keep my complaints to myself. Most people do a lot of complaining but they don't talk to the right person. Instead, they go home and complain to their spouses and their kids," he said.

While his sons knew better than to grow beards or mustaches, some of the younger boys let their hair grow a little longer in keeping with the style then. Marvin made sure they didn't take the look to an extreme, according to Keith's wife Mary.

"When we were going together in high school, long hair was popular. Keith's dad was very strict about long hair," she said. "If

Keith's hair was too long, his dad would tell the payroll department not to issue him a check until he got it cut shorter."

The children were also taught early on about one of their father's other pet irritations – the use of vulgar language. He believed the obscene words demeaned the person who used them for expression.

By example, Marvin rarely let an obscenity slip into his conversation. So when he voiced one by mistake, the episode was not soon forgotten. One of Marvin's friends, former turkey processor Don Pike, recalled one of those few times.

"Marvin was taking me on a tour of Bil Mar in early 1980 when he got mad about a wrench laying out instead of being put back in the maintenance area. He said: 'If I have told them bastards once, I have told them a dozen times to put that wrench back.' After that, I would go out of my way to use that word in a sentence just to remind Marvin that he was also human. Although Marvin didn't like me doing that, he couldn't help grinning each time I did."

Despite Marvin's lengthy list of dos and don'ts, his looming presence was not seen as a mean streak by his children. He truly had his children's best interests at heart. Just before one Valentine's Day, Marilyn sprained her ankle at Ovens School by tripping in a rut on the ball diamond. She didn't attend classes on Valentine's Day, so at noon her father took her to the schoolhouse to pick up her cards from classmates.

He surprised the older kids with some new bikes strapped to a load of Chris-Craft sawdust used for turkey litter and to insulate the first freezer building. With the same sense of excitement and surprise, he bought the younger kids a swing set.

The kids always looked forward to his Saturday night grocery trips while his wife was taking care of the young ones. He had a list of staples to buy but always brought home candy bars and potato chips for the children. When he was away from home on a sales trip, he would call from his long-distance destination to check on the welfare of the family.

Despite his brash exterior, the children knew their father could be very sociable. He was always the center of attention, whether at a family reunion or telling a story for after-church visitors to his home. His infectious enthusiasm was a hit at church auctions where he had a habit of bidding remarkable sums for ordinary objects when the bid was too low – $150 for a loaf of homemade bread or $400 for a wax job on a car. His softer side also allowed for some good-natured teasing by the children.

On one of those occasions, he kiddingly gave Gary, Jack and Bill Jr. a hard time about the way the boys were retrieving some horses that had escaped from the barn. The bareback animals galloped out into the pasture and the three boys, never having ridden without saddles, led the horses back to the barn on foot.

"What is wrong with you kids. Don't you want to be like the Lone Ranger [a popular TV action hero of the 1950s]," said Marvin, teasing them about being timid to ride bareback.

He told the boys it was easy to mount a horse without a saddle and proceeded to show them by making a running leap onto the horse from the back. The horse moved slightly after Marvin was in the air and he dropped to the ground, shoulder first, causing a severe dislocation. To this day, the family still jokes about the crash landing and Marvin laughs right along with them.

Gary, Don, Marilyn, and Jack ride Jim, a workhorse.

Riding horses was just one of the pastimes available to the children on the farm. They were eligible to join 4-H groups that promoted farm-related educational projects. And there was a field between the house and hatchery for playing ball. In 1953, their father presented them with another means of recreation when he bought 960 feet of frontage on Lake Michigan in Port Sheldon Township.

At the waterfront site, Marvin transformed a semi-truck trailer into a make-shift cottage. He outfitted the trailer with a screen door, steps, bunks and propane-powered lights, refrigerator and stove. He built a 16-foot Chris-Craft boat, from a $350 kit, with the help of his brother-in-law Dale Bekius, who worked at the boat plant after leaving Bil Mar. Gary and Jack, who also worked on the boat, bought the kit with money they earned from raising turkeys and selling them to Bil Mar. Marvin, giving in to his perfectionist tendencies, didn't pay much attention to the directions in piecing the boat together. If the directions called for one screw in a spot, he put in two. If one coat of linseed oil was required, he layered on six.

Nancy with her 4-H horses.

The DeWitt children and their friends used the boat mostly for skiing. The kids enjoyed the lake outings, yet they never remember their father sitting down to relax there. He was always busy with an ax, saw and bulldozer, using them to clear and clean up the property. In later years, the family moved a mobile home out to the site as a replacement for the truck trailer. Marvin's daughter Nancy and her husband Bob Haveman, lived in the mobile home on the property after they were first married. They have since built their home there.

If friends of the DeWitt kids enjoyed their lakefront visits, they found the family household on 96th Avenue to be even more hospitable. The DeWitt home became a gathering spot for young people in that area.

Marvin's house was also a focal point in the life of his nephew Bill Jr., who lived only a half mile away across the field on Polk Street. Bill was close in age to Gary and Jack, and that meant they played, worked and attended school together. Bill considered them more like his brothers than cousins. Between working and hanging out with Gary and Jack, Bill spent more waking time at his uncle's house than at home. He thrilled at all the activity there and enjoyed his aunt's cooking and baking, especially the sugar and cinnamon cookies made from leftover pie dough.

"There was always something going on at Uncle Marvin's house. Aunt Jerene was always baking – homemade powdered sugar doughnuts, cinnamon rolls, pies, and pie-crust cookies. It was the place to congregate because of the farm, the activity, and all the people over there. Uncle Marvin and Aunt Jerene made you feel welcome."

Marilyn confirmed that their home was a popular place for so many young people.

"My parents' way of life, their care, their love, and their presence in some way reflects God's steadfastness. We could count on the stability of our world. Their way of life was like a rock, the way you picture God as being a firm foundation. We had a sense of belonging to a family and being cared for. Home would always be there. You didn't have to worry about that. I think our friends sensed these things," she said.

Among the visitors to the DeWitt home were girlfriends of the boys, some of whom became their wives. Occasionally they were shocked by Marvin's casual behavior. After working all day, he would shower in a second bathroom near the home's rear entrance. He had the habit of walking from that bathroom to his bedroom in his underwear or pajamas without checking to see if the kids had any friends over. Often-times they did. However, it was the kids who were embarrassed, not Marvin, who thought of himself as the king of his castle.

Keith's wife Mary was one of those visitors caught off guard by his less-than-grand entrance from the bathroom.

"It didn't matter who was visiting. He would walk out in his pajamas or underwear. He didn't seem to care," she said.

Visitors to the DeWitt home could also find themselves the object of his sense of humor. Gary's wife Joyce was the target at one mealtime before she married into the family. The DeWitts, at Marvin's urging, had coaxed her many times to eat turkey eggs, a family favorite. Raised on chicken eggs, she made it clear there was no way she could stomach eating a turkey egg. Family members were just as determined she could. They found a small one resembling an egg from a chicken and cooked it up for her. They didn't let Joyce in on the trick until she had eaten the egg and voiced satisfaction with the taste.

"That day, I not only ate a turkey egg but also some crow. They all had a good laugh over that one," she said. "The family is serious when it comes to business, yet they also know how to have fun."

Practical joking aside, it didn't take long for young visitors to the DeWitt home to know who was in charge. One young fellow was warned repeatedly by Marvin not to park his car in front of the family's garage. Marvin came home one day to see the car blocking his access to the garage again. He drove the back end of the car off the driveway and into a ditch. The lesson must have sunk in. The young man never parked in front of the garage again.

Even adult visitors weren't spared the "gospel according to Marvin," recalls Joe Cotton, a commodities broker from Boston who sold unprocessed turkey products for Bil Mar, like drumsticks and wings.

"He had his rules and you felt bound to follow them. One time, I forgot and lit up a cigarette in his kitchen," Cotton said. "He didn't say anything. Though he did give me a look that made me feel uncomfortable enough to put it out."

Overall, visitors found Marvin to be friendly. But they remained intimidated by his overpowering personality.

To this day, Jack's wife Mary is still in awe of the man's self-confidence. If Marvin doesn't understand an idea, he will question its credibility. And if he feels something is wrong, no amount of persuasion will sway him otherwise.

"Dad can be very blunt, aggressive, controlling and demanding. He seldom changes his opinion. He doesn't need to seek anyone's approval. He is truly a self-made man," she said.

Mary said he is also someone who doesn't hesitate to express his disapproval, even if it means bruising someone's feelings.

He did just that one Sunday after church, by directing his displeasure toward Mary and her use of make-up. Marvin believed it was excessive, yet he didn't come right out and say so. He preferred a more flippant approach to make his point.

"What happened to you? Did your stove blow up in your face this morning?" he asked very seriously.

Mary replied in the negative and wondered why he would ask such a question.

Marvin, with a chuckle, shot back: "I thought something like that might have happened because of all the make-up smeared around your face."

Mary was taken back by the sarcastic comment. She grew up in a family where her father was very quiet and seldom spoke his mind. But she also believes such comments from Marvin are not mean-spirited or intended to hurt.

"You always knew where you stood with him as to what he believed was right or wrong. He says what he means and means what he says. And he tends to get away with saying things like that because he does it in a kidding way, " Mary said. "Sometimes you didn't like what he said or did, though you still sought his approval. There is something about him – maybe his strength of character – that draws people like a magnet."

Bob Haveman, one of Marvin's sons-in-law and now chief financial officer at Johnson Controls [formerly Prince Corp.] in Holland, also found out how blunt he could be. Haveman, who grew up on dairy farm, was dating Nancy DeWitt and working part-time at Bil Mar while attending Davenport College. One summer, he decided to work on a construction job instead of returning to Bil Mar, much to the displeasure of Marvin who wanted to groom him for an office job at the company should he marry Nancy. Marvin told Haveman more than once that he was making a mistake by not sticking with Bil Mar while attending school. When Haveman showed up with Nancy at a Bil Mar picnic, Marvin let him know he wasn't welcome.

"Marvin was dishing out the food and as I walked up to him, he said I shouldn't be there. I wasn't part of Bil Mar anymore. His remark made me feel very uncomfortable and I am sure I resented it at the time," Haveman said. "I learned early on that he spoke what he felt; he didn't hold back. You knew where he stood. He has no hidden agendas. And you never had a reason to question his ethics. If you take the time to get to know him, you find someone who can provide you with a lot of wisdom, insight, and advice. If you listen closely to the man, you can learn a lot from him."

By getting to know Marvin, Haveman also discovered his bark was worse than his bite. He experienced the caring side first-hand when his mother was stricken with cancer during his senior year in high school. Haveman's family did not have medical insurance and his father had to sell the dairy cows to pay the mounting treatment bills. On a visit to the DeWitt household, when Marvin was present, Haveman tearfully related his concern about his family's financial situation. Not long after, Haveman's father was offered a job at Bil Mar's feed mill.

"From the first time I met him, I always viewed Marvin as being a very dominant person, very action-oriented, a true entrepreneur. He was sometimes loud and gruff, like any other self-starter," Haveman said. "He also has a sensitive side, and I saw that the day I broke down and cried when telling the DeWitts about my family's misfortune. I felt that Marvin was there to listen and understand."

Joyce DeWitt, Gary's wife, was also struck by the sensitivity he could show toward family members. Pregnant with her first child, Joyce became very ill. Marvin wondered if the illness had something

DeWitt family portrait: From left, back row: Don, Marilyn, Nancy, Gary and Jack. Front row: Jerene, Merle, Keith, and Marvin.

to do with the well water pumped into a mobile home next to the hatchery, where Gary and Joyce lived after they were first married. He had the water tested for contamination, although no problem was detected.

Marvin seldom revealed his soft side when it came to instilling work habits in his children. Growing up on a turkey farm, the DeWitt children found work to be as natural as leisure time was to city kids. The work ethic was not only a part their genetic make-up. Their father, always seeming to be in motion, also led the way by illustration. A demanding sort, he did not tolerate idleness if someone was supposed to be working. When their father was around, the children always felt they had to be doing something, even when their chores were done.

"I can remember doing some reading after I finished my chores one time," Marilyn said. "When I saw him coming into the driveway, I went out to the kitchen and found something to do. I always felt as if I should be doing something when he was around. That is how ingrained the work ethic was in us. The message from Dad was 'you aren't worth much, if you are not working at something.'"

Keith still remembers his father's top work commandment: do it right the first time, or don't bother doing it at all. And his father had subtle ways of reminding his youngsters of that edict. At the age of 10, Keith was sweeping the garage floor by pulling the broom toward him. His father walked by and asked the youngster what kind of broom he was using. As Keith replied "push broom," he instantly saw the error of his ways and began to use the broom as intended.

"I developed a strong respect for what he knows and what he stands for, and that carries on to this day," Keith said. "Even now, in my early 40s, I still wonder what Dad is going to think. I still want to do the right thing by him, make the right decision."

For Jack, his father was the best possible role model for developing a work ethic.

"Dad was always a good guy to work with. He could work twice as hard as anyone else. He showed us how to work," Jack said. "Doing by example is still the best way of teaching. Dad was never one to tell you to go out and do something that he wouldn't do."

Marvin didn't reserve his high work expectations only for his children. Even future son-in-law Tom Norman was given a taste of his strict work ethic.

On his first visit to the DeWitt home, Marvin put Norman to work shortly after his arrival. After Marilyn introduced her fiancé, Marvin said "You can't just sit around and do nothing while you are here" and then led him to where the DeWitts were working on a new freezer addition to the plant.

Although he grilled the work ethic into all his children, only the boys were encouraged to follow their father into the family business. In the male-dominated business world of the 1950s, daughters did not receive the same encouragement as sons to excel at a career.

Marvin interested his boys in the business at an early age. He expected them to learn different facets of the operation long before they moved into management positions. Even the early jobs, he reasoned, would teach his offspring practical business experience and accountability.

Keith (shirtless), Merle and Nancy load turkeys.

"I gave them jobs early on. I wanted them to learn responsibility and know they would be rewarded if they worked hard. It was a good learning process. I gave them room to make their own decisions, as long as what they were doing worked," Marvin said. "I wanted them to be strong-willed and have the ability to think for themselves. I wanted them to be leaders, instead of followers. I wanted them to be competitive, even among themselves. Then they would always give their best effort."

They started, at the age of 7, in the hatchery, where the busy period was from February through June. At a young age, another one of their chores during the fall processing season was to spread the feathers and innards on the fields so the material could decompose. As they grew older, the youngsters were expected to participate in the winter breeding operation, using artificial insemination. In the summer, they tended to turkeys on the family's outdoor range and worked in the farm fields where feed crops were planted. In the fall, they eviscerated turkeys and cleaned equipment in the processing plant.

Marvin started paying his children 60 cents an hour for company-related work when they turned 14. That let them know there would be a reward for a job well done. They were allowed to earn chore-related money even before that age, if they wanted to raise their own turkeys and sell them to Bil Mar. Most of the children – even Nancy, who preferred farm chores to working in the house – took advantage of the opportunity. Gary, at 12, and Jack, at 9, started raising turkeys in 1953. They used $350 from their first flock of 300 turkeys to buy the Chris-Craft boat kit. The brothers raised turkeys until they were in their early 20s, tending more than 5,000 at one point.

As the boys grew older, they also started making long-distance deliveries of poults and dressed turkeys to Chicago, Detroit, Pittsburgh, Milwaukee and Dayton. They would work all day and then drive at night, staying at their destination only a few hours to unload before heading home. To stay awake, they sometimes popped the mild, over-the-counter stimulant No-Doze. Their only regret about farm chores is that their regularity prevented them from participating in most organized sports at school.

"It seems like when all of my friends were out goofing off, I was doing chores. We were always taking care of animals, and not just turkeys. We also had cattle and horses, and those types of chores had to be taken care of before and after school," Gary said. "When it came to chores, dad could be very demanding and would chew you out if a mistake was made. You knew what your boundaries were with him. You knew how you were expected to behave. He gave instructions on what to do, yet he gave you latitude on how you could accomplish the task – like a dog on a long chain. We worked hard but were always rewarded. Dad was generous when it came to that."

While none of the girls in either Marvin's or Bill's family joined the business, all seven boys ended up working for their fathers. They included Marvin's boys, Gary, Jack, Don, Merle, and Keith, and Bill's sons, Bill Jr. and Ray. Having so many family members involved in the business was one of the reasons Bil Mar was able to make smooth transitions from one growth stage to the next, such as the construction of a plant dedicated to processing.

Processing turkey in the first plant.

CHAPTER SEVEN

BUILDING A PLANT

By 1958, Marvin was itching to push the business to the next productivity level by constructing a modern processing plant.

For 20 years each fall, the DeWitts had processed their turkeys in any available space they could find in several buildings on the farm. That method was no longer economical when the volume of turkeys increased.

But Marvin not only wanted to build a new processing plant that would accommodate the growing business. He also wanted its construction to conform with tougher processing standards being drafted by the United States Department of Agriculture (USDA). The proposed rules required the federal inspection of processing plants that were selling meat across state lines. When the new processing plant was built, the DeWitts were selling oven-ready turkeys, both fresh and frozen, mostly to retail markets in a number of states.

The DeWitts, with the help of a construction crew, built the plant in 10 weeks, working from 5 a.m. to 10 p.m. every day except Sunday. Everyone in the two families pitched in where they could. Gary, Bill Jr. and Jack – all strapping teenagers – worked full-time on the project. Even Bill Sr.'s girls, Julia and Shirley, and Marvin's daughter Marilyn painted rafters before they went up. To no one's surprise, Marvin's involvement in the project went deeper than anyone else. Like the house he built for his family in 1949, he drew up the rough plans for the first dressing plant. He bought a welding machine and most days was out on the construction site before the regular construction crew arrived. He also operated construction equipment.

Frank DeWind was one of the workers on the construction crew under the direction of Square Deal Construction in Borculo. DeWind, who later joined Bil Mar in 1971 as maintenance supervisor, remembered Marvin wasting no time on the job site.

"Marvin was somewhat of a pusher and he wasn't afraid to push himself or his own children as hard as anyone else. Marvin hauled the wheelbarrow and tossed blocks like everyone else," DeWind said. "After we put up the new building, Marvin said he expected the business to grow 10-fold. At the time, that sounded impossible to me. I just grinned when he said it. Yet his predictions all came true. It may have taken a year or two longer than he anticipated, but it did happen. When he said something, he meant it. He wasn't wishy-washy about anything."

Racing to get the plant built before the killing season started was not without mishap. Bill Sr. was seriously injured while using a tractor bucket to lift some plywood to the plant roof. The load shifted in the wind and the boards crashed onto the tractor. Bill was hurt when he jumped off the tractor to avoid being hit by the load of boards. He fell against a plow hooked up to the tractor and broke his pelvis, putting him out of commission the rest of the summer.

His son Bill Jr. escaped serious injury while helping to tear down the old homestead barn, in which the first turkeys were raised. He was among a group using sledge hammers to knock down supporting timbers when the second floor caved in on him. He was saved when his body ended up between the two-by-six floor joists instead of being crushed by them.

The plant was completed Sept. 20, about two weeks after the killing season normally commenced. The new plant joined the brooder house, battery room, hatchery and two-story quonset barn. Marvin's mother was proud of her sons when the dressing plant went up. By the time of her death, a year later in the fall of 1959, she no longer had any qualms about whether they would succeed.

Marvin's decision to move ahead with the new processing plant was yet another example of his foresight in running the business.

The turkey business had boomed throughout the 1950s. The boom ended in 1960 with a nation-wide production peak of 127 million birds, a total surpassing consumer demand. The overproduction led to a drop in prices and a crash in the industry, forcing many small producers out of business. However, the squeeze on smaller producers went beyond market prices. The USDA finally issued the proposed inspection rules, which increased the cost of processing. It was a move Marvin had anticipated two years earlier when he constructed the processing plant.

The opening of a processing plant supervised by the USDA marked the first time in Bil Mar's history that someone outside the DeWitt family circle would have a say in the day-to-day business operation. The USDA's stated mission is to insure that products are wholesome, disease-free and unadulterated. On-site USDA inspectors had the right to reject an entire turkey or a part of the bird due to disease, injury, or any irregularity. They also had the power to shut down the operation based on their interpretation of agency regulations.

Marvin knew the USDA's presence was necessary for the growth of the business. Given his independent nature, he wasn't going to bow before every interpretation. If a situation presented a clear cut case of right or wrong, he chose the correct way. If there was a gray area, due to the ambiguity of a regulation, his decision was based on how the company could do something more efficient and economical without compromising product quality.

"The USDA regulations were good at first. They brought some consistency to everyone who was in the business. Then the government kept adding rules for every aspect of the operation, well beyond the original intent of the law. When we opened the plant, the USDA rule book was 12 pages long. Now there are books full of regulations and some of them are petty. Our whole operation was set up to give the customer the best product when they needed it. The USDA regulations sometimes interfered with that," Marvin said. "The USDA had the power to shut down the plant, and I sometimes resented that. Some of the inspectors went by the letter of the law, even when common sense said they shouldn't. When that happened, we weren't afraid to dispute USDA interpretation of regulations. I had plenty of nose-to-nose arguments with inspectors over their rulings. And if I really disagreed with something, I took it all the way to the United States Secretary of Agriculture.

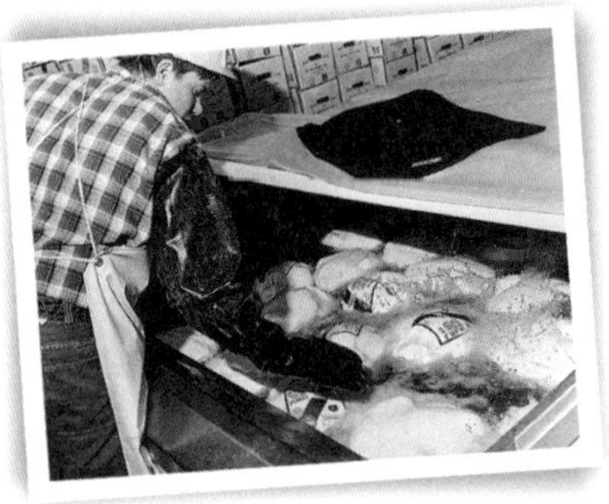
Turkeys are frozen in tank full of brine water.

"I started a business in the days when there wasn't much interference from government agencies. I was brought up a certain way and I ran my business according to those principles. Others didn't, and that is where the regulations come from. Good, honest operators like us also had to follow the same rules. That is something I had to learn to accept. It wasn't easy because they were always changing the rules. My feathers could get ruffled pretty easily. I have always been quick on the draw and quick-tempered."

Cornelius "Casey" Staal was one of the USDA inspectors in Marvin's line of fire. Although Bil Mar had a nationwide reputation for being combative with the USDA, he requested transfer from a Plainwell packing plant to Borculo in 1974. He wanted the challenge of working at a plant that did more complex processing. Staal stayed at Bil Mar for 20 years, developing a relationship of trust and mutual respect with the DeWitts. Staal was not easily intimidated. He also wasn't as hard-nosed as some of his fellow inspectors.

Staal was convinced that the DeWitts wanted to manufacture a product of the highest quality. Yet they didn't always agree with the USDA on the best way to achieve that goal. When the two sides did disagree, Staal said, the DeWitts could be trusted to do their best to comply once there was no other recourse. The USDA agreed with Staal's assessment of the family's trustworthiness in the the early 1980s, when Bil Mar was the largest processor in the poultry industry to be approved for the agency's voluntary Total Quality Control program. Under the USDA-monitored program, a company was allowed to assume full responsibility for inspection by creating its own quality-control team.

"Every time the USDA tried to push something new on the DeWitts, the family went straight to the top of the bureaucratic chain in Washington, D. C., to complain. They were a tough bunch to deal with. However, when they decided to ignore a directive, they were blatant about it. They didn't try to hide or cover up their actions," Staal said. "I attempted to reason with them to solve their problems. Though many times, they still fought to get their own way. I could understand their frustration over the growing number of regulations. The way the DeWitts saw it, every new USDA rule was just another way the government was interfering in their business. What they didn't understand is that every rule that came through had been violated in principle somewhere in the food-processing industry. Despite the combativeness, I liked Marvin and his sons. They had their reasons for what they did. They weren't just trying to be ornery. I had many opportunities to transfer elsewhere, but I think I would have been bored to death. At Bil Mar, there was never a dull moment."

Bil Mar's construction of the processing plant also opened the door to other regulatory scrutiny, like the monitoring of waste-water discharge.

In the earliest days of the business, the company ran the waste water from the processing operation onto the ground and it seeped into Pigeon Creek. The natural run-off allowed most of the waste to decompose in the ground. As the business grew, Bil Mar was required by the Michigan Department of Natural Resources to develop a series of lagoons to allow more elaborate filtration of the waste water before it was discharged into the creek. In the first lagoon, equipped with a water-churning aerator, most solids settled out. The water was then pumped into a second holding lagoon. There it was further filtered through seepage into the ground before discharge into the creek. The company was allowed to spray some of the waste water from the second lagoon for irrigation on surrounding cornfields.

Because of the waste-water system's erratic process, Bil Mar was cited a number of times by the DNR for not operating within the limits of its discharge permit. Most times the citation regarded overflow of the lagoons. Usually an overflow occurred during times of heavy rainfall. The first lagoon could also become plugged with excess turkey debris. That is why Marvin was so adamant about clean-up crews picking up bits of meat and stray feathers with a shovel for disposal in waste containers instead of hosing the waste off the floor into the sewage drain.

One time, Marvin bumped heads with the DNR when he attempted to stop waste water from running out of the second lagoon and into the creek during a rainstorm. He was using a bulldozer to build a higher dike around the lagoon when the machine slipped into the lagoon. To get the bulldozer out, he had to empty waste water into the creek. For his unsuccessful effort, Bil Mar was fined $25,000 by the DNR.

"As the business grew, regulations changed and we did our best to change with them. We didn't go out of our way to cause pollution problems. I always tried to do the right thing," Marvin said. "I am not saying I never made any mistakes or didn't cause any problems. When there was a problem, I tried to work with the DNR one-on-one through my elective representative to reach a compromise."

Operating a plant devoted to processing presented Marvin with challenges beyond just having to contend with governmental regulations. He also had to find enough workers to fill all the new positions required by the growing operation. Before the plant was opened, Bil Mar had relied on family, friends and neighbors to handle the chores associated with the turkey business.

Recruiting production workers outside that tight circle would not be easy. The cold and wet conditions necessary to maintain a high degree of sanitation in a food plant were not attractive to many production workers.

Like the Heinz pickle plant in Holland, Bil Mar first recruited outside workers from among Hispanic migrants working at farms in the area. The migrants, some of them from Puerto Rico, knew of others in their homeland anxious to work in this country. Bil Mar initially hired more than 100 temporary workers from that country by sending them plane tickets. The DeWitts would pick them up in Detroit and then transport them with an old school bus to Borculo. After the busiest part of the processing season ended, they would go back to their homeland.

To house the seasonal workers, Bil Mar converted the battery-coop building into a labor camp – 10 rooms, with four beds to a room, gas burners for cooking, and portable shower stalls. Bil Mar also set up some bunk beds in the office/hatchery building. The DeWitts used the school bus to take the seasonal workers grocery shopping on Friday and Saturday nights. Weekend activity in the seasonal camp could become a little like the old Wild West, with knife and gun fights. A camp resident, scared of getting mad and hurting someone after he started drinking, once gave Jack his pistol.

In the late 1960s, the search for seasonal workers led Marvin on a long-distance journey to Puerto Rico that almost landed him in jail. Marvin headed for Puerto Rico, not knowing he needed a permit to solicit workers. In one Puerto Rican town, Marvin asked a shopkeeper where he could find a certain individual who could put him in contact with prospective workers. After Marvin left, the store owner contacted police who began looking for him. Marvin, through one of his contacts in the country, heard the police were in pursuit and he decided to leave the country instead of hassling with the Puerto Rican legal system. He was on the way to the airport when police nabbed him in a taxi held up by a funeral procession. Marvin was detained until he could appear before a judge to pay for the permit, which he used to legally solicit workers.

Bil Mar also worked with employment recruiters in Texas. Bill Sr. made a few worker expeditions to southern Texas but with little success. The prospective employees were always eager to get on the plane leaving El Paso. However, along each airport stopover on the way back to Michigan, most of them disappeared.

As more illegal immigrants came to the U.S., they heard from friends and relatives in the area that Bil Mar needed employees. In the 1960s, Bil Mar did not have a human resources department. The hiring chores were left up to Marvin, Gary and Jack. At that time, immigration rules did not prohibit hiring illegal aliens. The only time a business could be prosecuted is if company officials were suspected of assisting their illegal entry. Employers were not required to prove whether an employee was in this country legally, and prospective employees did not have to show proof of citizenship to secure a job. The prospective employees only had to present a green card, proof of an alien's admission for permanent U.S. residency. Sometimes the cards were phony. The law left it up to the government to determine whether someone was an illegal alien. And that task fell to the U.S. Border Patrol, which conducted a number of surprise raids at Bil Mar in search of illegal immigrants. Usually word about the presence of agents in the plant spread quickly among the workers, prompting illegal immigrants to hide in the sprawling building or head out the back door into the cornfields. Frustrated with such evasion, the border patrol one time arrived in force, along with deputies from the Ottawa County Sheriff's Department, and surrounded the plant. They caught a number of illegal workers who were attempting to flee and arrested Jack DeWitt, who was plant manager. He was accused of aiding the escape of illegals and obstructing the work of the border patrol. He was exonerated of all charges in a U.S. District Court hearing in Grand Rapids.

"We were desperate for workers back then. If they fell through the door, I would pick them up. And if they could stand on their feet for awhile, I would hire them. We didn't ask a lot of questions. We let them prove themselves, " Marvin said about Bil Mar taking advantage of the lax immigration laws.

Workers were not only needed for the processing plant. Extra hands were also required for outdoor turkey raising. Up until the late-1960s, when the first environmentally controlled grow-out buildings were constructed, the turkeys were only raised outdoors on range land. With that process, the turkeys were moved outdoors to fenced enclosures after the eight-week brooding period.

In the earliest days of the business, the range was on the DeWitt homestead property. In the 1950s, with the business continuing to grow, Marvin started scouting the area for more range land. He heard that the federal government was going to release hilly land it had acquired on 136th Avenue, about five miles from the DeWitt farm. Marvin purchased his first 120 acres of range land from the federal government by trading some property he acquired through a bankruptcy sale. Over the years, Marvin acquired more than 2,000 acres of property, most of it in Olive Township, by swapping land with the federal government. Today, the DeWitt family is one of the largest landowners in Ottawa County.

Joe Cotton, a broker of Bil Mar products, said Marvin never missed an opportunity to buy land, even in times of someone's grief.

"One time, I went with him to make what I thought was just going to be a condolence call on a widow," Cotton said. "Part of the visit was for that reason but Marvin was also interested in buying the family's property. Before we left, he was taking out his checkbook. Marvin gained something by buying the property and the woman profited by selling it at a time when she needed extra money."

Bil Mar van among the range turkeys.

Growing the birds in the sand hills, as the range land is referred to by the DeWitts, was arduous work. The turkey fences had to be moved every two weeks after the ground became saturated with manure. Feed, and even water in the earliest days, had to be transported to the hills. At Bill's farm, the brothers put an 800-gallon tank in a tree and pumped water out of his well into the container. From the overhead tank, they filled a 500-to-600-gallon water wagon. That was taken to the hills, where it was dumped into 100-gallon drinkers. The tanks were turned upside down and the water flowed by gravity into troughs. The chore was made easier in later years when the DeWitts used a gasoline engine to pump water out of the Pigeon River to fill the water wagon in the hills. After electricity was run out to the hills, pumps drew water from the creek into the tank truck. Later, they dug a well on the property and water was pumped through plastic piping to automatic watering fountains.

The DeWitts bought prepared feed from a variety of sources in the earlier days of the operation. The feed was a mixture of corn, soy bean meal, bone meal and animal fat. They also made some feed on-site in a small mill attached to a brooder house. In 1961, they expanded the on-site feed-making operation by converting an old storage building into a mill. That on-site feed mill was abandoned in 1966 for a more automated system in the reconverted Harlem feed mill on U.S. 31, north of Holland, at Van Buren Street. Purchased by Bil Mar in 1965, the new mill site was alongside a rail siding that allowed hopper delivery of bulk ingredients, including the corn needed to supplement the grain grown on company farms. Bil Mar's feed mill operation was supervised by Marvin's son Don.

Bil Mar automates the Harlem feed mill on U.S. 31.

Even with an automated mill operation, the feed still had to be hauled out to the hills until range rearing was phased out in favor of environmentally controlled grow-out barns. In the earliest days, feed was transported by wagon in 100-pounds bags. To fill the feed trough, a worker walked alongside with an open bag balanced on his hip. Later, the DeWitts rigged up an auger-equipped grain-avator on the back of a truck to dump feed into larger range feeders, each holding 2,000 pounds.

Always a stickler for detail, Marvin would inspect the range operation on Sundays and then return on Monday mornings to let his employees know what they were doing wrong. He would adhere to the same fault-finding inspection routine after the processing plant was built.

"One thing that really stood out in my mind is that dad tried to be the best he could at whatever he did," Gary said. "That was the theme of operation for the whole company – we had to have the best quality. Dad demanded quality and looked out for the small things that went into that. On Sundays, he would go out to the hills to check the turkeys. On Monday morning, he would start butt-chewing, telling the help what he had seen wrong – from the spilling of feed on the ground to not adjusting the water flow properly."

Turkeys are fed on the range.

One of many rumors about Marvin's hard-nosed operation of the business was inspired by range rearing. Many employees in the processing plant believed that Marvin took the seats off all the company's tractors because he didn't want farm workers getting too comfortable. The truth only applied to the tractor used in the hills, where workers were constantly getting on and off the machine as part of their duties. Marvin believed taking the seat off was prudent. It only got in the way of a job that didn't require much sitting.

Besides the labor intensity of range rearing, the DeWitts had to cope with problems related to weather, predators, theft and disease. There was also the occasional panic attack among the birds caused by a low flying airplane, which they perceived as a large hawk. To escape the flying intruder, the birds would pile up in the corner of an enclosure trying to escape. The result was mass suffocation.

Egbert "Eg" Kuyers, the second full-time employee at Bil Mar, has no trouble remembering the worst storm in the hills. It was late fall in the early 1950s, while Marvin, Bill Sr., and Kuyers were attending a turkey-grower meeting in Saginaw, on the east side of the state. They left Saginaw in a howling snowstorm, knowing they were in danger of losing most of the flock on the range to freezing winds. Once back at the farm, it took them nearly a half hour to reach the hills, a trip that would normally take about 10 minutes. Some turkeys took refuge in the woods and they were withstanding the storm's onslaught. Many others were near the point of freezing. Bil Mar workers had to transport the birds from the range back to the safety of the barns. To accomplish the task, they worked from 7 a.m. the day the brothers returned from the convention to 4 a.m. the next day – nearly 24 hours straight. They still lost 1,500 turkeys. And it wasn't only a snowstorm that could decimate a flock. Near-freezing rains could take a share of birds, which lost body insulation when their feathers were soaked.

Predators also caused range loses. There were problems with roaming dogs, and keen-eyed owls and hawks. Humans would also find their way up to the hills to snatch a few turkeys. In one instance, a couple hundred birds weren't stolen but killed as a cruel prank. The three culprits were caught months later when an off-duty sheriff's deputy overheard them bragging about the vicious deed at a tavern. They were ordered by a judge to work for Bil Mar to pay off the debt. To thwart human predators, Marvin regularly patrolled the hills and also put down spiked 2-x-6 boards along the main trails as weekend deterrents.

When the Bil Mar crew wasn't battling Mother Nature and predators, they had to be vigilant for diseases – common among turkey flocks from the time they enter the brooder coops. Turkeys are susceptible to more than a dozen diseases, along with internal and external parasites such as worms, lice, mites, fleas and ticks. Marvin didn't confine his concern about poultry diseases to his flocks. He was more than willing to share what he knew about disease problems with agricultural industry groups, including chicken growers. One time, he paid for blood tests of his flocks as a way to learn more about a disease fatal to chickens yet harmlessly carried by turkeys.

Caused by a bacterium, fowl cholera was the disease the turkey growers feared most. The disease is highly infectious, causing the birds to become sick rapidly. They usually die without showing any symptoms. The disease produces hemorrhages on the surface of the heart, lungs, intestines, or in the fatty tissue. The birds may also have swollen livers. It was a cholera epidemic in the late-1960s, along with a push to year-round slaughtering and processing, that cinched the decision by the DeWitts to begin building climate-controlled grow-out barns. Minnesota turkey growers were the first to use the windowless houses for the finishing process.

Rearing birds in confinement has several advantages over the range – protection against predators, thefts, adverse weather conditions, and losses from soil-borne diseases. More birds can also be raised in a smaller area, lowering labor costs and acreage requirements. Raising them inside eventually allowed the industry to enter a year-round production cycle not determined by weather conditions.

Marvin had the first growing houses constructed in 1967. Rearing turkeys in the hills was phased out by 1988.

In the mid-1970s, Marvin heard about turkey farmers using even more efficient grow-out barns in Minnesota, and he decided to take a look for himself in the middle of winter.

Going along for the ride was a small caravan of Bil Mar associates in three cars, including Jacob "Jake" Voetberg, the farm manager.

Marvin's entourage ran into a blinding snowstorm just outside of Chicago.

However, he encouraged the group to forge ahead, having already reserved motel rooms in Minnesota. If they didn't go on, he would have lost the money paid in advance for that first night of lodging, a prospect that did not sit well with his frugal nature. As weather reports told of temperatures dropping to 30-degrees below zero, some members of the group expressed concern. Voetberg, riding in the same car as Marvin, attempted to assure the others by pointing to him as their leader and navigator.

"I told them not to worry. Moses was leading the way and he would get us to the Promised Land," Voetberg said.

Moses was a nickname Voetberg coined when Marvin vented his

ire at the temperamental hatchery incubators by exclaiming "Holy Moses," instead of swearing. Marvin didn't like the nickname at first. He thought it might be poking fun at a Biblical figure. Though he knew the name was going to stick when one of his nephews slipped and called him "Uncle Moses."

Finishing turkeys indoors didn't eliminate all the problems for a turkey grower. There were still diseases to battle. And, like the brooder houses, the grow-out barns were subject to damage from high winds and heavy snow. Both types of barns could also be affected by electrical failures that shut off ventilation fans. One such failure in a grow-out barn resulted in the suffocation of 10,000 turkeys and led to the installation of an alarm system that alerted farm employees at their homes of a power outage. In later years, the fans in the grow-out barns were replaced by a system of spontaneous ventilation using natural air flow in and out of the barns.

Setbacks in the turkey business weren't confined to the birds. Marvin was dealt his first major financial difficulty in the business – denial of a bank loan – when he sought money to pay contractors who had built some brooder houses. The DeWitts never had much money in their pockets during their many expansion phases. They did have net worth and a good credit history by never falling behind in their bank payments. And that is how they were able to borrow the money needed to continually expand the business.

"I was a strong advocate of paying the bills on time and not borrowing money unless we needed it. Today, many businesses borrow a little bit more than what they need. We tended to run our business more conservatively," Marvin said about his pay-as-you-go philosophy.

Paying the company's bills was on Marvin's mind in the early 1960s when he headed to First Michigan Bank & Trust Co. [later FMB-First Michigan Bank, now Huntington Banks] in Zeeland, expecting to obtain a loan like he had so many times before.

The bank had been cautioning him to put the company's books in order by providing a more detailed accounting of Bil Mar's various operations. At the time, the company only employed the services of a local bookkeeper. Marvin hadn't heeded the bank's advice. He had been too busy overseeing and promoting the business. He believed his reputation as a good credit risk would suffice for one more loan. It didn't.

A new loan officer, unfamiliar with the DeWitts' operation or first-rate business reputation, denied the request based on the casual accounting procedures. Dejected, Marvin left the bank vowing never to do business there again. As he was leaving the bank, another employee suggested to him that he consider doing business with his former employer, Old Kent Bank. After seeking counsel of his trusted friend and advisor, Dr. Carl Hoyt, a district agricultural agent for MSU's Cooperative Extension Service, he approached Old Kent about a loan. The bank agreed to set up a financial package, if he would enact more sophisticated accounting methods. Bil Mar hired the CPA firm of Touche, Ross & Co. [now DeLoitte & Touche] to produce audited financial statements.

Marvin and Dr. Carl Hoyt, a poultry specialist from Michigan State University, look over a load of frozen drumsticks destined for Germany.

Phil Vanden Berge, a one-time partner at Touche, Ross who became chief financial officer at Bil Mar, was involved in that early auditing. He remembers meetings at Bil Mar with a very nonchalant Marvin, who was not above whacking flies with a flyswatter in the middle of a business discussion.

"In the earlier days of the business, Marvin's practice was that he went to the bank in Zeeland and secured another loan when he ran out of cash. It worked because they always knew he had receivables. As the business began to grow, the bank no longer saw that as enough rationale to approve a loan," Vanden Berge said about the bank rejecting Marvin. "From a financial standpoint, the business was very fragmented with its various farming operations. The bank told Marvin he needed to develop a more formal relationship with them so they would know exactly what he had for collateral. He had always conducted his business with the bank on a handshake. He had been given a loan based on the strength of his character. The bank wanted to base a loan approval strictly from financial statements. And he was unable to provide them."

Despite setbacks, the business kept growing in Marvin's image – fast and furious.

He didn't waste a lot of time making or sharing decisions. There was no hand-wringing and gnashing of teeth. A realist, he is one of those rare individuals who truly lives in the present. He doesn't seem to worry about the future and he doesn't look back with any regrets. Marvin accepted things for what they were when there was nothing he could do to change the outcome. On the other hand, nothing stood in his way if Marvin perceived he could influence the result.

Bil Mar employees load frozen turkey parts for train delivery.

Friends recounted an incident that says a lot about his willingness to concede the inevitable. One of the family's horses broke out of a fenced-in area and was run over by a car on 96th Avenue. Marvin knew he couldn't save the animal, which had suffered severe injuries. He got a rifle, put the animal out of its misery with a single shot, and hauled the carcass away with a tractor for burial. He showed no emotion, no remorse. He knew what had to be done and he did it. In his mind, there was no sense making a big thing out of what happened. There was nothing anyone could do to reverse the situation.

His former minister, the Rev. Mike Van Buren, recalled an event that illustrates Marvin's tenacity to alter the course of events, when possible. After the new Ottawa Reformed Church was built, the old structure was torn down and piled in the parking lot. One of the congregation members was contracted to salvage what he could from the rubble and then haul the rest away. In Marvin's estimation, the clean-up process seemed to take forever. The longer the process took, the more irate Marvin became. The pile not only took up valuable space in the parking lot, according to Marvin. The mess also detracted from the new church. He talked to the church member about speeding up the salvage job but the slow pace continued. No longer willing to accept such procrastination, Marvin showed up one night at the church lot with a bulldozer and a truck to haul the pile away.

"There comes a time when you just have to step in and finish the job. I don't like things that are left unfinished. I have always been a person that sees a problem and wants to fix it immediately," Marvin said.

He ran the business with the same resolve. He got an idea. Talked to Bill. And then went to the bank to arrange a loan. Their wives were always updated on the business operation because they also had to sign their names to the bank loans. However, the decision to do something had already been made. When it came to running the business, Marvin skirted the democratic niceties.

And that included the biggest decisions affecting the company, like the DeWitts' entry into further processing – cutting the bird into boneless pieces and cooking the meat to manufacture an assortment of turkey products. Of all the decisions in the company's history, further processing was the one that transformed Bil Mar into a national player in the turkey-processing business by creating a year-round operation.

Further-processed turkey products.

CHAPTER EIGHT

THE BIRTH OF BIL MAR FOODS

Marvin's decision to enter the further-processing market followed a routine visit in 1960 to one of his customers – Watson Turkey Products in Blackport, N. J.

At the time, the DeWitts were selling poults to farmers, and fresh and frozen oven-ready turkeys to restaurants, stores, hotels, food distributors, and other processors, like Watson's. Bil Mar also sold frozen holiday gift turkeys to businesses.

What Marvin saw at Watson's was an eye-opener – a turkey deboning and roasting operation. Only one other processor in the nation was cooking turkey, Northwestern Turkey Products in Philadelphia.

Marvin was so intrigued by the process that he immediately talked to company owner, Irv Watson, about a deal. Marvin proposed paying Watson a licensing fee in exchange for allowing Bil Mar to use the process. Marvin was willing to give Watson 5 percent of the net income for the total number of turkeys Bil Mar processed using the cooking technique. Watson insisted on 5 percent of the gross income.

Marvin left New Jersey without an agreement, yet he was determined to move Bil Mar into that next stage of processing. He saw further processing as a way to increase turkey production by being able to offer parts of the bird on a more year-round basis – like the pork and beef industries – instead of just during the Thanksgiving and Christmas holidays when whole birds were the staple. The attraction of a further-processed product for consumers would be its year-round availability and cooking convenience.

In the Midwest, Marvin had always been on the cutting edge in the turkey business. He was the first to freeze turkeys, both conventionally and with a quick-freeze method that used brine water to keep whole turkeys from turning red. He was one of the first processors to hatch his own turkeys and operate an on-site feed mill. Seeing how further processing was taking off out East, he wanted to introduce that method in the Midwest.

He couldn't do it without Watson's help, at least indirectly. In January, 1961, he paid a $10,000 fee to one of Watson's employees, Joe Belinski, to show the DeWitts how to accomplish further processing. Talking Belinski into revealing the cooking process was another example of Marvin's ability to find knowledgeable people who could teach him how to advance his business. He never claimed to have all the answers about the turkey business. However, he was willing to pay the price for the information.

While Watson might have admired Marvin's ability to persuade people, he didn't appreciate that skill when it came to one of his trade secrets. Hearing about Marvin's ploy after Belinski arrived at Bil Mar, the incensed Watson took a plane to Grand Rapids and drove out to the plant in Olive Township. He stormed into the building and chewed out Belinski before leaving in a huff. Subsequently, Belinski was fired and he went back to Northwestern, owned by his cousin. Ironically, Watson had hired Belinski away from Northwestern to teach him the further-processing technique. In turn, Belinski's cousin learned the method of further-processing turkey while serving as a cook in the Navy. Northwestern became part of Jerome Foods, of Barron Wis., which is still a major player in today's turkey industry.

Jerome makes deli and food-service products, and is best known at the retail level for fresh turkey parts sold under the "The Turkey Store" brand. Watson's, never pushing further processing as hard as Bil Mar, eventually went out of business.

When Marvin decided to go with an idea, like further processing, other members of the family and his employees solidly backed him. They trusted him to lead the company in the right direction because of his gift for extraordinary common sense.

Gary and Marvin promote further-processed products at trade show.

"Marvin was shrewd in that he knew a good idea when he saw one and knew how to adapt it to his operation. He never claimed to be the smartest person in the world. He was smart enough to know when something would work for him," said Bob Haveman, one of Marvin's sons-in-law. "He also asked a lot of questions about things he didn't understand. He was willing to talk to different people, learn from them, and put what he learned into practice. His extremely good common sense, coupled with a willingness to work hard and take chances, is what really propelled him to entrepreneurial success. A lot of people work hard and have common sense, though they never achieve what Marvin did. They simply are not risk takers. They stay in a rut and never change because they lack the third component necessary to be a true entrepreneur."

Marvin agreed that his willingness to take risks was key to the continued success of the business.

"I really believe that when its all boiled down, our competitors didn't change with the times. Had we not gone to further processing, we would have been out of business like so many other growers who minimally processed. The turkey business changed, and we changed with it. We went from New York-dressed to oven-ready frozen to further processing. We went from serving a holiday market to serving a year-round market," Marvin said. "The key to business success is the right timing for the right product. We did that enough times to be successful. That is not to say all of our product ideas were original. Someone was already roasting turkey before we did. We just improved on the idea.

"I took things as they came while running the business. When a problem would occur, I saw it as a challenge to overcome. When an opportunity would arise, I grabbed hold and ran with it. I never backed away from anything, if I believed it would succeed. I was blessed with a natural ability to look at something and know whether to take a chance on it. To me, that is the definition of an entrepreneur."

Further processing set Bil Mar apart from the hundreds of other processors in the nation. Bil Mar was the third company in the country to follow through on further processing, behind Northwestern and Watson's, and the first further processor to run a fully integrated operation that also hatched and grew turkeys. In the early 1950s, there were were nearly a dozen turkey-processing plants in Michigan. They included several in the Detroit area; one each in Alma, Breckenridge, and Hamilton; and three in Zeeland – Bil Mar, Central Farms, and Zeeland Poultry Processing Co. owned by three DeWitt brothers not related to Marvin.

There were also a number of growers who operated small processing operations. Bil Mar became the lone survivor in the state by the early 1970s, thanks in large part to Marvin's vision.

"Uncle Bill should get credit for starting the company by coming up with the idea for the growing operation. He worked hard and was with dad every step of the way," said Marvin's son Gary. "It was dad who promoted the business and forged ahead with new ideas. He is a visionary. He could see the future of the industry, and the future was in further processing. He got Bil Mar out of whole turkeys, and moved into boning and roasting."

To institute further processing, Marvin bought two used baking ovens and put his son Jack, who had just graduated from high school, in charge of the project. The first product was a five-to-seven-pound white-meat turkey roll marketed to food-service customers, such as restaurants, schools and hospitals. The product was rolled in foil and then cooked on the rotating racks of the gas-fired ovens. After cooking, the product was wrapped in a Cryovac plastic bag, placed in ice water, and then put into a cooler to await distribution. Even Marvin's oldest daughter, Marilyn, who was attending Hope College in Holland, pitched in to make the new product.

Like any new venture, further processing was not without its mistakes or regulatory headaches. With Belinski's tutoring, the company made its first 1,000 breast-meat turkey rolls. Marvin considered freezing them but Belinski convinced him to put the new product in the cooler. He said "customers would be beating down the doors to get at them." They didn't, and the DeWitts ended up tossing a lot of spoiled turkey rolls. After that, Bil Mar made the rolls based on a customer order. There was also a lot of experimentation with spices and cooking processes to come up with a product that was neither too dry nor too moist, and easily sliceable.

Packaging for one of first further-processed products.

Marvin was very protective of the turkey roll, almost as if it was a new child. Bertha Geertman, who worked 21 years in production for Bil Mar, recalled his fondness for the new product.

"I remember making turkey rolls by hand and then putting them into the oven. Marvin was very particular about that turkey roll because it was the first processed product he put out. It was his pride and joy," she said. "In those early days of further processing, Marvin was more worried about quality than quantity. His name, and that of his brother, was on the product."

He honed the advertising message for the new product to a single theme – convenience.

"The original compact turkey. Boneless and waste less. It is ready to slice, ready to serve, ready to eat, without cooking, without fuss or bother," said an early product brochure.

Vacuum sealing roasted turkey rolls.

Marvin and Gary literally knocked on the doors of restaurants to spread word of the new turkey roll. Gary took on the task during the summers while attending Central Michigan University. Hoping to snare a customer, they would pack turkey rolls in an ice-filled cooler, put them in the back of their cars, and drive to diners throughout southwest Michigan. Once Bil Mar established a solid customer base, the company relied on distributors, like Gordon Food Service in Grand Rapids, to deliver the products. At one point, 80 percent of the turkey roll sales were to restaurants.

Making turkey rolls, by cutting off the breast of the bird, immediately presented Bil Mar with a new challenge – what to do with the dark-meat parts of the bird, like the thigh. The solution was to come up with other processed products. Bil Mar soon offered food-service customers a combination white- and dark-meat turkey roll. The company also presented a smaller, uncooked version of the turkey roll, known as a light-and-dark meat turkey roast, to the retail grocery market. The two-pound, combined-meat product was a first for the industry and marked the company's entry into the retail market with a further-processed product. Bil Mar also developed a three-and-a-half-pound all-dark roast for grocery shoppers. Other dark meat parts not used for cooking – such as wings, necks, and drumsticks – were frozen and sold in bulk, mainly to grocery stores.

The further-processed products were praised by Michigan newspapers as the latest in convenience foods. The Detroit News said:

"You no longer have to cook a whole turkey to get the makings for sandwiches."

The Grand Rapids Press gave the new products credit for expanding the turkey-growing business.

"Growers of this traditional holiday-time meal have long been plagued by overproduction and a limited market that reaches its peak only at Thanksgiving and Christmas. But with the introduction of new products by the DeWitt brothers in Borculo, the turkey-raising industry in Michigan is becoming more of an all-year affair. The compact, roasted boneless turkey roll resembles a precooked ham in appearance."

The turkey roll received particular attention from Bil Mar's peers. In 1963, the roll was named Ottawa County's Product of the Year as part of the annual Michigan Week celebration. The roll was subsequently picked as Michigan's Product of the Year.

While the relatively new turkey-cooking process received its share of compliments, further processing did draw some criticism. The roasted turkey roll barely hit the market when the product came under the scrutiny of the USDA. The federal watchdog agency questioned whether the 152-degree cooking temperature was enough to kill staphylococcus and salmonella bacteria. As a safety measure, the agency proposed increasing the temperature to 170 degrees. Marvin and others in the turkey industry believed 152 degrees was sufficient and protested that raising the temperature to the higher level lowered the quality of the meat by shrinking and drying out the product.

In challenging the USDA, Marvin turned to Dr. Carl Hoyt, a district agricultural agent for Michigan State University's Cooperative Extension Service who served Ottawa County.

"If I had a question about poultry, I would check with Carl. He knew as much about our business as we did. If he didn't have the answer, he got the vets from MSU to help me out," Marvin said about Hoyt's valuable assistance to Bil Mar. "He was never on the Bil Mar payroll, yet he was an asset to the business. Carl was welcome at Bil Mar at any time. He had permission to walk right in. He was somebody I could trust."

Hoyt wrote to the National Turkey Federation about setting up a committee to discuss the proposed regulation change with the USDA. Hoyt also contacted a microbiologist at MSU to test the Bil Mar rolls at various temperatures. The MSU study showed the temperature of the rolls climbed after the ovens were turned off at 152 degrees and that there was no trace of bacteria. The national turkey organization awarded a grant to MSU and Purdue University to replicate the study, convincing the USDA to only the raise the cooking temperature to 160 degrees, instead of 170. The moisture conservation resulted in a tastier, meatier product.

Even without the regulatory pressure, implementing further processing was a bold move in the early 1960s. The DeWitts were not only going up against the whole-bird holiday tradition of consumers. Cooks at restaurants and hotels believed it was more economical to roast an oven-ready turkey for slicing than to buy the precut, precooked boneless turkey parts. Bil Mar had to convince them that they saved money with processed turkey in the long run. According to the sales pitch, with processed turkey they were paying only for usable meat – not bones, scrap, and skin, which made up more than 50 percent of the turkey. Having a turkey processor prepare the meat under controlled conditions also reduced the shrinkage resulting from cooking the whole bird.

First further-processed products.

Marvin quickly realized he was going to need a very talented salesman to convince food-service customers that the relatively new process was a better buy. That salesman, Mickey Manaster, literally came knocking on Bil Mar's door in 1965.

Manaster had once worked for one of Bil Mar's customers, Culinary Foods, a Chicago convenience foods company owned by his uncle, Joe Manaster. Mickey was working for Becker Meats in Milwaukee when he approached Marvin about being a master broker for Bil Mar products outside of Michigan. He formed a group of salesmen, known as Mickey Manaster & Co., who worked with brokers around the country. Those brokers, also known as manufacturer representatives, dealt with food distributors who sold multiple brands.

The arrangement would prove to be one of the most beneficial relationships ever forged by Bil Mar. Up until further processing, most of Bil Mar's turkeys ended up in the retail markets. Manaster would reverse that sales trend. With his aggressive group of salesmen, Manaster made Bil Mar products a nationwide brand among a wide range of food-service customers – hotels, restaurants, schools, prisons, hospitals, in-plant cafeterias, and early grocery store delis like those operated by Jewell Foods in Chicago.

Manaster suggested many new product ideas, like the roasted split breast, roasted thigh set, and roasted whole breast. In the early days of further processing, creating products was not an easy task without technical people on staff. Bil Mar had to rely on experts at Michigan State University and equipment manufacturers who were passing along technical information from one company to another as leverage in making a sale. Food-service turkey products introduced later by Bil Mar included cooked rolls, diced pieces, smoked breast, patties, pastrami, salami, and cooked wings and sliced pieces with barbecue sauce.

Marvin (far left), his son, Gary (center) and his brother, Bill (second from right) receive outstanding supplier award from Gordon Food Service officials.

In 1971, Manaster recommended that Bil Mar make frozen main dishes in bulk for some food-service customers, such as Gordon Food Service, and frozen dinners for others, like the airlines and hospitals. In response, the company started a convenience-foods division, manufacturing such frozen dishes as lasagna, beef stew, stuffed cabbage, chicken fricassee, turkey and dressing, macaroni and cheese, roast pork, salisbury steak, spaghetti with meat balls and sauce, ham steak, and baked filet of cod.

In addition to its regular food-service offerings, Bil Mar developed a gourmet specialities line. The products included such upscale items as chicken Kiev [butter-filled], turkey/chicken/veal cordon bleu [filled with smoked ham and Swiss cheese], and Rock Cornish game hen. The list also included dinner and dessert crepes [thin, light pancakes made with a batter of egg and flour] and appetizers like ramaki [chicken livers and water chestnuts wrapped in bacon].

"Anyone can make a product but you have to be able sell it. That is where Mickey came in, "Marvin said about Manaster's important role in the growth of the business. "He was also coming up with new ideas for products. He would ask us if we could make something and we would bring that idea to life. We were able to follow through because we had a lot of faith in Mickey."

Gary DeWitt, Bil Mar's former chief executive officer and president, also praised Manaster for his role in helping Bil Mar move beyond its Midwest roots.

"We trusted Mickey's judgment when it came to new products. He was the kind of salesman who knew the food business and the needs of customers. We developed brochures and flyers around those products," Gary said. "Mickey would say 'you buy the equipment, you make the product, and I will sell it.' Based on his recommendation, we would build the freezers and a building, and buy the equipment before we had the sales locked up. Mickey and the DeWitts were alike in that we were both risk takers. The word 'no' was not in our vocabulary. Our operating philosophy was that there is nothing that can't be done. We always said that if something smells good, sounds good, and looks good, then do it, even if it looks risky. We built the business by taking chances with people like Mickey."

Bil Mar makes airline meals.

One super salesman was not enough for Marvin, however. The company also needed a strong leader for sales in Michigan and that turned out to be Charles "Chuck" Curtis. Marvin had no trouble finding Curtis, who had built a cooler for Holland-based W.H. Porter Inc. at Bil Mar, and was a fellow member of Ottawa Reformed Church. Marvin was impressed by Curtis and his diverse background – a degree in environmental health and sanitary services, and experience in marketing and sales. While at Porter, Curtis helped develop a sanitary panel designed for a food plant.

"I knew I wanted to work for Bil Mar after I got to know the family through the church we both attended. They were wholesome, sincere people. They had good values and practiced their religion in the way they lived their lives. They had built that business on honesty and integrity. They appreciated what their employees did and they rewarded them. I stayed there a long time. The job was so interesting, and I was encouraged to use all of my talents and education," Curtis said.

At Bil Mar, his knowledge would prove invaluable in a number of areas. Curtis, who had helped design municipal water systems on one of his jobs, assisted Bil Mar with its water and waste-water challenges. The company was always drilling wells to find scarce sources of water in the area. The water was pumped into a reservoir for sand filtration and later chlorinated before use in the plant. Waste water was treated by an unpredictable on-site system consisting of lagoons. Incoming and outgoing water concerns were not alleviated until Bil Mar tapped into the city of Wyoming's Lake Michigan water line between Zeeland and Borculo in 1978, and constructed an on-site waste-water treatment plant in 1985.

Curtis also directed the operation of Bil Mar's employee discount store from the opening in 1973 in the former hatchery building until it was firmly established. The outlet was subsequently opened to the public and named the Country Store. Curtis worked with Gary to develop the company's product brochures. He also helped develop some of the new further-processed products.

His main task at Bil Mar involved working with Michigan food distributors, like Gordon Food Service. Under Curtis, Bil Mar sales in the state shot from $1 million in 1972 to $30 million in 1979. Of that 1979 total, $16 million represented sales to GFS, now one of Bil Mar's largest customers. In working with GFS, Curtis was responsible for getting Bil Mar into the beef-product business in the mid-1970s when the food distributor's main supplier of beef products went bankrupt. Bil Mar, purchasing whole-top rounds and rib-eye roasts from meat packers, continues to make red-meat products for GFS and other customers.

Gordon Food Service, like Bil Mar, was not a big player in the food industry in the early 1960s when the two companies started working with each other. They grew together, starting with a roasted turkey breast. They are now ranked among the nation's largest in their respective industries.

Paul Gordon, GFS board chairman, said he has never had anything but the highest regard for the way the DeWitts conducted their business, especially their insistence on quality and customer service. He remembered a sign on Marvin's desk that spoke to the quality issue. The sign, reminding visitors that the lowest price didn't guarantee the best product, said: "I have no quarrel with those who sell for less; they know what their product is worth."

Gordon said Marvin and his sons treated their customers like they were the most important people in the world, going out of their way to meet their demands. He is still impressed with Marvin's down-to-earth operating style.

"I took some of our customers over there one time for a tour of the plant. We pulled up, and there was Marvin driving a front-end loader. I told my guests that he was the CEO of the company. They thought I was kidding. They thought he was a maintenance man," Gordon said. " I always found him to be very approachable. If we had a problem with a product, all we had to do was call him and things would be taken care of.

"We would also see something out in the market and suggest Bil Mar try making it. They would research it and then would produce it. They worked very hard to get us the product we needed, acting more like a partner than a supplier. We didn't stick with Bil Mar just because of their loyalty and customer support. The Bil Mar name was synonymous with quality. The DeWitts are also good people, who conduct their business in an honorable way. I only wish all of our suppliers could have treated us as well as the DeWitts. If they did, our business would be even bigger than it is today. "

All the new business generated by such sales people as Manaster and Curtis required multiple additions to the processing plant built in 1958. And Marvin was up to the task, according to Chuck Stehouwer, who audited the company's finances starting in 1968 on behalf of Touche, Ross & Co. and for a short time was a Bil Mar executive.

"Marvin wouldn't think twice about expanding the plant if he thought he could sell more product, like the preplated airline and hospital meals pushed by Manaster," Stehouwer said. "For Marvin, an expansion was just a matter of extending a wall, putting in a cement floor, and adding another section of roof for a walk-in cooler or oven. In his mind, it was that simple. He didn't waste a lot of time thinking on how to get things done. When he decided on something, he went with it."

A make-shift crane positions prefabricated walls for first plant addition.

In 1965, Bil Mar increased the volume of turkeys it could roast by adding an oven room onto the plant and buying larger, smokehouse ovens from Herrud Meats [now Thornapple Valley] in Grand Rapids. The new walk-in ovens made the roasting process more efficient, allowing product to be put on racks and rolled into position for cooking.

For that first expansion of the processing plant, Marvin experimented with a new construction process using pre-built concrete walls. He had first observed the building method while visiting his daughter Marilyn and her family, who were living in Colorado. Using pre-built walls was unheard of in the Midwest. To form the walls, concrete was poured into a steel form lying on the ground. After the cement set overnight, the form was tilted up and then pulled away from the new wall to get it ready for another pour. At first, Marvin hired a crane operator to lift the formed walls in place. He cut that expense by purchasing a used telephone truck and having Frank DeWind, his maintenance supervisor, rig it with pulleys and a winch.

As part of the 1965 addition, an office was put on the processing plant and administrative functions were moved out of the hatchery building. Another major addition included a new kill plant built in 1969, where turkeys were brought by truck from company-owned farms and those of contract growers. The killing process has remained virtually unchanged since then. Turkeys are placed feet first on shackles attached to a conveyor system that leads to the kill room. Their heads are dipped into a water trough where they are electrically shocked into unconsciousness. Their throats are slit by a miniature rotating blade. Hanging upside down, they are gravity-bled. The carcasses are then run through a hot-water scalder and a series of pecking machines to remove the feathers.

The kill-plant addition was followed by the construction of a frozen-foods plant in 1971, when overall annual sales at Bil Mar approached the $10 million mark – double the 1968 total.

With the frozen-foods addition, the plant was divided into three assembly-line processing sections known as P-1, P-2, and P-3. In P-1, which included the kill room, the entrails from carcasses were removed, and the neck and feet cut off. Nothing is wasted in the manufacturing process. Those parts of the turkey not used for consumer products – such as blood, entrails, and feathers – are sold to rendering plants for manufacture into feed.

"There was a saying around Bil Mar that we used every part of the turkey, except the gobble," Marvin said.

After evisceration, the meat went to P-2 where it was removed from the bone, shaped into further-processed products, cooked, and chilled. In P-3, Bil Mar made entire frozen meals and entrees for the food-service market. The meals were frozen solid in five to seven minutes by subjecting the entire package to a quick-freeze, liquid-nitrogen bath in excess of 300 degrees below zero Fahrenheit.

The new plant additions prompted Bil Mar to establish a quality-control program. To accomplish that goal, Marvin went in search of a microbiologist. He found one – Charles William Stout, better known as Bill. He had 12 years of sanitation experience at Eckrich, a sausage maker in Ft. Wayne, Ind.

The victim of a downsizing in 1970, Stout connected with Marvin through a corporate headhunter who had come across his resume. Marvin called Stout about the possibility of coming to work for Bil Mar. Before the two began to discuss the job, however, Marvin said he had to ask Stout two questions. The first was "have you got a beard?" The question was related to Marvin's discomfort toward men with facial hair.

His second question of Stout, "do you smoke?," had to do with his opposition to a habit he considered dirty and unhealthy. Stout, who considers himself a staunch conservative, answered "no" to both questions.

Satisfied with those negative responses, Marvin said: "Now we can talk about the job."

When Stout took the job in 1970, as one of the first college-educated professionals on Bil Mar's staff, there was no test kitchen or microbiology lab. Marvin took Stout on a tour of the plant, which culminated in an empty section with four walls and a floor. Marvin said one part of the section would be occupied by a test kitchen. In the other part, he said, Stout could establish a laboratory to conduct bacterial tests on raw incoming material, finished product samples, and equipment after it was broken down and cleaned each day. The lab, to assure uniform product manufacturing, would also conduct chemical analysis for such elements as fat, moisture, salt, protein, rancidity, calories and enzyme activities.

Besides sanitation concerns, Marvin had another reason for hiring Stout. He liked the idea of having an employee with expertise in microbiology who could go head-to-head with USDA inspectors when they fussed over a regulation.

Of all the changes brought on by further processing, none was quite so visible to the public as the company's adoption of a new name in 1966 when its many operating divisions were incorporated into one parent firm, Bil Mar Foods – the title of one of those divisions. In the early 1960s, for auditing purposes, the DeWitts came up with names for several operating divisions – Bil Mar Turkey Farms, Bil Mar Foods, Bil Mar Realty, and Bil Mar Feeds. Up until the corporate name change, the company had been operated as Bill and Marve's Turkey Farm & Hatchery with products sold under the Bil Mar label. The Bil Mar Foods corporate name better described the company's further-processing operations.

The incorporation also produced a subtle change in the company's ownership. In a system of cross-gifting, Marvin and Bill endowed all of their children with stock in the company. However, the stock did not represent negotiable assets, given Bil Mar's privately held status.

"It gave us all a piece of the action, a sense of ownership that was powerful, even though the assets were not liquid," said Marvin's son Gary. "Ownership is a powerful psychological incentive. You tend to take care of things better when you own them. Dad and Uncle Bill were generous in sharing the company with the next generation. That was very important in the continuing success of Bil Mar. The families who don't get along in business are usually those in which the first generation keeps financial control of the business."

By the time the incorporation went into effect, the emphasis on further-processed products – made on a year-round basis – was beginning to cast a shadow on Bil Mar's seasonal whole-turkey business, once the company's sales leader. By 1967, only 30 percent of Bil Mar's output was in whole birds [a product discontinued in 1979]. The rest of the birds were being used for immediate fabrication or frozen for later thawing and processing. The company would sometimes have to buy batches of frozen birds from other processors to meet production goals.

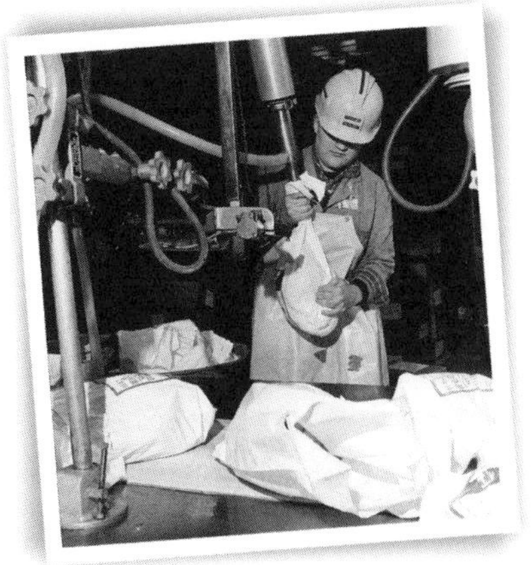

Vacuum bagging whole turkeys.

The increasing demand for further-processed products was the catalyst for Bil Mar to finally switch from seasonal to year-round schedules for slaughtering turkeys. In turn, the company increased the number of environmentally controlled grow-out barns to keep up with the slaughtering operation. Unlike the range land, the barns were not subject to the whims of Mother Nature.

The year-round activity boosted the ranks of full-time employees at Bil Mar from 125 in the early 1960s to 225 in the late 1960s. And in the 1960s, Marvin was still doing much of the hiring. He had a knack for hiring the right people, giving them firm direction, and then getting out of their way – until something went wrong.

On those occasions, employees were hammered by the demanding and perfectionist side of Marvin's personality. Yet overall, he was fair, honest, loyal, and generous, according to employees who were proud to say they had earned his respect.

As a natural-born leader, he had an ability to motivate others not only with his long-range vision but by his day-to-day example. Some employees talk about him in almost reverential terms, admiring his tenacity and willingness to jump into a situation no matter how difficult or dirty.

Marvin on a daily tour of the plant.

CHAPTER NINE

HANDS-ON BOSS

Marvin was never comfortable sitting behind the desk in his office. He spent most of his time in the plant in places where he thought his attention was needed. He seldom used the services of a secretary, preferring to set his own appointments and write his letters in longhand instead of dictating them. He did not concern himself with titles, even though he could lay claim to a number of them – co-founder, president, and chairman of the board. Yet if someone asked him about his company standing, he usually referred to himself as Bil Mar's sewer, water, refrigeration, and maintenance man.

That unpretentious attitude was reflected in his typical work outfit – khaki shirt and pants, and knee-length rubber boots. Wearing a suit and tie was a rarity. When he formally dressed up, employees knew he was probably scheduled for an outside meeting with a lawyer, accountant, or banker. Some long-time workers would jokingly ask him if he was suited up to attend a funeral.

"He was not a figurehead who dressed up in a suit and tie, sat in an office, and greeted visitors. You could frequently see him walking through the plant, driving a bulldozer, or delivering gift turkeys at Christmas to area plants when there was no one else to drive the truck. Sometimes he was more like an employee than an employer, " said Marge Boersen, Bil Mar's former computer operations manager.

A hands-on type of boss, Marvin never asked anyone to do something he wouldn't do himself. As a teenager, Ed Hanenburg learned that lesson one cold and rainy October night in 1957.

Hanenburg – now a land developer and a farm owner with large dairy, beef, and pork operations in West Michigan – worked part-time at Bil Mar during the killing season.

Marvin, Hanenburg and a group of other workers had just finished a long shift late in the afternoon, and the teenager was one of the last to clean up. The phone rang and it was Marvin's wife. She said a customer had called for a rush order of turkeys. Marvin asked Hanenburg if he would stay over to help him. The young man had plans to go out that night and he knew it wouldn't be a small job. He agreed, however, out of respect for Marvin. To get the turkeys, the pair had to drive to the sand hills in rain that turned to sleet. They didn't finish the job until 10 p.m. And although Marvin never said so, Hanenburg sensed that his help was appreciated. After the job was finished, Hanenburg stood in awe of Marvin's persistence in satisfying a customer, after a work day that had stretched more than 14 hours.

Over the years, Bil Mar gave work to a number of teenagers, like Hanenburg. Under today's strict child-labor rules, Marvin would have been found in violation many times over for the number of hours put in by the high school boys. But the youngsters enjoyed the extra spending money and Marvin believed he did a service to the community by exposing the youngsters to his tough work ethic.

"I used to be real tough on how I wanted things done, especially with young workers in training. I wanted to give them training they would remember, like being here everyday, being on time, and doing their best while they were here," he said. "They might have not liked the way we did things. But those kids needed an education on what work is all about. It helped them to be better people later. "

One of the those kids, Bernie Schipper, worked part-time at Bil Mar in the mid-1960s. He learned the hard way about Marvin's inclination for being tough, yet fair.

Schipper's first job was sanitizing the killing facility, which meant moving feathers out of the blood tunnel and into barrels. He also cleaned equipment, like scalders and pickers.

Schipper ran into trouble when he graduated to sanitation in the processing part of the plant after those shifts concluded for the day. At the end of his night shift, he was supposed to look for packaged turkeys that had fallen out of brine troughs used for quick-freezing the birds. One night, he found a couple on the floor and walked out of the plant with them. Not knowing what he was going to do with them, he sold the birds to some of his friends.

Marvin found out about the theft and fired the youngster. Schipper had been a good worker up to that point, and Bill DeWitt Jr. had taken a liking to him. When Schipper called Marvin about coming back to work at Bil Mar, Bill vouched for the lad. The final decision was up to Marvin.

He had the boy come to the plant with his parents to apologize, reimburse Bil Mar for the birds, and promise to never cheat the company again. Marvin believed Schipper was sincere about having learned his lesson and hired him back. Schipper didn't betray Marvin's exoneration. Thirty years later, he is now a product manager at Bil Mar and still regards Marvin as his mentor.

"He was always inspecting the work you did, and always demanding you do a better job. If you missed something, he would let you know about it. Sometimes that could be a little irritating," Schipper said. "In time, you developed a respect for him because you knew he would work hard to get a job done the right way. He was not afraid to go out in the plant and get dirty."

When Marvin walked through the plant, he commanded attention. Employees knew that his demanding nature required him to make sure things were working right.

Building the operation from scratch, he was quick to pick up on the smallest detail – a dripping faucet, an air compressor leak, or a light left on in a freezer. If, at a particular moment, he didn't know about something out of whack, he eventually would find out. The company never grew too big that he couldn't keep tabs on almost everyone and everything.

There was a standing joke among employees that he made daily head counts to make sure people were doing their jobs. Some workers moved to another part of the plant when they saw him coming through on one of his inspection rounds. The rest became more alert about the task at hand.

Turkeys move down the boning line.

"He was very much in charge when he walked through that plant," said Sheri DeWitt, who met her husband Merle while working at Bil Mar. "I remember when he used to move through the plant, and someone would say 'here comes Marvin.' As he passed, it was almost as if everyone was standing at attention."

There was justification for all the apprehensiveness. If Marvin found something not to his liking, he was quick to criticize with little regard for diplomacy or tact. He also didn't hesitate to reprimand someone in front of others. Every day, it was a mid-morning tradition for supervisors to congregate in the break room. The reward was a free doughnut and coffee from the company. The punishment could be a tongue lashing from Marvin, who knew he could connect with all the supervisors in one place and at one time.

"Everyone knew that no matter where they worked in the plant, their performance and work areas were subject to criticism by Marvin DeWitt. And that included salespeople. Marvin didn't believe in salespeople spending much time in their offices. He wanted them on the road," said Larry Baker, a sales representative at Bil Mar for 14 years. "Some employees thought his complaints about small things were penny-wise and pound-foolish. Marvin believed the dollars took care of themselves when you watched the pennies."

Marvin didn't confine his criticism to job-related behavior. One winter, before a shift was to begin, he spotted an hourly worker spinning his car in circles on the icy company parking lot. Marvin went out to the lot and told the employee the behavior was dangerous and would not be tolerated. The worker, a fairly new employee, didn't recognize Marvin and disputed his authority by saying "you're not my boss." Marvin went back into the plant, brought out the employee's supervisor, and had him fired on the spot.

Marvin also had no qualms about chiding an employee who ran afoul of his pet peeves, like smoking. He lectured employees on the dangers of smoking to the point of ridicule. He especially disliked pipe smokers who took even more time away from the job for the habit – constantly cleaning the pipe and filling the bowl with tobacco every time they wanted to light up. He was forever offering employees a cash bonus if they would quit smoking for a year. One of those who took him up on his offer and quit for good was Bill Chaddock, who still manages Bil Mar's computer operations. Chaddock credited Marvin's encouragement as the main reason for snuffing out a 25-year habit.

Marvin's style of management was from the old school where authority flowed from the top down, instead of the teamwork approach so popular today. Very control-oriented, he intuitively managed people and situations by the seat of his pants. His methods probably would not receive a passing grade from the Dale Carnegie School of how to win friends and influence people. He believed someone had to call the shots and ultimately be responsible in order to maintain a successful business.

At Bil Mar, he was that someone. To reinforce his no-nonsense image, he even installed a witty – though revealing – sign at his private parking spot in the company lot. The sign warned "Don't even think about parking here."

"Dad never took a Dale Carnegie course or a management course on how to deal with people. He mainly ruled by his overpowering personality. He demanded perfection and he demanded quality," Jack DeWitt said. "His style of management was one of his own invention. He was driven and just didn't know any better when it came to dealing with people. He was on a mission."

When it came to criticism, Marvin was definitely an equal opportunity employer. No one escaped his wrath, even his sons. Some employees still wince today when talking about some of the verbal attacks he made on his offspring.

Marvin admitted he was harsher with his sons. They grew up in the business and had no excuse for making the same mistakc twicc. He also didn't want anyone to accuse him of favoritism. He took a similar attitude toward salaried employees. He considered them part of the family's inner circle and, like his immediate family members, expected just a little bit more from those employees.

"Anytime you are around Marvin, you are on edge – almost to the point of intimidation. You are always wondering 'is he going to be critical of what I am doing or not doing.' That doesn't mean he was nasty. There were just so many stories about how he ruled with an iron fist and how demanding he was," said Larry Baker, who was considered a part of the family's inner circle. "That was his style of management. You knew he wouldn't ask you to do anything that he wouldn't do or couldn't do himself. You knew he had already done that task before and probably went beyond what he had to do. I always tried to reach his level of expectations. I always had respect for what he had accomplished and how he accomplished it. His work ethic was amazing."

In today's highly sensitive business climate, in which any slight can trigger a lawsuit charging harassment or discrimination, Marvin recognizes that his aggressive style of management would be out of sync.

"I was not a people person, in the sense that I didn't take a lot of time to think about someone's feelings or self-esteem. They had a job to do and I was paying them to do the job. If they weren't doing the job right, I let them know about it. If I chewed someone out, I didn't take them to one side and quietly tell them about something," he said. "When I saw them is when I thought about something, and that is when I talked to them – even if it was in front of 10 other people. I wasn't trying to demean anyone in front of their fellow workers. I just didn't have time to coddle someone."

As hard as he could be on people, the criticism was a one-time thing. He did not hold a grudge. He would vent his feelings about a situation one time and never bring it up again. He was not a person to rub something in.

"Marvin was a hard taskmaster, even with his own boys. He could get mad in a hurry. If you ran into him the next day, he would be jovial again," said Neil Wagenaar, Bil Mar's chief accountant from 1970 to 1988. "He didn't hold grudges. You might have felt intimidated at the time he was mad, yet you also knew you wouldn't be haunted by your past mistakes. When it came to past actions, Marvin's memory was as short as the fuse for his temper."

While Marvin's criticisms could be frequent, his compliments for a job well done were almost nonexistent. He rationalized that complimenting an employee for doing something right wasn't necessary. He was paying them to do a good job, not for poor performance. If he was silent about your performance, you knew you were doing a good job. To his way of thinking, not yelling is complimentary.

"The only time I said anything to an employee about their work is when they were doing something wrong. I didn't have time to comment if things were being done right. I had to look for things going wrong, so they could be corrected immediately. If things were going right, they were taking care of themselves. I am not saying that withholding compliments was the best management style. That is just the way I handled things."

One outside witness to his tough management style was Preston Kool, a friend, former mayor of Battle Creek, and the owner of a group of car dealerships in West Michigan. Kool was invited to the plant to critique his friend's leadership technique after Marvin observed him reading a management textbook. With Kool in attendance, Marvin started a meeting of managers by complaining about a floor drain upside down in the plant. One of his sons asked him why that made any difference since the drain was still operable. Marvin said "the difference is that there is a right way and a wrong way to do things." Upset that his authority was questioned, he told the son to correct the situation at that instant. The son said he wasn't going to leave the meeting for something so trivial. Marvin said he would find someone to accomplish the task, and then the company wouldn't need his son around anymore. The son complied. Kool found the experience unsettling but not out of line for Marvin.

"I felt the exchange was harsh and that it would have been wrong for me to have talked to an employee like that. That was Marvin's style, his way of getting things done. He didn't know any another way. It worked for him when it probably wouldn't have worked for most other people," Kool said. "Up to that point, he had always done things his way and that is how he had become successful. He lived by the same principles he expected his employees to follow, including his sons. He didn't ask them to do anything that he wouldn't do himself. From my perspective, Marvin didn't need any management training."

As the self-assured leader of the company, Marvin valued his opinion before those of others. That doesn't mean he wouldn't change his mind on an issue or was blind to new ideas.

He tended to turn down an idea on the first go-around. For some employees, the experience could be frustrating, and they didn't approach him again. He only wanted to make sure the idea was really something the person believed in. He figured that someone really trusted the concept if they kept knocking on his door. The lag time also allowed him to make a clearer evaluation before making a decision. He had an uncanny ability to sort through conflicting information and generally come up with a correct response or solution to a situation. It was a trait he passed along to his sons.

Dr. David Pyle, Bil Mar's first on-site veterinarian and the company's former executive director of corporate farms, clearly recalled the trying process of convincing Marvin to accept a new idea.

"One time, we disagreed over how many times to reuse the litter in the barns. He wanted it used over and over to save money. The ammonia smell got so strong it was affecting the health of the birds. You could barely stand to walk into a turkey barn," Pyle said. "It took a while to convince him, though he finally gave in. His initial attitude on a lot of things was that 'we had always done things that way, why should we change.' By the same token, once he believed you were right about something, he would back you 100 percent."

Marvin's self-assured attitude did not sit well with all of his employees. Those who could look past the gruff exterior of the man saw a hardworking employer with a vision of how he thought things should be – not a mean-spirited person who would deliberately run someone down to achieve his goal.

"He was self-assured and some people found that abrasive. He could be rough and gruff, and seemed to have an attitude of knocking people out of the way to reach his objectives. However, his motivation for succeeding was his own pride and self-satisfaction. He wanted to go to bed at night and be proud of himself," said Kevin McKenna, who worked 13 years in product development and industrial sales at Bil Mar. "He didn't base his decisions on attempting to make you look bad or making him look good. I really think his motivation was pure and real. He was just trying to get something done right in the quickest way possible. He never intended to hurt anybody. He was tough, overbearing, impatient, and quick-tempered. He was not, however, a mean-spirited person."

Further-processed products on oven rack.

If Marvin's tough and pervasive demeanor in the plant was legendary, so was the concern he showed for his employees He saw himself as being responsible for their livelihoods and was always willing to help them. He gave them advances in pay to help them over rough financial times. He afforded them time off for family business. No matter how busy he was, he took time to hear out an employee. If he couldn't answer a question, he found someone who could. He made sure a non-English speaking employee was paired with someone bilingual until they could speak the language. As a result, long-time employees felt as if they were part of his extended family.

"Marvin and his sons went above and beyond what they had to do as an employer," Marge Boersen said. "They were more like friends or neighbors than bosses. Marvin took time to talk to the workers. He knew their names and seemed to know about their families. He showed a real interest in them."

Bertha Geertman, who retired from Bil Mar in 1986 after 21 years as a production worker, fondly remembered the helping hand he extended after her husband died. Left with four children, she needed a job to support her family. Marvin walked up to one of her sons in the hardware store in Zeeland and said his mother could have a job at Bil Mar whenever she was ready to work.

The thoughtful acts continued after she went to work for Bil Mar. One morning, Marvin asked Geertman if she planned to attend a reunion at a school where his wife had also been a student. Geertman said she would be unable to attend because her shift wouldn't end until well after the event had started. He expressed regret and said he would be attending with his wife. That was about 11 a.m. An hour later, her supervisor said she could leave work at noon with Marvin's blessing – only if she promised to attend the school reunion.

Chuck Curtis, who formerly led Bil Mar's sales effort in Michigan, remembered Marvin repaying his employees for a job well done, even during tough times like the early 1970's gas shortage and recession. The slow times cut into the company's profit margin and it was not able to give the traditional cash bonuses to management workers. Curtis still received a bonus from Marvin – the use of a company car and credit card for a family vacation in Florida.

Through the years, Marvin also developed a reputation for fairness among his employee, regardless of their age, sex, nationality, or abilities.

"I admire Marvin. He had a basic respect for people no matter what their level of expertise. He never put himself above anyone else and he treated people the way he wanted to be treated. He was particular about the way he wanted his business to be run. He also realized it took people to run that business. He did not forget them," said Mary Delrue, Bil Mar's executive director of manufacturing. "There are some people who say the DeWitts didn't treat women fairly. I never found that to be the case. I think that belief comes from the fact that the DeWitt girls never got involved in the business. Once the DeWitts knew you could do a good job, it didn't matter what color or sex you were. You were accepted as a part of the DeWitt family."

Marvin took many employees under his wing if they showed initiative. One of them was José Mancilla, a retired Bil Mar production worker who hired on during the 1963 killing season. Mancilla, who came from Mexico in 1960 as a migrant worker, was hired at Bil Mar after working in the apple orchards near Sparta.

Mancilla wanted more than seasonal work and talked Marvin into putting him on the year-round crew that was producing the company's cooked products. But even that job was only five days a week, and Mancilla soon let Marvin know he was interested in even more hours. Marvin offered Mancilla a Saturday job helping him do chores around the farm. Consideration from Marvin went well beyond the workplace, however.

Shortly after Mancilla was hired, Marvin found him a rental home closer to the plant. Mancilla had been driving to Borculo from his residence in Muskegon, where his wife's family lived. The landlord near the plant was reluctant to rent the house to Mancilla until Marvin said he would cover the rental payment if the employee was unable to pay. In 1964, Mancilla was working full-time at Bil Mar when his temporary work visa expired and he ran into trouble with the U. S. Naturalization and Immigration Service. With deportation hanging over his head, Mancilla sought Marvin's advice. Marvin contacted his lawyers at Warner, Norcross & Judd, who advised Mancilla to seek resident-alien status by returning to Mexico and filing the proper paperwork with the U.S. Embassy. While he was gone, his family stayed with relatives in Muskegon. Marvin lent the family money to make ends meet until Mancilla's return. Mancilla's resident-alien status was granted after Marvin agreed to sponsor him by promising to look out for his welfare. When Mancilla returned from Mexico, he wanted to buy a home for his growing family but didn't have the money for a down payment. Marvin not only helped Mancilla find an affordable home, he also loaned him the down payment and co-signed the bank loan. Mancilla became a U.S. citizen in 1982. Marvin also helped his brother and five of his friends come to this country.

In his actions, Marvin also showed a caring attitude toward employees whose lifestyles he could not abide, especially those afflicted with alcoholism. He kept them on the payroll so they would have an income.

"By giving them as many breaks as I could, I was not making an excuse for their behavior. I don't believe alcoholism is a disease, just like I don't think overeating is a disease," he said. "I was just trying to be as understanding as possible, mostly for the sake of their family who had a hard life because of the drinking problem. We had a number of problem drinkers working for us. When they were sober, they were faithful employees."

It was these acts of consideration that endeared many of his employees to Marvin. He knew how to treat his employees to the point where a loyalty was developed.

"People always respected Dad, even when he got a little carried away with his yelling and temper. You would work your buns off for him. You would give him your right arm. That is the kind of loyalty and commitment he inspired," Jack DeWitt said. "He commanded that kind of respect because he was recognized as the visionary, the mover, and leader of the company who adhered to basic Christian principles. We also knew that he would never give up. His persistence came from his faith in God. He had confidence in more than just himself."

The Rev. Mike Van Buren, former pastor of Ottawa Reformed Church, shared a similar perspective on loyalty shown to Marvin.

"His character strengths far outweigh any weaknesses he might have shown by being too blunt, too critical, or too task-oriented. He is a man of integrity. His word is solid. He has an unconditional love for his Lord, his family, his employees, his neighbors, and the community-at-large. He is one of the strongest men I know. He is the only man I ever watched break the head off a golf club just by hitting the ball. He puts everything he has into everything he does and that commands respect."

Out of regard for Marvin, many employees, like Jake Voetberg, spent their working lives at Bil Mar. Voetberg, now retired, has the distinction of being Bil Mar's longest-serving employee – 36 years, from 1953 to 1989. He was born in The Netherlands, where he had experience in farming and a degree from an agricultural college. Voetberg lived there until age 28 when he emigrated to America. His passage to this country was paid by Marvin, always on the lookout for additional workers. Marvin heard about Voetberg from Bernie TerHaar, who had a chicken farm in Drenthe, where Jake's brother worked. When Voetberg and his wife, Margaret, arrived in this country, they could not speak English. Marvin's mother helped them learn the language of their adopted country.

"I had a number of offers to work at other turkey farms but never took them because I was my own boss. Marvin would let me do what I wanted to do. Marvin and his whole family were good to me," Voetberg said.

In 1972, when Marvin was 52, he started backing away from day-to-day Bil Mar operations – 34 years after he began the business with his brother Bill.

By then, three of Marvin's five sons – Gary, Jack and Don – had been groomed for key management positions. Gary, as comptroller and office manager, was in charge of sales and administration. Jack, as production superintendent, was responsible for further processing, and killing and packing whole birds. Don – who always preferred working outside the plant in the fields, on the farms, and at the feed mill – was in charge of feed operations. Marvin's younger sons, Merle and Keith, were working in production. A son-in-law, Tom Norman, was hired in 1972 to do purchasing and inventory control, and later became facilities manager. He met Marilyn DeWitt in Denver, Colo., where she was teaching and he was working in the engineering department at a nuclear weapons plant.

In the early 1970s, Bill Sr. also started to back away from active involvement in the business and would retire by the end of the decade. His son Bill Jr. was named farm manager in charge of live birds and all contract growers. Bill Jr. also had responsibility for shipping live turkeys into the plant and production scheduling. Bill Sr.'s other son, Ray, was working in Bil Mar's maintenance department, specializing in refrigeration.

Although Marvin was no longer concerned with the minor decision-making of the business, nothing major occurred without his stamp of approval. He still attended all of the management and sales meetings.

"Dad still knew what was going on, even when we were put in charge of the day-to-day operations, " Jack DeWitt said. "He almost had a sixth sense about that business. He was tuned into everything, from the farm operations to the inner workings of the plant."

By giving up minor decision-making, Marvin was able to leave the business for sightseeing trips around the world and to hunt big game animals as a member of Safari Club International. Close to home, he donated time for service on the Zeeland School Board, Ottawa County Board of Supervisors [now Ottawa County Board of Commissioners], and the Ottawa County Road Commission.

"It was the first time in my years at the business that I felt I could take off when I wanted to," he said. "The boys were there to handle the day-to-day operation of the business, though I kept tabs on everything that was going on. It's not that I quit working. I just allowed myself to play a little bit more."

Marvin in his trophy room at Bil Mar.

CHAPTER TEN

BIG-GAME HUNTER, COMMUNITY SERVANT

Marvin's enormous appetite for life experiences led him to locales far removed from tiny Borculo – Mexico, South America, Russia, China, Australia, Antarctica, Africa, and the Panama Canal.

But the global sightseeing trips, accompanied by his wife and friends, didn't satisfy his hunger for adventure. They only inspired him to seek other thrills, like traveling to several continents in search of big-game trophies.

His entry into the world of big-game hunting came through contact with Don Prince, owner of Prince Bridge & Marine in Grand Haven and a fellow member at Ottawa Reformed Church.

Prince was a member of Arizona-based Safari Club International, one of the world's largest hunting organizations. Many of the group's projects involve wildlife conservation, public education, and protecting hunter rights. The organization also sponsors Sportsmen Against Hunger and SafariCare, which sends doctors and nurses to people in need of medical attention.

Prince established a friendship with Marvin when they worked on the church consistory and the committee to build a new church. Prince jokingly said they bonded because they were both stubborn Dutchmen. What they also had in common was a belief in hard work and honest business dealings.

Marvin was visiting at the Prince home one Sunday after church when Don and his sons began talking about an upcoming hunting trip to the Yukon. The discussion sparked Marvin's curiosity and led to his membership in Safari International.

"Marvin has a natural curiosity about things and a need to pursue things to their conclusion. I would describe him as a man with adventure in his soul. It was that sense of adventure that led him to the four corners of the earth," said Prince, who joined Marvin on his first safari in 1973.

Marvin also liked being out in the wild roughing it – brushing his teeth in water from a creek, not taking showers for a week, riding horseback, and sleeping in a sheepherder's hut in the mountains.

To get in shape for the first hunt in northwest Canada's Yukon Territory, he ran up and down 96th Avenue in front of his house near the plant. Right before the trip, he challenged two of Prince's sons to a foot race. Marvin, then in his early 50s, was keeping up with them when he pulled a hamstring muscle, causing him to take a fall. The injury did not alter his trip plans.

The first day of the Yukon trip, Prince, his sons, and their guides came back to the base camp around dark. They finished supper and were getting ready to bed down for the night when Marvin and his guide straggled in around 11 p.m. Marvin stumbled into Prince's tent and exclaimed: "What are you trying to do, kill me. You didn't tell me about all the rocks and boulders. This is rough country."

Marvin was obviously exhausted after a day of traversing the rugged Yukon country. Not one to give up, he awoke with everyone else at 6 the next morning ready for another long day of tracking and hunting.

Marvin hunts in Yukon territory of Canada.

"He took to the experience like a duck to water. I saw him climb up the sides of mountains when physically he shouldn't have been able to continue," Prince said. "But he would not give up his pursuit of a goal. It was no different than the way he built his business from scratch. He had that natural desire to succeed."

Before his big-game days, Marvin had little time for hunting. His hunting activities were mainly confined to the opening day of pheasant season, almost always with Bil Mar clients. Occasionally, he would engage in Michigan's fall rite of deer hunting. When the big-game hunting opportunity came along, he could devote time to the pastime. And like other ventures in his life, he hit the ground running and proceeded full tilt.

On the Yukon hunt, he bagged a dall sheep, a moose and a caribou. He shot the sheep, his first trophy animal, from a rock ledge 200 yards away from where the animal was grazing in a valley. He was so nervous, he couldn't keep the gun steady. For a sure shot, he had to wedge the rifle between two rocks. The gun's stock still bears those rock marks.

The next year, he journeyed to an island in Alaska, where he shot a brown bear. Two years later, in 1976, he embarked on a five-week safari to Kenya in Africa. Among the trophies he brought home were a zebra, ostrich, wart hog, Cape buffalo, and several types of antelope such as an eland, kudu, and impala.

By 1984, he had been on African safari three times. He returned to that continent for a fourth safari in 1997 with 21 male members of his family, only months after undergoing hip replacement surgery.

Marvin was still walking with the aid of a cane when he arrived in the central south African country of Zimbabwe, yet he never missed a day of hunting. Even on the last day of the hunt, when most everyone was wrapping up, Marvin sat most of the night in a blind waiting for a leopard to show up.

Marvin – known in hunting circles as one-shot DeWitt for his keen aim – has also taken big-game trophies in British Columbia, Mexico, Spain, the Bering Straits, New Mexico, Montana, Texas, and Wyoming.

Among his other trophies are black bear, walrus, musk ox, elk, pronghorn antelope, buffalo, rhinoceros, hippopotamus, hyena, baboon, giraffe, and sheep of the bighorn, desert, and stone variety.

To document his hunting trips, he had most of the trophies full-mounted or head-mounted. As the number of mounts grew, his office at Bil Mar became a big-game trophy room. After the plant fire in 1984, he dedicated a third-floor room in the company's new office building as a trophy room. At one time, a walk through the trophy room was part of the itinerary for special visitors on plant tours. In late 1998, construction was begun on a new building to house the trophies on Marvin's Stanton Street property. The building was designed by Marvin's grandson, Eric DeWitt, an architectural student at Lawrence Technological University. The relocation of the trophy room is part of an agreement between Marvin and Sara Lee Corp., which acquired the business from the DeWitt family in 1987. Like the room at Bil Mar, the new fireproofed building will have a special air-circulation system.

Harold Haas, Marvin's friend and a former poultry processor from the Detroit area, took the plant tour and kidded him about all the animals he had killed for his trophy room. Marvin quickly reminded Haas that he could not claim righteous indignation about killing animals. Haas had slaughtered chickens and turkeys for a living.

Marvin enjoys the thrill of the hunt, including the tracking involved and the challenge that comes from attempting to down a fast-moving animal, like an antelope. Though on the trail of a trophy animal, he was not blind to the scenery and native people around him as he tracked up mountains, through jungles, and across deserts.

"For him, the exploration, along with the planning and camaraderie, was just as important as the hunting aspect. He loves traveling, meeting people, and seeing new places," Prince said. "When he visited a place, he wanted to do and see everything that was possible. He was really fascinated by the different lifestyles."

And nothing stood in the way of traveling and big-game hunts. Before he had a heart pacemaker installed, his doctor strongly recommended he not attempt a trip that was to take him 5,000 feet into the mountains. He ignored his physician's advice and forged ahead with his plans.

He was only injured once on a big game hunt when he fell out of a tree while hanging bait for a lion. Marvin had shot an impala to use as bait, and his guides were not hanging it the way he wanted. He climbed up the tree to show them how it should be done and a branch broke underneath him. He fell on a limb when he hit the ground, badly bruising his leg. The injury, however, didn't slow him down for a minute.

His ability to ignore pain in pursuit of a goal has been recounted many times by friends and business associates. When he was putting up barbed-wire fencing around the homestead property, a roll of wire sprung back and cut a foot-long gash in his leg almost to the bone. He scoffed at the idea of taking time away from the task at hand to seek medical assistance. Instead, he poured an antiseptic, tincture of Merthiolate, into the wound until it started boiling. Then he bandaged the leg and went back to work.

"He can be a tough person, a throwback to the days when people really had to struggle to survive. Those were the days when medical treatment wasn't as readily available, especially for those in rural areas," said Jim Bultman, newly installed Hope College president and former president of Northwestern College in Orange City, Iowa, which has received major donations from Marvin and his family. "In Marvin's younger days, they sustained a lot of injuries and they couldn't afford to run to a doctor all of the time. His generation took a lot of risks and was largely self-sufficient."

Besides big-game hunting, Marvin took up another recreational pursuit in the 1970s – golf. He was introduced to the game by Preston Kool, a friend and West Michigan businessman. Marvin brought to the game of golf his highly competitive spirit, which was a little unrefined for the gentlemanly sport. He would shout "miss it" to break the concentration of a fellow player about to take a swing, reminiscent of the days when he rattled batters behind the plate as a softball catcher. His early attire also didn't conform to golfing etiquette. He wore tennis shoes, knee-length tube socks, and an old pair of shorts and a T-shirt. Marvin realized he didn't fit the picture of the stereotypical golfer and enlisted Kool to polish his image so he could someday play at private clubs.

"One day he asked me if I would teach him how to play golf better. I told him I wasn't a golf pro and suggested he take lessons from someone who was. He wasn't asking me how to play the game of golf better but how to be a better player in terms of golfing etiquette," Kool said.

Kool was also responsible for getting Marvin involved overseas for more than just big-game hunting and sightseeing. In 1972, the pair performed some mission work on behalf of International Development, a Washington, D.C.-based organization with ties to the World Evangelical Fellowship. The group was attempting to link American entrepreneurs with foreigners who wanted assistance in starting businesses. Kool knew of a Nigerian who wanted to work in the poultry business. And he couldn't think of a better mentor than Marvin.

Marvin presents Howard Miller clock to Dr. Earl Butz, former U.S. Department of Agriculture Secretary, during appearance in Zeeland.

"I needed someone with vision who was knowledgeable in the poultry business and not afraid to fail. That person also needed the desire for doing exciting things. Marvin fit that bill perfectly," Kool said.

Under Marvin's supervision, the Nigerian interned at Bil Mar for six months. With the learning phase completed, Marvin and Kool accompanied the man back to his native country to set up a poultry business. The enterprise never succeeded due to the political turmoil in that African country. During his stay in the war-torn country, Marvin ignored warnings not to stray from the base camp, especially after dark. He was oblivious to the chaos around them. His curiosity about the country and its residents outweighed any fear he might have had about possible dangers.

Within three weeks, it was obvious that the poultry venture was not going to work unless the two American businessmen were willing to pay bribes demanded by local officials. Unwilling to support the corruption, the two men decided to leave the country. The night before they left, Marvin, Kool and the Nigerian joined in prayer. Before they finished, all three men were in tears. Marvin and Kool had grown to like the ambitious young man and they were sad that things had not worked out.

In the 1970s, Marvin's activities weren't limited to overseas trips and Bil Mar operations. He also made time in his busy schedule for further community service, which began with his election to the Zeeland Public School Board. He felt a need to give back some time to a community that had served his business and family so well. He was also driven by an insatiable desire to learn how things work, in this case the systems of local governing.

"Even though the business and other activities took a lot of my time, I also felt it necessary to get involved in the community. When you get involved, you see things from a different perspective," he said. "I brought my conservatism and common sense to all the boards I served on. I think I had a good handle on the hidden costs of running those operations because of my business experience."

He first ran for Zeeland's public school board with the idea that he could have some impact on the educational process. He served at a time when rural one-room school districts were consolidating with their larger urban counterparts across the state. He supported the change, which allowed for bus runs out in the country where kids were walking upwards of two miles to the rural schools.

He was not the teachers' favorite pet on the school board. He was outspoken in his opposition to most pay raises for teachers. He believed they were overpaid for the amount of time they actually worked. He was also an advocate of a year-round school year, so the teachers would have to work more days and the buildings would not sit idle all summer.

During Marvin's tenure, the teachers also formed a union, which went against his independent grain. He's a firm advocate in people dealing one-on-one and believed the union hindered that process.

"The state tenure laws made it difficult to get rid of a bad teacher. The union just made it that much harder," he said.

In his deliberations, he tried to evaluate how the board's decisions were going to affect the Christian schools in the community. He recommended the public schools cooperate with them, when legally possible, for the benefit of education throughout the community.

Mel Baron, who served on the school board with Marvin, remembered him as being inquisitive and determined to make a decision based on facts instead of hearsay. He was also never afraid to speak his mind on an issue.

"Marvin DeWitt was a self-made man who didn't have many opportunities for schooling. That does not mean he was not intelligent," Baron said. "He was very capable of letting the board know what his thoughts were on almost any question, including whether a newly hired teacher met his approval. One of the issues we disagreed on was pay for teachers. I tried to impress upon him that teachers weren't being hired to cut gizzards out of turkeys. We were putting our children into the hands of people we had to trust."

Dr. Ray Lokers, former superintendent of the Zeeland school district, found Marvin to be a fair and open-minded board member, despite his opinionated nature. Marvin would relay complaints from parents about school operations to the district, reminding them that there may be another side to the story. If the complaint proved unwarranted after investigation, he would set the parents straight.

"You always knew where Marvin stood on an issue. That does not mean he was unwilling to accept other opinions if someone could present a convincing argument," Dr. Lokers said. "Marvin was not always on the winning end of a board decision. When that happened, there were no sour grapes on his part. When the board reached a consensus on a position, everyone, including Marvin, pulled together. Marvin knew what he wanted to do and where he stood, yet he was willing to back the board once it made a decision. There was no playing politics on the board. Marvin recognized that he was a member of the board and not the board."

Lokers also remembered him as a hard worker, especially prior to the consolidation of the rural elementary school districts. Before consolidation occurred, Marvin spent a lot of time talking to residents in the Borculo area to solicit their opinions on the operation of the Zeeland district.

"He was very concerned about the consolidation of elementary districts around us. He wanted to make sure that even though they were assimilating into our district, they would still be recognized as individual areas and that parents in those areas would have a say in the operation of the schools," Dr. Lokers said. "He didn't like the idea of those areas just being swallowed up and losing their identity after being autonomous for so long. That was a fearful thing for people in those areas, who had worked so hard at making their schools a success.

"Marvin was also concerned with the larger picture and what was best for the entire area during consolidation. There was a lot of discussion with other big districts in the area about where the lines were to be drawn for the new consolidated districts. It was quite a job to figure out what would be best for everyone, and the board that Marvin served on helped make those decisions."

While serving on the school board, Marvin was elected to the Ottawa County Board of Supervisors [now the Ottawa County Board of Commissioners]. Marvin quit his school board position in favor of the county board job after he was informed that serving on both was a conflict of interest. Looking to try something new, Marvin opted for the county board position. He felt comfortable with fellow supervisors who were hard-nosed conservatives like himself. He recalled that county departments would always inflate their budgets by at least 20 percent, knowing the board was going to take a fiscal knife to their requests.

Eunice Bareham was appointed to the board in early 1972 as the first woman member. Representing Spring Lake, Spring Lake Township, and Ferrysburg, she was a 46-year-old widow with four children to raise. She had come to know Marvin before her service on the board through her active participation, with her husband, Bob, in the Republican Party. Bob, who died in 1971, had been a former Spring Lake village treasurer and councilman. Marvin had long been a leader in the party.

She respected Marvin for his courage. He did not hesitate to speak his mind or fight for what he believed in. And he was never malicious in pursuit of a goal. He also exhibited a lot of common sense, which more than compensated for his lack of formal schooling. Like other male commissioners, his initial treatment of Bareham was condescending. At first, Bareham was referred to as "girlie." Male commissioners welcomed Bareham, saying it would be nice to have a woman board member who could be counted on to make sure coffee and cookies were available for meetings. That macho behavior soon faded when Bareham made it clear she was not going to be the board's waitress.

Ottawa County commissioners Peter DeKock (left) and Marvin Dewitt confer in the meeting room before the monthly session of the full board.

Marvin said he learned to appreciate women board members, who seemed to be more industrious than a lot of men – maybe in an attempt to prove themselves after so many years in the shadows of public life. A number of men on the board were afraid to talk back to women, probably recalling a popular refrain from their upbringing that boys aren't supposed to attack girls. Marvin treated women and men as equals. If he was sure about his position, he would talk back to both genders.

Bareham offered this recollection of service with Marvin on the board: "Of all the commissioners on the board, I had the greatest respect for his opinions and insight. That did not mean I was intimidated by him. I was not afraid to disagree with him. But those disagreements did not go beyond the board room. He never forgot to ask me how my children and I were doing after the death of my husband. There was no personal animosity as a result of our many disagreements, even after I became county treasurer. Marvin came across as being gruff and tough. He was not someone you would lie to or try to manipulate. You would lose on both counts. I always believed there is a man with a big heart behind that gruff exterior. If someone close to him was hurting, he would come through for them."

After county board membership was reduced from 21 to 11 commissioners, Marvin decided not to run again. Instead, he sought a six-year term on the county road commission, from 1977 to 1982.

Ron Bakker, former road commission manager, said Marvin was a "nuts-and-bolts kind of commissioner," who was not afraid to ask detailed questions, especially about purchasing pieces of equipment.

During Marvin's term, he convinced the commission to purchase diesel trucks, which were easier to start, cheaper to fuel, and needed less repair. The road commission also agreed to use a larger 12-foot scraper to cover more of the road.

"Marvin was always asking why we weren't doing things a certain way. If you had a reasonable explanation, he would accept it and become a strong proponent. If you didn't have an answer, he would keep pushing you for one and get you thinking about it," Bakker said. "He started with nothing, and got to where he was because he was interested in the details. Some of the commissioners would accuse him of talking too much and spending too much time on details. But we changed a number of things at the road commission for the better, either as the result of him raising the question or advancing an idea. He was not a polished politician or speaker. He didn't always use the best King's English. However, he was adept at getting his point across. He had a gift for logic and common sense."

Because his business was in a rural area of the county, Marvin knew the value of good local roads and worked closely with the townships to promote that goal – even when there was strong opposition, Bakker said.

"Often times, we were pressured by townships and residents

along a road to do a project in a manner that suited them better by keeping a road narrower or saving some trees. Some of the commissioners would attempt to compromise. Marvin was not much for compromise when it came to the standards for a good road. He was looking 20 years ahead. He would not cheapen a project for the sake of compromise. Some other commissioners would say that a compromise wasn't all that bad and they could live with it. Not Marvin. He was a strong believer in maintaining the standards he thought were right for that road. He would not bend unless you gave him a good reason for bending.

"After serving with him on the road commission, I could understand why he was so successful in business. He was not one to give up. There were many tough times in his business when a lesser man would have thrown in the towel. We faced a number of tough issues during his tenure on the road commission. If he believed in something, he would never back off. It didn't matter that there were 20 or 30 angry people at a public hearing. Marvin could not be scared off if he believed his course of action was in the long-term best interest of the community. He would implore people to think in long-range terms."

By his example, Marvin inspired his children to pursue community service. All of the children have played active roles in their respective churches, in such capacities as Sunday school teachers, youth club leaders, deacons, and elders. Marilyn has served as an elder delegate to the Holland Classis of the Reformed Church in America and a women's representative to the Zeeland Classis of RCA. Marilyn also assisted in the RCA hurricane relief effort in 1995 in St. Thomas, Virgin Islands. Jack helped build a church in the Dominican Republic. Don serves as a Stephens Minister, a lay ministry of care giving.

Gary and Jack have been involved in trade associations. Gary was president of the Michigan Allied Poultry Association and served on the USA Egg & Poultry Council. Jack served on the technical and regulatory committee of the National Turkey Federation. Gary has also been elected to public office on the Zeeland Public School Board.

The children have given volunteer time to a variety of organizations, including service on boards. Gary has served such organizations as Holland Community Hospital, Old Kent Bank, Camp Geneva, Michigan Independent Family Agency, and Pine Rest Christian Hospital. Marilyn's service list includes Ottawa County Probate/ Juvenile Court's CASA (Court Appointed Special Advocate) program, Good Samaritan Ministries, Macatawa Area Coordinating Council, Ottawa County Mental Health Board, Resthaven Patrons Inc., and Western Theological Seminary Alumni Council.

Jack's list of community involvement includes the Holland Township Planning Commission, Zeeland AMBUCS (American Business Clubs), coaching Little League baseball, and board service for Northwestern College, Paragon Bank, AD Bos & Co., Quincy Street Meats, and HEDCOR (Holland Economic Development Corp.). Don serves as a board member on behalf of Youth for Christ in Holland and Gospel Communications International Inc. [formerly Gospel Films]. He is also involved in Motor Racing Outreach. The nationwide organization provides a traveling chapel, spiritual counseling, Bible studies, and child care for NASCAR drivers, their families, and pit crews. The outreach organization provides similar services at boat, truck, and motorcycle races. Don's community service also involved coaching Little League and Rocket Football.

Nancy has been a 4-H leader, president of the Parent Teachers Organization at Roosevelt Elementary, and a volunteer for CASA. She has also given time to boards governing Camp Geneva, Hope College's Village Square [representing Reformed churches in the Zeeland Classis], and Wedgewood Christian Youth and Family Services in Grand Rapids. Merle is a graduate of the Holland Leadership Program sponsored by the Holland Area Chamber of Commerce.

Unlike his children, Marvin took his community service one step further by becoming active in the political process long before he started serving on public boards.

He joined the Republican Party in Ottawa County in the 1950s, when the business was still struggling to make ends meet. His support in the 1950s and 1960s helped lay the solid foundation that supports today's party activity in the county.

He could always be counted on for a donation, even during tough business times. He hosted a number of fund-raising picnics for politicians out in front of the plant. And he donated turkeys for party raffles.

"Marvin came through in the 1950s when $50 was hard to come by. He still managed to find a way to contribute to the party. In the Zeeland area, Marvin's name was the first you thought of when it came to the Republican Party," Bareham said.

He was not content to support the party out of his own wallet. He strongly encouraged his salaried employees to give party donations, believing that having friends in politics was smart business. The strong-arm tactic met with disapproval from some of the supervisors. Marvin, however, took the criticism in stride.

"I know some of the salaried employees were not happy that I twisted their arms to give donations to the Republican Party. I figured that I paid them well and those contacts would pay off for the business – and their futures – in the long run," he said. "I also felt it was a way to get people thinking about the political process. It is not easy to get money out of the Dutch for politics, though I was always encouraging my friends to contribute."

From the start of his political involvement, Marvin had no intention of becoming a power broker. He did want to cultivate some friendly contacts in high places because his business was so heavily regulated by the government. Over the years, he asked for a few favors, yet tried never to abuse those relationships.

"Making friends with politicians squared with my philosophy of talking to the person in charge when there is a problem. It doesn't hurt to know people in higher places when you have a problem," he said. "Our representatives wouldn't do anything wrong or unethical for us. They would help us when they could. If I had been a better letter writer, I probably would have asked for more help from all kinds of people."

Michigan Sen. William Van Regenmorter (R-Allegan, Ottawa, and Van Buren counties) confirmed that Marvin did not use his position in the Republican Party to exert undue influence on officeholders.

"Marvin has always conducted himself very, very professionally, and with great integrity. Other than occasional requests for ordinary legislative information, one incident of him requesting help comes to mind," Van Regenmorter said. "Some years ago, Bil Mar had a devastating fire that destroyed most of the facility and put many of the employees out of work temporarily. Marvin called me to express his deep concern about those employees. I called several banks in the area that agreed to make arrangements to relax payment schedules for home mortgages and other financial dealings. Calling about concerns for others is typical of Marvin."

Marvin's many recreational, community, and political activities in the 1970s did not preclude him from finding time to promote the business. In 1971, he hit the road with his friend Dr. Carl Hoyt to honor a returning prisoner of war from Vietnam and drum up some favorable publicity for Bil Mar.

John Sexton, a former Vietnam prisoner of war, is personally treated by Marvin to a Bil Mar turkey for his first Thanksgiving at home.

The release of John Sexton, of Warren, Mich., came just before Thanksgiving and the young man said he couldn't wait to feast on the holiday dinner with turkey and all the trimmings. Hoyt contacted Marvin about having some turkeys shipped to Sexton's family. Marvin thought they should personally deliver the birds. They also called the Michigan Pork Producers to supply a couple of holiday hams. Sexton and his family accepted the turkeys and hams graciously, welcoming Marvin and Hoyt like old friends. They were impressed that the president of such a large company would personally make the delivery.

Also with an eye on furthering Bil Mar, Marvin deepened his participation in organizations with connections to the business. He became a board member for the largest such group – the National Turkey Federation.

As a representative of NTF, he was involved in the failed attempt to enact a national turkey marketing order in 1958. Passage of the order, by NTF members, would have provided marketing controls at the hatchery level, and a mechanism for raising funds to support promotion and research programs. The intent of the order was to maintain a balance between the industry's production capability, and its ability to expand markets and create profits. Approval of the order, which Marvin recommended to local hatchery owners and turkey growers, would have occurred at a time when the industry was starting to evolve from seasonal production to one of a year-round basis. The NTF believed that passage of the order would have given smaller hatchery owners and growers a better chance of competing with larger ones. The proposed order was defeated nationwide and the aftermath is evidenced in the consolidation of the industry, and the declining number of NTF members since then. In the late 1950s there were 5,000 members versus about 800 today.

It was also Marvin's involvement in the NTF that earned him an invitation to deliver the annual Thanksgiving Turkey to the president of the United States in the fall of 1975. His opportunity came during the presidency of Gerald Ford, a former West Michigan Congressman who Marvin knew on a first-name basis from his active involvement in the Republican party.

After his nomination for the honor, Marvin raised four turkeys in a pen behind his home near the plant. For the presentation, two of the turkeys were live while the other two were processed and frozen. The day before the ceremony, Marvin and his wife were accompanied to Washington, D.C., by Dr. Howard Zindel, chairman of the poultry science department at Michigan State University, and his wife, all of whom stayed the night in a hotel with the two live turkeys. As the night wore on, the turkeys became restless in their new surroundings, and Marvin put them out on the roof of the hotel to peck and scratch the night away.

The President is always photographed with one of the live turkeys in the White House Rose Garden. The second turkey was brought along as a back up in the event something happened to the other one. The President never eats any of the national turkeys, either live or frozen. After the presentation of the bird, the two live turkeys are donated to a petting zoo. The two frozen turkeys are donated to charities.

Marvin (far left) presents 'National Turkey' to President Gerald Ford.

Marvin's moment in the national spotlight was overshadowed somewhat that morning by then-California governor Ronald Reagan's announcement that he was running for the Republican presidential nomination in 1976. Suddenly, the news media were more interested in the impending political struggle between Ford and Reagan than the annual delivery of a turkey. Before the presentation, Marvin's displeasure with the timing of the announcement was tempered when President Ford called out his name in the Rose Garden crowd and asked how things were going in Borculo. After the turkey presentation, Marvin and his wife were given a private tour of the White House.

"I felt that the whole experience was quite an honor. That wouldn't have happened had I not been involved in the national federation. I was always involved in all the turkey associations and poultry meetings," Marvin said. " It was a way to become acquainted with people in the same industry and learn some things. It was also a way to be on the ground floor when it came time to setting rules and regulations for the industry."

The White House presentation wasn't the only honor bestowed upon Marvin in the 1970s. In 1977, Marvin and his brother Bill were the recipients of the Distinguished Service to Agriculture award from MSU's College of Agriculture and Natural Resources.

In presenting the award, MSU said: "Starting with 160 acres of land and a few buildings in 1938, the brothers have built Michigan's largest complete poultry rearing and processing industry, consisting of 3,000 acres, more than 50 buildings, and over a million birds annually. This large family operation is noted for many innovative advances within the industry and their production of an excellent product for consumers. They are noted for their humanitarian work, notably in Nigeria, and for their generous and constant support of local civic and church programs. Throughout the years, they have been extremely cooperative in furnishing MSU poultry sciences faculty and students with material to conduct academic studies. They have been leaders in the Michigan Turkey Association, Michigan Allied Poultry Industry, the National Turkey Federation, and have served on boards in all of these industry organizations."

Although his many outside interests might have taken Marvin physically away from the Bil Mar plant on 96th Avenue, his mind was never very far from the business he had co-founded.

No matter how long he had been away from the plant, he could walk back in and seem never to have missed a thing that had transpired. No matter where he was in the world, he stayed in contact with his son Gary about any pending decisions.

"Marvin always amazed me. When he returned after four or five weeks from one of his trips, he knew more details about what happened at the plant than I did," said Tom Norman, one of Marvin's sons-in-law and a former facilities manager at Bil Mar.

Chuck Curtis, who once handled Michigan sales for Bil Mar, was also amazed at Marvin's ever-commanding presence over the business.

"Marvin haunted the halls of Bil Mar even when he was not there. That is how strong his presence was," Curtis said. "He always had more control of the operation than what most people thought. He was constantly phoning in when he was away. And he would come in for meetings at least once a month. If it came down to making a hard decision, he would be there to help make it."

And in the mid-1970s, Marvin made some major decisions, including the introduction of a retail line of products, under the Mr. Turkey brand, and the purchase of a second plant in Iowa.

Mr. Turkey character represents
Bil Mar's retail line.

CHAPTER ELEVEN

ENTERING THE RETAIL MARKET

As Bil Mar moved through the 1970s, the company became a significant player in the food-service market where white-meat turkey products were its top seller. Retail sales, involving mostly dark-meat parts, were almost an afterthought.

Marvin preferred to concentrate on the food-service niche. Unlike retail, selling products to hospitals, restaurants, schools, prisons, hotels, in-plant cafeterias, and airlines requires a minimum of capital outlay for marketing, advertising, and packaging.

He was also aware that consumer tastes were changing and retail sales were waning for the bulk wings, thighs and drumsticks, and two-pound and three-and-a-half-pound roasts.

So as the white-meat business boomed with food-service sales, Marvin and his sons were left wondering what they would do with the increasing amount of corresponding dark meat. The company needed a new market for dark meat. And that meat had to be presented in a more convenient product form than bulk parts and roasts.

When the DeWitts first contemplated a full-scale push into the retail market, they only thought of repackaging some of the bulk retail items in smaller quantities, and adding a full line of smaller turkey roasts and turkey with gravy.

In looking around the industry, however, the DeWitts found some companies beginning to take the retail experiment one step further – processing dark-meat parts to create products as substitutes for pork and beef items, like hot dogs and luncheon meats. The DeWitts believed that was the next hot market for turkey and decided to jump into the retail business in 1977 with the Mr. Turkey line of products. Their timing couldn't have been better. Bil Mar entered the retail turkey business early and was well-established when consumers – concerned about heart disease – demanded low-fat alternatives, like turkey, in grocery meat cases. Bil Mar's solid retail business is what also enticed the Sara Lee Corp. to acquire the family-owned company in 1987.

"The secret of being successful in business is being able to react to change. If the salesmen said the market was demanding a certain product, we worked hard to manufacture that product. We were always ready for change," Marvin said. "That is why we went into the retail business, even though we were geared more toward food service. Turkey is lower in fat than beef or pork, and we came out with a lot of new retail products to meet that demand. We were in the right business at the right time, and we took advantage of an opportunity – just like we did when we made the first roasted turkey roll as a convenience product. You have to be alert to what the market wants and then provide it."

Bil Mar's planned move into the retail arena, just a few steps behind its largest rival, Louis Rich, was quick to catch the attention of the turkey industry. Turkey World magazine devoted a lengthy article to the proposal.

"Bil Mar Foods in Zeeland has made quite a name for itself in the food-service market for turkey products. And a few dollars, too. There will be no let up in that, but the company now is expanding into the retail market with a full line of convenience turkey items packaged the way supermarkets will sell them and the way housewives will buy them," said the lead in for the article. "It is an added-value program for Bil Mar Foods – a program born of necessity and opportunity, and a program from which Bil Mar, the turkey industry, and consumers will all benefit... A prime reason Bil Mar decided to go retail is that supermarkets simply don't handle bulk products any more, such as 30-pound boxes of byproduct items like drums, necks, wings and tails. The company would not be able to market dark-meat byproducts with as great a return as it is expecting to receive by doing even more further processing. Bil Mar decided that if it wanted to sell more dark turkey meat, it would have to be packaged the way supermarkets and housewives want it."

By adding a retail division, Bil Mar had come full circle in its 38-year history. The company started by selling minimally processed New York-dressed turkeys to retailers. Bil Mar then moved into the wholesale food-service market with frozen turkeys and further-processed products. The introduction of Mr. Turkey products put the company solidly back into the retail arena.

"Before we went to further processing in the early 1960s, we didn't have to worry about dark meat. It was sold along with the rest of the whole turkey," Gary DeWitt said. "After we went to further processing, we were mainly a food-service company. And food service mostly wanted the white-meat products. That left us with the rest of the turkey to deal with. The question of what to do with the dark side of the turkey and how do you add more value to that portion was really the foundation of retail."

But convincing consumers to buy turkey other than for Thanksgiving and Christmas was not an easy sell, even though Bil Mar had some limited retail success in the off-holiday season with its turkey roasts, frozen turkey parts, and whole birds for Sunday dinners. By tradition, consumers were conditioned to think of turkey as a one-dimensional product. They mainly bought the meat during that five-week holiday period, when 70 percent of all turkeys were sold and consumed. To abolish that mind-set for good, the DeWitts hired Warren Waters to lead the new retail division. Waters, former national sales manager at Ralston-Purina, had been recommended by long-time Bil Mar customer and friend, Harold Haas, principal owner of City Poultry in Detroit. Waters was in the market for a new job when Ralston-Purina was sold.

"I had a better offer from another past associate before I started with Bil Mar. But I decided to go with the DeWitts. The family was genuinely nice and I felt I would be more comfortable there. They were also given the highest recommendation from Harold Haas," Waters said.

Waters was responsible for developing a line of nationally branded, dark-meat turkey products for the retail market. From the start, everyone involved realized that a retail product needed a catchier name than Bil Mar. Coming up with a brand name and logo was a collaborative effort. Beverly Curtis, wife of Bil Mar sales executive Chuck Curtis, suggested the company put a cartoon character on the new retail products and came up with a Super Turkey sketch. From that suggestion, Waters worked with a Detroit advertising firm to create a variety of cartoon characters to represent the retail products. There was Mr. Turkey, with a top hat, cane and tuxedo, who would promote pre-packed turkey parts, turkey roasts, and turkey slices with gravy. Mr. Sausage, a piggish-looking character, was to sell turkey breakfast sausage. Mr. Hot Dog, a walking hot dog with a chef's hat, was to advertise turkey dogs. Mr. Sandwich was supposed to attract shoppers to the turkey ham, salami, pastrami and bologna. Mr. Burger was going to be on the packages for turkey chuck wagon patties.

In the end, Mr. Turkey was selected as the best character to symbolize all of the retail products because he represented the main ingredient. Having one character would also make it easier for consumers to identify Bil Mar retail products.

There was a momentary glitch in using the Mr. Turkey character as a logo. A patent attorney discovered that another company – a small poultry processor in southern Indiana – was already using a similar turkey character. Marvin, who had sold poults to the company over the years, contacted the owner and bought the rights to the logo for $10,000. Proud of the company's heritage, Marvin insisted the Bil Mar name be on the Mr. Turkey package. The designers complied with his request by having the tuxedo-clad turkey standing in front of a barn inscribed with Bil Mar.

Waters started from scratch in creating the retail division. Bil Mar was doing very little in the retail market compared to the food-service business of the company. Retail products mainly consisted of frozen whole turkeys, frozen turkey dark-meat parts, a two-pound dark/light meat roast, and a three-and-a-half-pound dark roast.

Starting from scratch was not an inexpensive proposition, however. The biggest difference between food service and retail was the amount of money a company had to invest for product promotion.

With food service, Bil Mar had a minimum of advertising and marketing expenses. The company only had to deal with brokers and food distributors. Product development followed a predictable process. Many food-service products were custom-made at the request of Bil Mar's master broker Mickey Manaster or a food distributor, like Gordon Food Services. With retail, a company had to invest a considerable amount of money upfront for advertising and marketing to convince the end user, the consumer, to buy the product. The tricks of the retail trade included in-store product demonstrations and coupons. The initial marketing strategy was to reach consumers in areas representing about 50 percent of the population – the Midwest, Plains States, the Southeast, Southwest, and Washington and Oregon in the Northwest.

Warren Waters leads retail division.

"Retail was a new culture for Bil Mar. For the first time we had to get into the communications business. We had to figure out a way to reach consumers so they would go into a store and purchase our products," Gary DeWitt said. "That also pushed us into the area of promotions. We would give stores a discount of cents off per pound so they would promote it in their ads."

Marketing was only one piece of the retail strategy. Bil Mar was also faced with a new production challenge – how much product do you manufacture when you don't know how well a new product will be accepted in the more-volatile retail market. Retail distribution presented its own difficult juggling act. The delivery time was shorter than for food service, sometimes a five-day period from the order to the shipment time. Instead of dealing directly with supermarkets, Bil Mar sold the retail products through distributors like Park Poultry in Canton, Ohio, General Produce in Milwaukee, Wis., City Foods in Detroit, and Will's Poultry in Buffalo, N.Y. They became Bil Mar's sales agents in major cities because they had good contacts with supermarkets.

"Selling retail was a real learning process after so many years in food service. There was the challenge of consistent on-time delivery of the right amount of product. Sometimes orders were short and sometimes more was delivered than ordered. And if a product wasn't produced correctly, you had the problem of shortened shelf life or high bacterial counts," Gary said. "The new retail culture also forced us to make sales projections based on what salespeople thought they would sell. But we always remembered that most sales people are far more optimistic when it comes to predicting what kind of sales they can generate. We tried to produce just short of what we thought would sell. That way, we were never forced to discount too much if we had overproduced. If we were a little under prediction, we were never afraid to purchase raw materials from the outside to take up the slack in production."

Bil Mar also had to invest substantial dollars in conceiving a broader line of products to entice consumers spoiled by numerous choices in the marketplace. To come up with so many new turkey products – like ham, luncheon meats, hot dogs, Polish kielbasa, smoked sausage, breakfast sausages, patties, and Canadian bacon – a research and development group had to be established. The group would also be responsible for product modification and new packaging.

Bil Mar's first research and development director was Joe Gaskill, who worked on the development of turkey ham and hot dogs. Gaskill was followed by Dr. Phil Weiner, who was Bil Mar's longest-serving research and development director.

"I was impressed by the enthusiasm of the DeWitts, especially Marvin, and their innovative ideas. Marvin was a dynamic person who saw opportunities and was not afraid to take chances. He instilled that same philosophy in his sons," said Weiner, who received a doctorate in food science from Michigan State University and worked for an Eckrich plant in Indiana and a Sara Lee meat company known as Kahn's in Ohio before joining Bil Mar. "I liked the non-political style at Bil Mar. The politics of my old job is one of the reasons I left to go to Bil Mar. The DeWitts didn't need a lot of meetings to decide on a course of action. If you wanted to question something new, the time to do it was at that meeting. When the meeting was over, everyone was expected to be on board. I also appreciated the family's ethical style, and the high standards they set for themselves and everyone else. Bil Mar proved to be a very excellent environment to excel."

Promotional material for Bil Mar's retail product line.

The hiring of Weiner proved to be another fortunate move for Bil Mar. He was the company's first research and development person with extensive red-meat knowledge necessary for the successful formulation of turkey-meat imitators, like pastrami and bologna. He also brought to Bil Mar new methods of cooking, seasoning, and moisture retention – all designed to lower the product cost while extending shelf life.

With Weiner's help, Bil Mar expanded its customer base by fabricating a lower-cost turkey product through a process of emulsification. As an example, Bil Mar tore apart a whole breast, chopped it into smaller pieces, mixed in a percentage of water, formed the new product, and then cooked it. The mixing action extracted the natural proteins to the outside of the meat. The combination of the protein and a small amount of salt added for flavor bound the meat together, like glue, during the cooking process. The finished product – known in the industry as a further, further-processed item – resembled a whole breast without the muscle texture.

"We needed someone like a Phil Weiner to look at the complicated processes for cooking and cooling cycles, and then concentrate on how best to manufacture turkey. Arriving at the beginning of Bil Mar's retail history, Phil was the author of our retail product line," Gary said.

Even with top-notch sales and R & D employees aboard, the retail effort at Bil Mar jumped off to less than an enthusiastic start. It lacked the wholehearted support of some key personnel in the company. Mickey Manaster, the company's top salesman, was dead set against investing in a retail program. He believed the company's best bet was to focus on its rock-solid food-service business. Jack DeWitt, Marvin's second oldest son and plant manager, also questioned why the company should stick its neck out with a retail program when things were going so well in the food-service market. Lining up in support of retail were Gary DeWitt, by then president of the company, and Waters, who would lead the effort. Marvin, chairman of the board, initially questioned the need for such a program like he did any new idea. He eventually convinced himself there was value in entering the consumer market and gave his blessing.

The disagreement over the worth of the retail program eventually took its toll on the company. The grumbling would drag on for eight years until Manaster, retail's biggest detractor, left the company. Jack's support for Manaster and Gary's backing of Waters would only intensify a natural rivalry between the two brothers.

Despite the simmering retail disagreement, the program was launched with much fanfare on TV and radio, and in newspapers and magazines. The retail line marked the first time Bil Mar would advertise on television, which gave birth to an animated Mr. Turkey – the debonair turkey character who wore a top hat and a tuxedo on all of the retail packaging.

Bil Mar hired Rene Zendejas, a famous puppeteer, to bring the Mr. Turkey logo to life as the company's retail spokesperson. The creativity of Zendejas was put to the test in making a life-like turkey who could talk, roll his eyes, turn his head, wiggle his fan tail, and demonstrate products with his hands – all at the same time. To achieve that sense of versatility and realism, he decided against a conventional hand puppet or a stringed marionette. He devised an inverse marionette, with cables concealed inside a three-foot-high Mr. Turkey body.

The puppet required two operators, who had to lie on the floor out of camera range during filming to manipulate the intricate controls that would give the movement characterization. The voice of Mr. Turkey was supplied by an actor who was picked from an audition held on both the East and West coasts. The voice had to represent a friendly but authoritative figure who could sell families on the nutritional advantages of Mr. Turkey. Three separate commercials – for turkey franks, ham, and luncheon meats – were shot using the puppet as the main character. He appeared with actors in typical dining scenes on a set designed like a home kitchen. Zendejas' vision of Mr. Turkey was right on target with the consumer. The Mr. Turkey character was receiving fan letters shortly after the commercials aired.

Two Mr. Turkeys attend Tulip Time Festival.

The media was quick to pick up on the advertising message that promoted turkey as a new multi-faceted food instead of just a 25-pound, golden-brown bird resting on the Thanksgiving dinner table.

A Grand Rapids Press article couldn't have been more flattering if Waters had written it himself: "The trend is moving away from turkey as just the holiday bird. It is now served in many forms through the year, and a leader in the field is Bil Mar Foods. Other products, in addition to the company's regular line of whole turkeys, turkey parts, roasted breasts, thighs and rolls, include salami, bologna, pickle and pimento loaf, pastrami, breakfast sausage, ham and hot dogs. Turkey meat is mild in flavor, high in protein, and low in fat and cholesterol. When combined with appropriate seasonings and sometimes smaller amounts of pork or beef, turkey meats, such as cold cuts, can duplicate or surpass the flavor and quality of many other cold meats, according to company officials. They said the meat is also more economical to produce – taking just three and a half pounds of grain to convert into a pound of meat. The ratio for pork conversion is four to five pounds of grain per one pound of meat, while beef requires seven to cight pounds of grain."

Bil Mar's marketing campaign was also bolstered by university studies, showing the nutritional superiority of turkey over red meat.

A Cornell University researcher, who directed studies on the comparative protein, fat, and vitamin content of turkey and other meats reported that "turkey heads the list of lean meats in high-protein and low-fat content."

The report noted that each 100 calories of turkey meat supplies about 15 grams of protein, while each 100 calories of lean pork and lean ground beef supplies about 12 grams of protein. Also three and a half ounces of turkey meat supplies only about 176 calories, while a like amount of hamburger supplies 286 calories; porterhouse steak, 455 calories; pork ham, 289 calories; and lamb rib chops, 407 calories.

Marketing turkey franks.

The low-fat, low-calorie craze among consumers didn't really take off until the mid-1980s. But those early studies helped set the stage for turkey's rise in popularity at the grocery store.

Touted along with turkey's nutritional advantage was its lower per-pound price than red meat. Turkey products are generally less expensive than red-meat products because it costs less to raise turkey. Turkeys are slaughtered at a younger age, about 30 to 34 weeks for toms, and the cost of feed for turkeys is less expensive than feeding beef cattle.

Turkey's low-fat, low-cost advantage over red meat still couldn't overcome the skepticism some consumers exhibited toward the new retail products.

Promoting turkey lunch meats.

"The problem in most people's minds is what will the turkey product taste like. They want a hot dog to taste like a traditional hot dog, not like turkey," Waters said about the fickle consumer. "The same goes for the other products that turkey companies are trying to substitute for beef and pork products."

Gary DeWitt, interviewed about the turkey dog shortly after its introduction, said consumers fell into two camps when it came to accepting the new product. They either disregarded it or embraced it.

"For one group, the thought of eating a turkey hot dog and having it taste like a pork or beef frank is beyond them. The concept turns them off and they won't even try it. The other group is more willing to try a new product, especially one that contains a third less fat and calories than beef or pork wieners. They find that the taste is comparable to beef and pork franks," he said.

The secret to winning over consumers through their taste buds relied on the manufacturing process. The new retail products had to be made in the same manner as the corresponding red-meat product, including the use of spices and other ingredients. Fortunately for Bil Mar, the mild taste and the lean consistency of turkey meat easily absorbs the flavor of spices and other ingredients.

"It really doesn't matter whether you start off with beef, or turkey or pork. A beef hot dog and a turkey hot dog taste exactly alike because they are cooked the same way," said Weiner in an interview shortly after the products were introduced. "The process of curing, smoking and cooking are the same procedures used with other meat, such as turning pork into ham. We don't put anything in the turkey to make it taste like red meat. The meat used for turkey products comes from the same part of the turkey as it does in other red-meat products. For example, turkey ham is made from turkey thigh meat, just like traditional ham comes from the pig thigh. Look at the labels for turkey and pork ham and you'll see the ingredients are basically the same."

Just cooking turkey meat like red meat didn't assure instant success for the new products. Some of them went through a lot of experimentation to capture the right consistency for quality and taste. All the DeWitt families were enlisted to be taste subjects for the many product prototypes.

"It was hit-and-run and learn-as-you-go in the early days. We lacked the knowledge to produce these new products with consistent quality," Gary said. "For example, the first hot dogs had a tendency to turn green after they were shipped to customers. We took care of that problem by using fresher meat, and by being more consistent when mixing the ingredients and while running the product through the smoking process."

Even with all challenges, the new retail products were arousing the public's curiosity – much to the displeasure of red-meat companies who were beginning to lose some business to the turkey processors, like Bil Mar.

The National Pork Producers Council and the American Meat Institute decided to challenge the new trend in 1980 by suing the USDA to prevent the turkey industry from using the word "ham" on turkey ham products. With the help of the National Turkey Federation, the USDA had finalized a regulation providing for a product made from skinless, boneless turkey thigh meat to be labeled turkey ham. The red-meat group first responded by presenting the USDA with a petition asking that the regulation be withdrawn and that the use of the word be limited to products derived from the hind leg of a swine.

The petition was denied by the USDA and the two red-meat groups filed a law suit against the agency in a federal district court, contending that ham was synonymous with pork products. Supporting the USDA, the NTF gained equal standing in the litigation by obtaining intervener status. The NTF and USDA argued that the definition of a ham is the thigh of an animal, which could apply to the turkey as well as the hog. The court, however, ruled against the USDA, which declined to appeal the decision. Having legal standing as an intervener, the NTF appealed the decision to a federal court of appeals, which decided in favor of turkey processors.

The decision had far-reaching consequences. Had the two red-meat groups prevailed in setting aside the turkey ham label, they would have had a legal precedent to challenge labeling for other red-meat equivalents such as turkey bologna, pastrami, salami and franks. Such legal wrangling could have proved disastrous for the turkey industry's retail efforts.

For Bil Mar, the annual growth following the creation of the retail program symbolized Marvin's willingness to be innovative. His attitude, in turn, fostered a high level of creativity among employees. There was a sense of freedom and an openness to exploration that led to discoveries, according to Kevin McKenna, who started working at Bil Mar in 1979 as a product development chef. That year, Bil Mar posted $75.8 million in sales, triple 1976 sales of $25.8 million. By 1984, the 1979 figure had doubled to $169.8 million.

Semi-truck bears Mr. Turkey logo.

"The growth was fantastic because there was a can-do attitude. There was no question of whether something should or shouldn't be done, but how were we going to do it. It was Marvin who created that atmosphere," McKenna said. "You were always allowed to have an opinion. You were allowed to strive and go as high as you could go. I felt like a free agent, empowered to make things happen. I felt like I could make a difference."

The birth of the retail program wasn't the only major growth development in the 1970s. Marvin engineered the purchase of Bil Mar's second production facility, a bankrupt processing plant in Storm Lake, Iowa. Bil Mar also constructed a state-of-the art feed mill on U.S. 31, between Holland and Grand Haven.

But with expansion came growing pains for the family-run company. The early 1970s gave birth to a union among hourly production employees and the hiring of the company's first outside consultant to provide advice on personnel matters. The union formation and consultation did not sit well with Marvin, a man who prided himself on his family's ability to operate the company with a minimum of outside assistance or interference.

Bil Mar plant in the 1970's.

CHAPTER TWELVE

GROWTH AND GROWING PAINS

Like most drives to form unions in manufacturing plants, the organized labor movement at Bil Mar started with some grumbling among production employees.

As production supervisor, Jack DeWitt was one of the first in the family to hear the rumors of unionizing because of his close relationship to hourly workers on the plant floor.

When asked about their concerns, employees told Jack they wanted more company-paid benefits, such as health insurance. He relayed the requests to his father Marvin and brother Gary.

But the feeling among the DeWitts, especially Marvin, was that employees were already being fairly compensated.

The employees were given a yearly bonus fitting their performance and responsibilities, and the company's profit margin. They were eligible for a company-sponsored profit-sharing plan, based on

15 percent of yearly profits. The company offered paid holidays and vacations, a free holiday turkey, and an extra check at Christmas. And the workers were among the highest paid in the poultry industry, including unionized plants.

Marvin and his sons also rejected the idea of a union. It crimped their personal, one-on-one style of management.

"The union tied our hands as to how we could treat our employees. With a union, I could no longer favor a good worker or reward someone for an outstanding job," Marvin said. "The union also had some say as to how you promoted and disciplined someone. You had to have a file full of complaints before you could dismiss someone. The union rules were set up around a system of seniority, not someone's ability to do a job. I didn't feel a union was necessary for a worker to get ahead on his job."

A number of employees didn't share Marvin's attitude. The work force at Bil Mar in the early 1970s was changing in response to the company's growth. To fill a growing number of positions, the company had to cast a wider net for workers. And they lived in such places as Muskegon and Grand Rapids, where unionization is more common than the Holland/Zeeland region.

The commuting employees expected more in the way of benefits and wages than Bil Mar was willing to offer. Some of them were also put off by the domineering way in which the company was operated by Marvin and his sons. Those workers saw the formation of a union as a way to equalize the conflict between management and employee rights.

To them, all the power was tilted in favor of the DeWitts. There was no human resources department with guidelines for hiring, training, promotion, raises, and firing. If there were personnel chores to be done, Marvin or one of his sons handled them. The informal system had suited the DeWitts for more than 30 years and the family didn't see a need to change.

"The DeWitts were not slave drivers, despite dad's reputation for being rough and gruff," Jack DeWitt said. "We had a personal style of management. Our attitude toward employees was straightforward – you help me out and I will help you out."

Frustration with the DeWitt's style of management and the family's reluctance to increase benefits led some hourly workers to approach representatives from the nationwide Teamsters union. Marvin felt betrayed by the union talk. He had always been protective of his employees, considering them a part of his extended family. Now, some of them were saying the DeWitts were no longer capable of taking care of them.

The DeWitts believed they might have thwarted the union drive had they been more aggressive in presenting their side of the issue. But the normally brash family was leery about a process that involved a federal agency, the National Labor Relations Board, and potential charges of unfair labor practices.

When a vote on forming a union was finally set, Marvin proposed one last tactic to change the minds of hourly employees. The DeWitts bought $120 worth of groceries and displayed them on the production floor. The value of the groceries was equal to what an employee would pay annually for union dues. The groceries were even raffled off to employees. The strategy failed to impress a majority of hourly workers who voted to join Teamsters Local 406 in Grand Rapids.

Gary said the family had to accept some blame for why the union was formed.

"The union came about when we weren't paying attention to some of the things that sparked interest in it. We weren't communicating properly with employees, and we were not training supervisors on how to work with employees," he said. "There was no formal system of listening to employee concerns, and our hiring procedures were less than complete when it came to explaining the operation to new employees."

With the union formed, negotiating sessions between the DeWitts and Teamsters representatives led to the signing of a three-year contract on Jan. 31, 1972. Unionized employees gained additional wages, benefits, and more say in the plant operation. The DeWitts won major concessions on the contract's scope.

The union agreed to DeWitt demands for a multi-year contract, which would diminish the frequency of disruptions in production due to possible strike action. Only production employees, about half of the company's 500 hourly and salaried workers, were represented under the contract, weakening the power of the union in the event of a walk out. Excluded, at the insistence of the DeWitts, were hourly support staff whose absence could have quickly paralyzed the operation. Support staff included workers in such areas as maintenance, clean-up, material handling, and freezing/cooling.

The expiration of the contract every three years, on Jan. 31, was timed by the DeWitts for the company's slowest period of the year. It would also be the coldest time of the year for anyone assigned to outside picket duty.

While the DeWitts bristled at the idea of a union, in hindsight they acknowledged some positives resulting from the experience. For the first time, Bil Mar and its hourly employees operated under a more formal relationship. Employees were held accountable not only by management but by a set of formalized guidelines enforced by the union.

"For the first time, there were certain rules and procedures that both management and hourly workers had to follow. It did give us a framework to follow in our relationship with each other," Marvin said. "In some ways it made the operation go more smoothly. Everything had to run more like clock work. You were required to post jobs. There was some consistency in pensions, insurance, and sick leaves. Although I think the union brought some needed organization, I still preferred the one-on-one contact with employees. The union took some of that away."

The birth of the union convinced Gary that the family could no longer control every detail of the growing operation, especially personnel policies. In the wake of the union vote, the DeWitts – for the first time in their history – hired a consultant for advice.

On the recommendation of a friend in the industry, the DeWitts chose RSI (Retention Systems Inc.) of Alabama to set up the company's first personnel department.

"After RSI, I was always quick to bring in a consultant if I thought we needed some extra help and advice," Gary said. "I hired consultants when I didn't know how to do something, when I didn't have the time, or when I didn't want to do it."

As expected, Marvin resisted the idea of bringing in RSI to tell the DeWitts how to run their business. He was a big believer in doing things for yourself, and his style of management focused more on what you could see and hear when it came to running the plant. Yet he also knew that an entrepreneur can only build a business to a certain point before enlisting outside help.

When he did give in to the idea, a Bil Mar supervisor – only half in jest – suggested he take a vacation until RSI finished its research because he would resent someone poking into his business. Marvin stuck around and even came to appreciate RSI's recommendations.

"I wasn't real keen about the RSI study. A friend of ours out East said it was something we should check into. I figured we knew what we were doing when it came to hiring, retaining, and firing people," Marvin said. "Hiring RSI turned out to be a good idea after all. We learned a lot about how to handle people in a more formal and consistent manner. It gave some structure to our management operation."

RSI recommendations focused on how to motivate and treat employees fairly. RSI also suggested regularly scheduled meetings as a way to keep the line of communication open between hourly and salaried employees. The first step in that process was to establish a personnel department and hire a director, not related to the DeWitt family, to oversee its operation. RSI also stressed more formal training for supervisory personnel. Time clocks were abolished and supervisors filled in master time sheets for hourly employees. There were incentives implemented for outstanding attendance, like giving employees the day off for a birthday or work anniversary. Employees wore different-colored hats to identify their level of responsibility – red for top managers, green for supervisors, white for office workers, orange for quality control, blue for maintenance, and yellow for production. And the company's first employee newsletter was printed in December, 1975, initially as the Bil Mar Bulletin and later as The Gobbler Gazette. After the RSI review, employee turnover and absentee rates dropped.

Allowing RSI into Bil Mar was like opening a home to fresh spring air after a long winter. The outside perspective inspired the

DeWitts to make other changes in the operation, like bringing aboard a staff of professional managers to further spread out the responsibility of overseeing the growing company. The change in management structure was absolutely necessary for Bil Mar to remain competitive and move to its next level of growth.

"After I started there, in 1972, I took a sheet of wrapping paper and put down who was responsible for what," said Tom Norman, Marvin's son-in-law. "The lines on that piece of paper zigged and zagged all over the place. I found out that some people were responsible for doing the same job. Marvin wasn't much impressed with organizational flow charts. He said 'If there is a job to be done, we just do it.' We had to get more organized as the company grew from $15 million to $100 million in a very short time [from $15.8 million in 1973 to $113 million in 1981]. We needed to hire more managers to keep up with the pace. And as the size of the work force grew, supervisory responsibilities had to be more clearly defined."

For the management transition, the company eventually turned to Cliff Crocoll, another consultant, in 1977. Crocoll came from the Sligh-Lowrey Clock Co. in Zeeland on the recommendation of Warren Waters, who led Bil Mar's retail program. Crocoll's original task for Bil Mar was to streamline some of the production processes. Gary was impressed with Crocoll, though Jack was cool to him at first. He didn't seem to fit in with Bil Mar's style of management. He sported a beard, smoked, and peppered his conversation with obscenities – all traits foreign to the DeWitts. Eventually, Jack warmed up to Crocoll as he devised ideas to make the production process more efficient. With that task completed, Gary and Jack asked Crocoll to look at ways the management structure could be improved.

Unlike Gary and Jack, Marvin was not able to look past Crocoll's personal appearance and habits, and he took an instant disliking to the man. Normally, Marvin would not tolerate such traits on Bil Mar premises. He only endured them while Crocoll was a consultant and not on the payroll.

Their first meeting was to set the stage for their final encounter more than a year later when Crocoll was hired by Gary and Jack as

Bil Mar's general manager and fired shortly after at Marvin's command.

Marvin, whose hunting activities and civic duties were taking him away from the plant more often by the mid-1970s, wanted to meet Crocoll after hearing about him through the Bil Mar grapevine.

Marvin had barely been introduced to Crocoll when he said "I'm not used to dealing with guys who have beards." Crocoll sarcastically shot right back that he wasn't "used to dealing with farmers, either." The remark did not sit well with Marvin, who was normally afforded higher esteem.

Although Crocoll wasn't high on Marvin's list of likable people, he was instrumental in expanding Bil Mar's administrative base beyond the DeWitt family. He persuaded the DeWitts to start hiring professional managers, starting in 1978. First in line was Chuck Stehouwer, Bil Mar's long-time accountant from Touche Ross, who was hired as vice president of finance. He was followed by Tom Van Hall, also from Touche Ross, to oversee bookkeeping; John Gary, to supervise manufacturing; Fred Hjort for personnel; Lowrey Miller for purchasing; and Bill Chaddock, for computer operations. Within a year, Stehouwer left to return to his former accounting firm, yet remained Bil Mar's accountant until the company's merger with Sara Lee in 1987. He was replaced by Phil Vanden Berge, who credited Crocoll for Bil Mar becoming a more professionally run organization.

"At one time, Gary was president and ran administrative tasks, sales and most everything except manufacturing and farming. He would be involved in product technology and development. Jack ran the plant. And Bill Jr. ran the farms," Vanden Berge said. "In a sense, they were running these things autonomously. They all tended to do what they pleased in their own operation. Cliff challenged that arrangement.

"With the new management team, the days of the DeWitt family members having so much control over the operation were over. It had to be that way. The business was growing too big for them to be overseeing every detail."

The management changes recommended by Crocoll brought an unexpected dividend when Dr. Phil Weiner returned in 1980 as vice president of product development and quality control. He left Bil Mar in 1978, to take a position at a packing plant in Albany, N. Y. Previously, Bil Mar's limited management structure put too much responsibility on his shoulders for following through on a growing number of projects.

Gary and Jack, impressed with Crocoll's work to revamp Bil Mar's organizational structure, hired him as general manager without consulting their father. When Marvin found out, he gave them an ultimatum – either they fire Crocoll or start looking for another job. In short order, Crocoll was gone.

At the time, Gary was not pleased with his dad's abrupt handling of the situation. He soon learned that Crocoll was best suited to be a troubleshooter and not a day-to-day manager.

After he left Bil Mar, Crocoll continued as a free-lance consultant and alerted Gary that BEI (Blueberry Equipment Inc.), a prosperous South Haven company, was going to be sold. BEI was the nation's most diversified manufacturer of equipment for harvesting such specialized crops as blueberries, cranberries, grapes, and strawberries.

Gary, his brother Jack, Bill DeWitt Jr., and Vanden Berge formed a partnership to buy the business, which Crocoll helped organize on a consultant basis. Bill Jr. left Bil Mar in July, 1984, to oversee the operation, and Crocoll unsuccessfully lobbied for a general manager's position. Gary and Jack later sold their share of the business to Bill Jr. Gary and Jack backed away from BEI at the urging of their father, who felt they were focusing their attention on that business at the expense of their Bil Mar responsibilities.

"Cliff did a good job of organizing the blueberry equipment business, just like he did at Bil Mar. But he was no operations manager," Gary said. "He enjoyed fixing things instead of operating and developing things. He was a great troubleshooter. Yet he would get bored with day-to-day operations and not follow through on the details."

Organizational changes at Bil Mar in the 1970s didn't just involve management personnel. After some debate, Gary also persuaded his dad to hire another consultant, Food Management Inc., to institute a cost-accounting system.

The system determined the true cost of manufacturing a product by weekly analyzing the operation of all departments. At the end of a month, the company could match sales figures and production costs to calculate its real profits.

The discussion over cost-accounting occurred at the same time Bil Mar was beginning its retail program under the direction of Warren Waters. That the DeWitts had to discuss the worth of such a system amazed Waters, who was accustomed to buttoned-down corporate life at Ralston-Purina. He believed a cost-accounting system would be crucial for determining pricing in the volatile retail market.

Within a week of hiring on at Bil Mar, Waters attended his first management meeting at which cost accounting was the topic. A couple of consultants made their pitch for a better accounting system while Marvin and his son Jack expressed their reservations.

"That meeting was a good introduction as to how the company operated. It got pretty boisterous, with several family members pounding on the table to make their point," Waters said. "Marvin asked me what I thought about it, and I told him I hadn't been there long enough to make a judgment. I said ultimately you will do what they are talking about. If you are running a business, you have to know what everything costs. With a smaller, family-run business, you are able to keep tabs of what is going on and you do what's needed to be done to make a profit. You couldn't depend upon such an informal system as the number of products increased and the business grew. At Ralston, they had costing down to counting the rolls of toilet paper. I was flabbergasted when I realized what information wasn't available at Bil Mar."

By analyzing costs, other organizational changes followed at Bil Mar. The company improved purchasing procedures by seeking bids for materials and services, instead of basing those business contacts on friendships. And, on Gary's recommendation, the company created a computer department that made Bil Mar a data-processing leader in the industry. The early computer system kept track of feed costs, turkey growth, price of making a product, warehouse inventory, customer orders, sales, accounts receivable, accounts payable, and payroll.

Even with all of the changes, the company still operated day-to-day on an informal basis until the 1980s. There was no budget process. And little time was spent on strategic planning.

There were no formal board meetings. Business meetings, attended by DeWitt family members and other salaried personnel, were sometimes conducted over coffee in the plant's lunchroom. In a half hour's time, the group could easily make a $100,000 decision. Many of those decisions relied on Marvin's gut instinct. And nine out of 10 times, his instinct proved right.

Marvin's focus on the short-term, once derided by scientific management theorists as short-sighted, is enjoying a revival in some management philosophy circles. The trend, in which planning is not done much beyond the next quarter, is outlined in a book titled "Real Time," by Regis McKenna. The author says companies will have to conduct business in "real time," because "the competitive environment will no longer tolerate slow response or delayed decision making." The "real time" theory recognizes that the future cannot be predicted or controlled.

"I was never partial to making out a budget in the earlier days of the business. With a budget, you tend to follow through on your projections. That means that even if you don't need to spend money on something, you end up spending it anyway. Without a budget, we made decisions a whole lot quicker than they do today," Marvin said. "We made a lot of our business decisions during the morning coffee break. Some of the things we did were probably done in haste. We didn't believe in wasting a lot of time discussing an issue. Today, businesses have too many meetings. There is too much discussion and not enough getting done."

In the midst of all the organizational changes at Bil Mar, Marvin never lost sight of his primary goal – to produce more turkey products. To that end, he engineered the purchase of Bil Mar's second production facility, a bankrupt processing plant in Storm Lake, Iowa.

Marvin first heard about the Iowa opportunity in early 1977 while attending a National Turkey Federation convention in Miami, Fla. A group of turkey farmers in the Storm Lake area put their business, Vilas & Co., into Chapter 11 bankruptcy, which allows a debtor to ward off creditors while attempting to fiscally reorganize. At the convention, they approached Marvin about bailing them out by becoming their partner in Iowa's largest whole-turkey operation.

Before the convention was over, Marvin had Gary, Jack, Bill Jr. and Chuck Stehouwer visit northwestern Iowa to look over the operation, which included the processing plant, five grower farms, and a feed mill.

Marvin then visited the plant on a consulting basis to determine the possibility of turning the operation around. He took one look at the books and realized that just investing more money into the operation would be a losing proposition. The company listed $4.5 million in assets but $5.2 million in liabilities. Marvin made the right business decision by not becoming an investor. In the spring of 1977, Bil Mar was able to buy the Vilas assets for $1.6 million – or about two-thirds less than what the company was worth – after bidding through the bankruptcy court when the company went into straight bankruptcy. The business was renamed Bil Mar Foods of Iowa.

Marvin not only saw the Iowa purchase as a good business opportunity. He also liked the idea of saving the livelihoods of employees and area turkey growers.

Characteristically he made the decision to buy the plant without much consultation from other members of the family.

"Dad basically put the Iowa deal together without checking with the family. He just told us he was going to do it. I was a little disgruntled that he didn't fully consult us before making a decision. Yet he was always the man in power, the man in control. He was going to make a decision, whether it was right or wrong," Jack said. "Dad is from the old school of management where you tell someone to do something instead of talking about it. But you can't fault dad when it came to the vision he had about the growth of the turkey business. A lot of what

Marvin checks out the Bil Mar site in iowa.

happened at Bil Mar was based on dad's gut feeling. He was a visionary more than anyone else in the family. He had the guts, the determination, and will to succeed. He got the Iowa plant up and running the way he wanted it operated."

From the start, Marvin took a personal stake in the adopted business. First, he contacted the company's creditors – banks, feed suppliers, hardware stores, lumber yards, gas stations, vets – and assured them that Bil Mar could salvage the business. Then he turned his attention to the plant's 300 employees, who were unionized but had no contract agreement with the new owners. He asked them to forsake any union activities for one year, giving him the opportunity to prove he could treat them right. If after that period they weren't satisfied with their treatment by Bil Mar, the employees were welcome to bring back the union. He then rounded up the plant's six supervisors to talk them into staying with Bil Mar. Dan Torrington, a top salesman at the company, was named general manager – a position he held until 1984 when Bill DeWitt Jr. left Bil Mar and he came to Michigan to run the farm organization.

For the Iowa employees, the first impression of Marvin was one of bewilderment. He was the co-owner and founder of a company twice their size, yet he showed up in work clothes, instead of the expected business uniform of suit and tie.

After he started talking to the group, however, they knew he was a straight-forward type of person ready to roll up his sleeves and get down to the work of saving the business.

And they immediately learned he was going to apply his conservative principles to their operation. Greg Steenblock, then production manager and now director of manufacturing at Storm Lake, sported neck-length hair and a beard, a style left over from the 1960s. Marvin told Steenblock point blank that he would need to cut his hair and shave off the beard before coming back to work the next day.

At first, Steenblock was incensed. Who was this stranger coming into his workplace and taking him to task about his grooming habits. Even so, he returned the next day with shorter hair and a clean shave.

"I went ahead and did what he said. He seemed like someone

who could be trusted," Steenblock said. "He told it like it was. You knew exactly where you stood with him. He didn't pull any punches."

Marvin reorganized the business from top to bottom. His first task was to trim operational costs, including the closing of a brand new main office attached to the feed mill. Then came the investment of money for remodeling and new equipment to make the plant more efficient. The banking, accounting, and administration functions of the plant were moved to Michigan so that Storm Lake could be operated as a satellite corporation.

"There were a lot of inefficiencies throughout the operation. Dad went there to correct those," Gary DeWitt said. "His presence alleviated a concern by our lender, Old Kent Bank, that there would not be a DeWitt on-site and we would be overseeing that operation from 600 miles away. Dad personally trained the Iowa supervisors to operate it like we would."

Marvin walked the Storm Lake plant floor during the week for the first year of its operation to make sure things were going smoothly. Marvin believed he not only had the obligation to lead an organization. He also felt responsible for teaching others to be leaders.

"He believed that everything was measurable. He also believed that you can't manage a plant by sitting in some office, thinking that things will take care of themselves" Steenblock said. "I walked through that plant many times with him, watching him shut off the lights where they weren't needed. Sometimes we would be walking at a brisk pace when he would make a dead stop and ask me to listen. What he heard was the sound of water when it shouldn't have been running. Or the sound of an air leak from a compressor. He would say 'do you know how much that is costing you?' He paid attention to the details and made sure everyone else did. He said the larger problems were obvious. It was the small things that kept nipping away at your butt if you didn't watch out for them.

"When he went back to Borculo after the first year here, I was relieved. I said to myself, 'finally, he's out of my life.' I guess I felt that way because his constant presence here put a lot of pressure on me. A week after his departure, I missed not having him there for guidance. He taught me so many things about managing a business. It was pure hell while he was here, yet he never did anything without a good reason. He is the type of person you want to work for. You want to give him 110 percent."

Today, the Storm Lake facility is one of the largest employers in town, with more than 600 workers on the payroll. And the employees are still not unionized. Four years after the Bil Mar takeover, one of the employees came up to Marvin at a Christmas party and said "you asked us to give you a chance to show that you could take care of us in the right way. You have proven yourself." Over the years, there have been three unsuccessful attempts to bring back a union.

Steenblock said the union defeats had a lot to do with Marvin's people-oriented style of management. The employees always knew they could go directly to Marvin for assistance, if they had a problem with a local manager. They also admired his hard-working, honest approach to the business, and that he treated them fairly and respectfully.

"He really listened to what people had to say to him. His reasoning was that if they were going to take the time to stop and talk to you, it must be important to them and you should take the time to listen," Steenblock said. "He was very opinionated. Though it didn't always have to be Marvin's way. He would change his mind, if you presented a reasonable alternative in a straightforward manner."

Marvin's reorganization of the Iowa operation did not go unnoticed in the turkey industry. Turkey World magazine said "Bil Mar's magic turns Storm Lake around" in a headline topping a story about the recovery. The story said Marvin turned the company into a profit center in 12 months "with a few prayers, a good turkey market, and a no-nonsense, no-frills management philosophy."

"We cut $150,000 to $200,00 overhead immediately. There was waste in all areas of the operation. They did too much leasing of equipment and some of that was not being used. Much of the equipment, like the picking machines and live-bird unloading system, was outdated. And the processing building had deteriorated," Marvin told Turkey World about the situation he faced upon Bil Mar's acquisition.

The purchase of the Iowa plant paid off for Bil Mar in every respect. Overnight, the company doubled its production capacity. The DeWitts decided to leave 30 percent of Iowa's production in whole birds [a product phased out in the early 1990s]. The remaining birds were boned and the meat was shipped to the Borculo plant for further processing.

The additional Iowa capacity proved invaluable during two crucial periods in Bil Mar's history, the 10-month strike in 1981 and the devastating plant fire in 1984. Besides shipping meat to the Borculo plant, the Iowa facility sells excess raw turkey to other manufacturers and fabricates a raw boneless turkey roast.

The Storm Lake area was also the site of another first for Bil Mar – building contract-growing facilities as a third method of producing turkeys. Bil Mar was already operating company farms and contracting with independent growers. With contract farms, Bil Mar constructed a facility and supplied the growers with the turkeys and the feed. The growers supplied the labor.

After the Storm Lake facility was humming, Marvin had one more goal to accomplish before the end of 1977 – the construction of a computerized feed mill on U.S. 31, north of Holland.

Bil Mar's automated feed mill on U.S. 31.

Marvin, his sons Gary and Don, and Bill Jr. toured the country looking at different types of mill operations before settling on one that would work best for Bil Mar's growing operation in Michigan. The DeWitts built the structure in record time, using slip forms for pouring concrete so that construction could proceed 24 hours a day. Hydraulic jacks were used to move the forms up as the cement sections dried. Completed in 1977, the 16-story mill replaced the reconverted Harlem mill operated by Bil Mar since 1966 at the same site. The operation of the new mill was supervised by Don.

In the old mill, Bil Mar produced mashed and cracked corn mixed with soy bean meal, bone meal, and animal fat. No exact measurement was applied to that method of feeding, which produced inconsistencies in the amount and cost of feed needed to bring a bird to market weight. At modern mills, the ingredients are constantly adjusted by nutritionists to achieve the optimum nutrition needed by the turkeys. A well-balanced diet results in more efficient feed conversions at a lower cost than the former non-controlled feeding programs. Generally, it takes three pounds of feed to produce one pound of turkey meat.

The method of preparing feed at modern mills is also different than how it was formerly handled. Feed is now ground like flour for better absorption by the turkeys. The finer textured feed is heated up to 180 degrees to kill salmonella. The feed is then pelletized and cooled. In pellet form, all the vitamins and nutrients from the ingredients are concentrated for much more efficient feeding. The turkeys get what they need instead of pecking around for what they want. The energy-packed feed, coupled with selective crossbreeding and environmentally controlled growing conditions, has drastically reduced the growing time while increasing the size of the turkey. In the 1960s, it took 28 weeks to produce a 28-pound tom. In the 1970s, it took six fewer weeks to grow the same-sized tom. Today, it takes only 19 weeks to produce a 34-pound tom.

Environmentally controlled brooder house.

The new mill also gave Bil Mar improved capacity, allowing the company to buy larger quantities of raw ingredients at a cheaper price and to store more finished feed.

The Iowa plant and the new feed mill weren't the only projects keeping Marvin busy in the 1970s, a period when he supposedly was backing away from the business.

He opened a retail store to test the depth of the raw-turkey market. He entered into a cattle-raising venture with his friend and West Michigan businessman Preston Kool. And there was the experiment to more effectively raise a turkey.

In the mid-1970s, based on the sales popularity of raw turkey parts at its on-site Country Store, Bil Mar tested that market regionally to determine if such production should be pursued on a larger scale. As part of that analysis, Marvin opened a retail outlet – the Turkey & More Store – on 28th Street in Grand Rapids to sell individually wrapped packages of raw turkey. The two-year experiment, from 1976 to 1978, convinced the DeWitts there was a growing retail market for raw turkey. However, in the midst of starting up a retail program for cooked dark-meat products, the DeWitts were not willing to dedicate the assets needed to build a facility for the large-volume production of raw turkey parts. A companion investment would also have been necessary to create a separate sales and distribution program, requiring even shorter time frames for delivery and shelf life. The raw-turkey market is now dominated by The Turkey Store brand, owned by Jerome Foods.

Marvin produces turkey litter to feed livestock.

In the late-1970s, Marvin and Kool raised Charlois cattle with an innovative twist. Marvin devised a plan to feed turkey litter to the cattle as part of their diet. He figured it would be another way to dispose of the litter while at the same time reducing the cost of cattle feeding. The venture earned him a story in the April/1979 edition of Michigan Farmer magazine, entitled: "Poultry Litter Silage: The perfect match up on a turkey-beef farm." The story said: "Turkey waste comes from the growing houses mixed with soft-wood shavings. The raw waste tests 21 percent crude protein, so corn silage has been added as a filler. The mixture is stored in an oxygen-limited structure that processes it into palatable feed. Baled hay is also added to the mixture, which is fed to the cattle in the winter as a cheap and nutritious ration. The cattle are pastured in the spring after calving. " Marvin did not follow through on the litter silage experiment. He was just too busy with other activities, like globe-trotting and big-game hunting.

In November/1979, Turkey World reported on another of Marvin's enterprises – starting an independent growing program known as Turkey Acres, Turkey Acres II, and Land of Turkeys.

The story said he had "recently sunk $458,000 into an experimental grow-out operation featuring what he considers the most efficient design for modern-day turkey buildings... DeWitt is attempting to answer most all of the questions for prospective Bil Mar turkey growers who can model their setups after that of Turkey Acres."

Marvin's turkey-related experiments led him into the 1980s. He greeted the decade in his usual aggressive fashion by expanding the company's operations with a second acquisition. In March of 1980, he engineered the $3.5 million buy out of Pike's Turkey Farms in Garrettsville, Ohio. The processing plant was owned by Don Pike, an industry friend who didn't have the capital to expand.

Pike, impressed with Marvin's impeccable character, sold to Bil Mar even though another business suitor offered more money.

"I have heard some people say you can't sell a business to someone else and remain friends. Well, they haven't met Marvin," Pike said. "Another businessman offered me a half-million dollars more for the operation after Marvin made his offer. I stuck with Marvin because it all comes down to integrity and trust, the character of the people you are dealing with. He was one of the most respected and liked turkey growers in the country. He is absolutely, completely honest. I think he would have to read a book about lying before he could ever do it. He would tell the absolute truth, even if it meant hurting his own business.

"With Marvin, I knew my processing plant was in good hands. He has more common sense in his little finger than most Ph.d.'s have in their whole body. Marvin is a very unusual individual, and I mean that in a good sense. When God takes him someday, there won't be anyone around to replace him."

With the Ohio acquisition, Bil Mar's future looked very bright. Led by the food-service division and bolstered by the new retail program, sales topped $86 million in 1980 – a $77 million increase in just 10 years. The new management team was settling in. And, in the wake of the RSI study, the company was taking steps to assure that employees were content, including the opening of a company discount store and construction of a new cafeteria. Bil Mar subsidized the cost of operating the cafeteria to keep meal prices at or below cost.

The only dark cloud on Bil Mar's horizon was the expiration of the three-year contract with Teamsters Local 406. But the DeWitts had successfully negotiated three contracts with the production workers and didn't expect major problems.

Their optimism would prove to be short-lived in early 1981 when a dispute over a new contact led to the most violent and prolonged strike in the history of Ottawa County.

Company retail outlet sits in the shadow of the plant.

Strikers block a driveway at Bil Mar.

CHAPTER THIRTEEN

TANGLING WITH THE TEAMSTERS

Representatives of the Teamsters Union underestimated Marvin if they were counting on threats to gain contract concessions for production workers.

During the first bargaining session in early December of 1980, two months before the third contract was set to expire, union business agents from Local 406 warned of a strike if their demands weren't met. One of them fooled around with a switchblade knife in an apparent attempt to intimidate Gary, Jack and Bil Mar's personnel director.

The strike threat and crude behavior were true to the Teamsters' long history of playing rough. Marvin's reaction was true to his reputation of standing tough when challenged. The DeWitts, he declared, would not be bullied into signing a contract.

Unlike past negotiations with Bil Mar, union demands didn't

hinge on improved wages, benefits, or working conditions. The high-priority issues on the union's negotiating list reflected a determination to sustain membership and exercise more clout in the company's operation.

The union was demanding a successor clause in the contract requiring a new owner to recognize the Teamsters as a bargaining agent should the DeWitts ever sell the business. And they wanted union representation for more support personnel. Those goals were not surprising, given the union's loss of more than 500,000 members to trucking deregulation in the early 1980s.

The Teamsters also wanted unrestricted plant access for union business agents so they could more closely monitor plant operations.

The DeWitts turned a cold shoulder to union demands, which did not appear to represent the welfare of Bil Mar employees. The union, from the DeWitt's perspective, seemed more interested in its survival.

"Wages, benefits and working conditions were not major issues in that strike. It was mainly a power play by new Teamsters officials from Grand Rapids to flex their muscles," Gary Dewitt said. "They wanted more control over management decisions the way they exercised control on the East side of the state. They wanted us to bow down three times a day to the new union leadership in Grand Rapids."

Jack DeWitt perceived the union demands in the same context.

"The union basically wanted to run our business. They even sent in representatives from Detroit to head up union negotiations. They thought they could come in to little Borculo and walk all over the DeWitts," he said. "They wanted more power and we weren't going to give it to them. We stuck our heels into the ground and held onto what we had. We were not about to let someone from Detroit come in and take over our family-owned business."

The union and Bil Mar deadlocked in seven bargaining sessions in December and January, setting the stage for the Feb. 1, 1981, walkout by 420 production workers in a plant that employed about 800.

One week before the contract expiration, the media were still unaware of the battle to erupt at Bil Mar. The only newspaper article about the company reported on the opening of an employee cafeteria and health center. The story said: "Bil Mar has spent some of the financial fruit of its tremendous growth on its employees. A new wing houses a full-service cafeteria and a small health center – both aimed at making Bil Mar a better place to work. The addition also contains corporate offices and a research kitchen. The corporation subsidizes lunchroom operations in an effort to keep prices low. "

Giving no hint of the contract dispute, a company official was quoted in the article as saying "'The investment in a better working environment can only mean continued growth for Bil Mar. Satisfied workers produce efficiently and in greater quantity. A high level of production, in turn, fuels corporate growth.'"

Placard enlists support for Bil Mar strikers.

A week later, every media outlet in southwest Michigan was reporting on Bil Mar. And the news was no longer upbeat. Buffeted by freezing winds, strikers took up positions on the evening of February 1 at entrances to the plant on 96th Avenue. And the picketers were anything but cordial. They kicked at vehicles entering the plant, and tore down employee parking signs and burned them.

Ottawa County Sheriff's deputies were on the scene from almost the start of the strike to keep the peace between the two sides. Within days of the strike, there were arrests of union members for vandalism to vehicles entering and leaving the plant. The damage included dents, scratches, and broken windshields, headlights and antennas. Bil Mar executives were also the subject of headlines, denying charges by the union that the company was threatening some of its foreign employees with deportation if they did not cross the picket line.

On the strike's first day, a few production employees did cross the picket line out of respect for Marvin and his family. The defections, which would increase as the strike wore on, only served to heighten tensions.

"I could not go against the DeWitts after all the good they had done for me. I didn't want to turn my back on them," said Bertha Geertman, a production worker, about her motivation for crossing the picket line. "I did get some nasty telephone calls during the strike. They wanted to scare me from going into work. It was a very stressful time, but we decided to hang in there for the DeWitts. I consider the DeWitts my friends."

Strikers stand watch around warming barrel.

To counter some of the picket line abuse, the DeWitts organized daily car pools at various church parking lots near the plant. DeWitt family members, non-union supervisory personnel and support staff, and rebel production workers would pile into vehicles to form a convoy led by sheriff's deputies. At the high point, nearly 60 vehicles would cross the picket line together. Working employees felt more secure in groups than driving alone across the picket line, even in the face of continued name-calling, spitting, threats of violence, and damage to vehicles.

Marvin's constant presence served as an inspiration for those who dared cross the picket line. One employee said Marvin discerned the strike as the equivalent of a war. The union sympathizers were the enemy. The loyal employees were his troops. And he was their general.

Bil Mar management mapped out a strategy designed to keep production near prestrike level by enlisting supervisory personnel, support workers, and family members to serve on the front line of production. Among the volunteer troops were the wives of supervisors, like Nina Schipper and Deb Huyser, and Marvin's daughters, daughters-in-law, and older grandkids. Office personnel would work up to eight hours on the production line and then spend time on their regular paperwork.

The Borculo operation was also assisted by production lines at the company's Iowa and Ohio plants.

Production at Borculo dropped 20 to 30 percent when the picket line was first formed. Bil Mar's volunteer army – reinforced by salaried workers, union defectors, temporary employees, and workers in Iowa and Ohio – returned the plant to full production within six weeks.

"We had to regroup, look at what people we had and what we needed to do to keep the production figures from sliding any further," Merle DeWitt said. "Everyone was working on the line. Everybody did what they had to do. If you were requested to do it, even if it wasn't your normal job, you just did it."

Strikers on picket-line duty.

Kevin McKenna was one of the support workers called to serve on the production line. His regular job was creating products in Bil Mar's test kitchen. During the strike, McKenna never knew day-to-day what task he might be assigned.

"You would come into work each day wondering what job you would have to do, like boning. One time, I had to run a plastic-wrap machine 10 hours. The smell from the fumes gave me a headache. Yet there was no question about coming back to work the next day," McKenna said. "Marvin would work right alongside of you to get a job done. He earned a lot of respect for that. It was his example that kept us going during the strike."

When Marvin wasn't leading the troops inside the plant, he walked the picket line and talked to striking workers about the issues. He also held informal bargaining sessions with union business agents in their luxury cars parked along 96th Avenue. His message to the union was clear. The DeWitts would never buckle under the strike pressure.

The strikers responded with more harassment and destruction. They blocked driveways with large chunks of snow and ice. They wired entrance gates shut. They threw snowballs at the Country Store. They attempted to keep customers from entering the retail market. They made threatening calls to non-striking workers at their homes. And they reported several false bomb scares, causing the evacuation and search of the plant.

The strikers shot holes in office windows with pellet guns, slashed tires, defaced buildings with spray paint, and planted glass and nails in the driveways to damage the cars of non-striking workers. No one in the vicinity of the plant was immune to the damage. Also targeted were vehicles driven by Country Store customers, sheriff's deputies, and security guards hired by Bil Mar to protect company property.

Firebomb damages Country Store.

Marvin's nearby home was spattered with paint-filled baby-food jars. Two gasoline firebombs were thrown at the Country Store but only one hit its mark, charring the outside of the building. The fire, investigated by agents from the Federal Bureau of Investigation and the Alcohol, Tobacco, and Firearms bureau, was extinguished by security guards. On the same night, strikers reported retaliatory strikes by Bil Mar employees who slashed and punctured some of their tires. The firebombing backfired on the strikers when a fire marshal prohibited them from burning wood in open barrels to ward off the freezing temperatures.

As destruction to property increased, Marvin carried an ax for protection until the union complained to sheriff's deputies about him. He revealed the handle one night when picketers attempted to block entrance to the driveway of his home. He carried a loaded shotgun in his truck during drive-by surveillance of picket activity. He kept a loaded gun handy in the bedroom of his home, determined not to be driven away by the turmoil. Besides the paint spattering, the home was the target of rocks, boards, and threatening phone calls. A window in his car was broken with a rock one Sunday night as he returned from church with his wife.

Bil Mar strikers taunt co-workers who cross picket line.

"I got very little sleep during that whole mess. The picketers were there around the clock. I was just as determined to show them I would not be scared off by their tactics. That is why I spent so much time patrolling the property. I was not afraid of going to jail for protecting my property," Marvin said. "The union was lucky I was a church-going Christian. There is a lot more I could have done to fight them off but I tried to follow the Christian belief of turning the other cheek when struck."

Three weeks after the strike started, the union began to lose ground. At that point, 60 union workers had crossed the picket line to enter the plant and Bil Mar had hired about 70 new workers to replace the strikers. In the media, both sides blamed each other for not bargaining in good faith. The Teamsters placed ads in various publications asking other unions to boycott Bil Mar products as a show of support for the strikers. Bil Mar took out its own ads, seeking workers to replace the picketers. At the end of the fourth strike week, 131 Teamsters were crossing the picket line and 120 temporary workers were on the production line, equaling about half the 420 workers who had walked out. Bil Mar officials reported that plant production was up to 75 percent capacity.

By mid-March, the 6-week-old strike was not only taking its toll on the union. The sheriff's department had paid out more than $12,000 in overtime due to the strike, drawing citizen complaints about the use of tax money to keep a lid on a private dispute. The Finance Committee of the Ottawa County Board of Commissioners recommended Bil Mar foot the bill for having deputies at the site six hours a day. Payment, the committee said, was necessary to prevent depletion of the sheriff's department budget. The committee had also considered charging the Teamsters for overtime costs. That tactic wasn't possible because the union, unlike Bil Mar, owned no property on which the county could hold a lien for the bill.

Marvin appeared before the full board of commissioners to protest the proposed reimbursement by Bil Mar. He vowed the company would not pay the bill if assessed.

"This is a silly notion. It's not fair, not legal, not possible, and we won't stand for it," he said. "I feel I am entitled to police protection just like any other citizen. My taxes pay for it just like they do for the roads I drive on. I won't pay for the strike duty because it is the union causing all the problems, not us."

The board responded to his strenuous objection by deciding not to charge Bil Mar for the police service.

Marvin's appearance before the county board was followed in late-March by another stalemate in negotiations, which by that time were being meditated by the Michigan Employment Relations Commission and the National Labor Relations Board. Bil Mar and the union agreed there was no common ground to continue talks and no further meetings were scheduled. With no end to the strike in sight, the Teamsters decided to bring some new pressure to bear during the ninth week of the contract dispute. On March 31, the union brought in Teamsters from other locals to beef up the picket line and block the plant's five entrances.

Sheriff's deputies had been tipped off the night before about the union's plan after they were called to quell a rock-throwing spree by 70 picketers aiming at buildings and cars on Bil Mar property.

The next morning at 6:30, 15 deputies – equipped with riot helmets and yard-long batons – faced off with more than 300 picketers just as the first convoy of 25 cars arrived for work. Despite the police presence, picketers were able to block most movement onto plant property. Vehicles were bombarded with rocks, and struck with clubs and baseball bats. The

Deputies respond to threat of strike riot.

deputies called for reinforcement from their own department and other police agencies in the county. Within minutes another 30 officers were on the scene.

"It was virtually an uncontrollable situation. There were too many picketers and a lot of them were from outside the area. The situation had trouble written all over it," Sheriff Robert Dykstra told reporters after the melee.

The call for additional police assistance ended up averting what could have been a major battle between strikers and a group of night-shift workers from inside the plant.

After the first convoy was blocked, Marvin decided to counter the union's forceful tactics. Armed with a pipe wrench, he led a group of workers out of the plant. They brandished baseball bats, tire irons, and bolt cutters.

Marvin (far right) and non-striking employees arm themselves against Teamsters.

"The union brought in a carload of union members from Detroit, who were going to bust us up. They were determined not to let any employee into the plant that day. When that gang hit the picket line, our people came out of the plant," Marvin said. "We had been pushed around by the union too long and we weren't going to take it anymore, especially from a bunch of outside agitators. We were about to face off when the police reinforcements arrived. Ottawa called for help when it looked like there was going to be a battle."

The officers managed to separate the two groups just before the second convoy of non-striking employees arrived at 8:05 a.m. There were reports of vehicle damage, arrests and several minor injuries, yet the convoys got through.

The union's show of force convinced the Ottawa County Circuit Court to grant a temporary restraining order requested by Bil Mar lawyers. The order limited the number of picketers at any single plant entrance to three persons and no more than 15 at any one time. The order required that picketers be no closer than 30 feet to any of the plant's five entrances. Picketers were also prohibited from obstructing vehicles, threatening non-striking workers, carrying weapons, and trespassing on Bil Mar property.

The near riot was followed by a 30-minute negotiating session at which each side restated its unyielding position. It was to be the last meeting between the opponents. Bil Mar then sent letters to the remaining picketers, welcoming them back. By then, more than 260 of the 420 union members had returned to work. Those remaining on the picket line were getting $35, a gallon of milk, and a loaf of bread each week from the union.

Gloria Waterman was one of the strikers who returned to work after a couple of months on the picket line. She was against the strike from the start but felt compelled to walk out due to her union membership.

Vandalism mars strike.

"I would never had joined the union, only I had to because it was a closed shop. Right from the beginning, I couldn't see how our union dues were benefiting us. I felt it was wasted money," she said. "Wherever you work, you always feel like you are not getting enough. You always want more. That is no reason for going on strike. I never felt comfortable about walking out. The DeWitts were fair to us. They stressed family and church, and that fit into my beliefs. The union leaders just kept saying to hang in there, we'll get you what you deserve. We were standing out in the cold, and they were riding around in their big, expensive cars and drawing a pay check."

One last incident of vandalism in late-April convinced Ottawa County Circuit Court to issue a permanent restraining order against the strikers. More than $15,000 worth of damage was reported to tires and radiators on several semi-tractors and trailers at the plant.

Bil Mar sent notification to strikers that, starting May 4, the company would hire permanent replacements for those who had not returned to work. Replaced strikers would be put on a special list for re-employment if vacancies occurred in their former jobs or in equivalent positions.

By mid-May, 70 percent of the strikers were back in the plant. Petitions requesting the union's decertification were also being circulated.

The Teamsters, in a June 2 letter, made one last appeal for union members to band together in a show of solidarity: "As you know, we are going into the 18th week of our strike. The company would like to give their customers and their employees the impression that the union is gone. I sincerely hope that no one believes this. They have also indicated to you that the union would be voted out. This local union, as long as there is one person on the picket line and as long as we have a legal reason for being here, is not going to leave. We are appealing to those who have gone back in to return to the picket line on June 8. If all the members will unite, we will have a better bargaining position and will negotiate a contract to the benefit of all Bil Mar employees."

When there was no show of solidarity by union members, Bil Mar responded with a letter to the union that said it no longer recognized the Teamsters as the representative of the company's production workers. Bil Mar said more than half of the original union workers had signed a decertification petition. The Teamsters accused Bil Mar of wanting to break the union at the plant and filed charges of unfair labor practices.

The union did not admit defeat until December 18, 1981, in a letter to Bil Mar indicating the strike had been terminated – 10 months after the first picket line went up. Bil Mar responded to the formal end of the strike by declaring that the walkout was effectively over in mid-May when a majority of union members had crossed the picket line and returned to work in defiance of the Teamsters. The Bil Mar union was subsequently decertified by the NLRB.

One of the last strikers to cross the picket line was Deb Goerbig, a union steward. She now questions the union demands and the accompanying violence.

"With hindsight, I can see that we weren't being realistic about our demands. We thought things were going to happen overnight," she said. "Those who voted for the strike were basically after more wages and better insurance, not all the other issues being pushed by the union. I would never want to go through a situation like that again. It was violent and there were a lot of hard feelings while it was going on."

Despite the strike's duration, relationships between strikers and non-strikers smoothed over fairly quickly. The DeWitts didn't retaliate against any of the strikers. And the defeated strikers didn't perform any acts of sabotage upon return to the plant.

"When the strike was over, those who stayed out came back pretty humbled and quiet. I think they were treated very fairly by Bil Mar," said Gloria Waterman. "I never felt any great strain between those who stayed out and those who came back in, or those who chose not to go out at all."

With the strike ended, Marvin again shifted his attention away from the business and to a new role as a compassionate capitalist. In that quest, he shared a considerable amount of his Bil Mar wealth with colleges that advanced moral principles as part of their academic mission.

Marvin and members of his family attend ribbon-cutting ceremony for the DeWitt Center for Economics and Business Administration at Hope College's VanZoeren Hall.

CHAPTER FOURTEEN

COMPASSIONATE CAPITALIST

Marvin had always given 10 percent of his earnings to Ottawa Reformed Church, even in the days when the business was struggling to make a profit.

As his wealth grew in proportion to the business, he began to look beyond his church for organizations in need of assistance. The first recipient of his generosity was Northwestern College in Orange City, Iowa. The school, with 1,200 students, is one of three institutions of higher learning affiliated with the Reformed Church in America, including Hope College in Holland and Central College in Pella, Iowa.

Before Marvin invested in Northwestern, the school was financially troubled and the campus underdeveloped with a number of run-down buildings. He was alerted to the plight of the college by his former pastor, the Rev. Howard Teusink, the first minister at Ottawa

Reformed Church.

Marvin decided Northwestern could use his help more than Hope or Central colleges because of its deteriorating condition and lack of outside support. By joining Northwestern's governing board, he addressed the school's problems with the same level of energy he brought to any of his ventures. Some people question Marvin's interest in higher education, given his general lack of enthusiasm for academics. He is proud of the fact that he became a successful businessman without much formal schooling. He succeeded not with degrees behind his name but by working hard, never giving up, applying common sense, and hiring the right people.

He relished telling about the time he was aboard a plane on company business and exchanged some small talk with a young woman who was on her way home from college. After the woman learned he was the owner of a company, she asked him what college he had attended.

Marvin replied: "The college of hard knocks."

She asked him where the school was located, and he replied, with a hearty chuckle, that it was the school of experience.

Zwemer Hall at Northwestern College.

Despite his pride at being a self-taught man, time has changed his perspective about the worth of an academic education.

"When my kids grew up, the necessity of college wasn't as apparent, especially to those of us in my generation. As I got older, I realized that some people will always go to college because that type of education works for what they want to become," he said. "College years are a critical time in the lives of many young people, and I want to support those types of colleges that most closely adhere to my religious beliefs. Those colleges, like Northwestern, provide the type of academic atmosphere that I approve of."

Like at his church, he became Northwestern's largest financial supporter. He donated a half million dollars for the construction of the DeWitt Physical Fitness Center, which features basketball courts, tennis courts, a track, handball courts, and locker rooms.

He contributed a quarter million dollars toward the restoration of the college's original campus building, Zwemer Hall, built in 1894. It is now the college's administration building and listed on the National Register of historic buildings. He gave a quarter million dollars for the Bultman Center, a new intercollegiate athletic center for health, physical education, and intercollegiate athletics.

Bultman Center at Northwestern.

He was the catalyst and major contributor toward the construction of the schools's first chapel building in the mid-1980s when the farm economy in that area of the country was depressed. Most board members were against moving ahead with the $4 million plan. Marvin persisted. Due to the tough financial times, the college received an unusually low construction bid for the project. Marvin then presented the school with a quarter million dollars to complete the chapel fund drive.

Jim Bultman, Northwestern's former president and recently installed president at Hope College, asked Marvin if the college could put his name, along with his wife's, on the chapel. He declined, saying the chapel should have a Christian name. He did consent to have their names put on the chapel's music wing. He even got his children involved in donating to the

Christ Chapel at Northwestern.

project. While taking a tour of the nearly finished chapel with his son Jack, Marvin noticed old pianos in the music wing. He believed they were out of place for the new building. He turned in Jack's direction and told Bultman his son would be happy to donate a new baby grand piano. He also said the school could count on each of his other six children to buy a new piano for the music wing.

"He is a giant among men in so many ways," Bultman said. "Despite his wealth, he retained his modest, down-to-earth approach to life. He remains committed to his Christian faith and to his family. There will never be another person like him. I count it a special privilege to be a small part of his life. "

Marvin continues to watch out for the school's well being. He is honorary chairman of Northwestern's $20 million campaign for Phase III campus development. Marvin and his wife committed $1 million to launch the campaign and promised another quarter million dollars as a challenge gift should someone else donate $1 million.

When it came to the support of higher education, Marvin didn't confine his good will to Northwestern. He has also become a Hope College contributor. At the suggestion of Gordon Van Wylen, Hope president from 1972 to 1987, he financially assisted the renovation of the DeWitt Center for administrative offices and a student gathering place known as the Kletz. The Center was named after the DeWitt family who founded Big Dutchman Inc. Marvin, along with his family, also donated money for the DeWitt Center for Economics and Business Administration in VanZoeren Hall. Marvin also assisted his son, Gary, in the construction of the DeWitt Tennis Center, which provided the Hope tennis team an opportunity for year-round practice. The suggestion

Marvin and his son, Gary, contribute to construction of DeWitt Tennis Center at Hope College.

for indoor courts was made by Gary's son Dirk, a former member of the college team whose practice time was limited by outdoor courts. Both the VanZoeren Hall and tennis center projects were named after Marvin's family.

Van Wylen said his association with Marvin reminded him that there are many people who have achieved success without a college degree.

"Marvin is blessed with a number of natural gifts that more than make up for his lack of academic achievement, allowing him to create a vision and see it through. He's able to grasp all the realities of a situation, see the relationships between them, and then deal with all of them to accomplish his objectives. He has the unique ability to see the big picture but also not ignore the details. He can move back and forth between them," Van Wylen said. "Many people squander their natural gifts. Marvin didn't. He believes he has to use those gifts in the right way. He was called to live a certain way and he has. All of this is coupled with his Christian faith, which gives him a real sense of doing things with fairness and integrity. Marvin is a big believer in being himself and not being swayed by peer pressure. He has not let his life be guided by other's expectations. He has been true to his beliefs and his faith."

Northwestern and Hope, who honored Marvin's contributions with honorary degrees, have not been the only benefactors of his higher-education support. Grand Valley State University, a state-supported school in Ottawa County's Allendale Township, has also benefited from his gift giving. GVSU president Dr. Arend Lubbers, who also has a Reformed Church background, enlisted Marvin's support for the construction of a center for campus ministry. Peter Cook, chairman and majority owner of Mazda Great Lakes in Grand Rapids, initially donated $1 million toward the $2.5 million project, which became known as the Cook-DeWitt Center. Marvin followed with a $600,000 donation and a promise to solicit the remaining $1.6 million from family and friends. Marvin continues to support the ministry center's endowment fund. He also serves on the Grand Valley Foundation Board to raise money for other GVSU projects.

"He is not a person who can stay on the sidelines. Once he gets his feet planted into something, he is no longer a bystander or observer," Dr. Lubbers said. "He didn't just write a check for the ministry center. He was concerned about how the project would shape up and offered suggestions about construction and building materials. He was always looking for ways to use the dollar in the most efficient manner as possible. He was also adamant that the overall construction had to be of the highest quality. He was an interested and involved donor, and that interest is what I enjoyed. Here was someone who shared my enthusiasm in the project and I took that as a compliment."

Marvin's children follow his example when it comes to charitable giving. They donate money to a variety of causes and projects, most of them with a Christian bent. Among their favorite organizations are: Hope College, Western Theological Seminary, Northwestern College, Reformed Church in America, Focus on the Family, Camp Geneva Retreat and Conference Center, and Zeeland, Borculo and Holland Christian schools.

Other organizations on their donation list include Good Samaritan Ministries, Campus Crusade, World Vision International, Boy Scouts of America, Right to Life of Michigan, Prison Fellowship Ministries, Gospel Communications International Inc. [formerly Gospel Films], Rev. Schuller's Hour of Power, Youth for Christ, Children's Bible Hour, World Home Bible League, Bibles for Mexico, and Family Research Council.

Marvin talks with fellow board member at Northwestern.

Sometimes the family joins together in gift giving. The family's latest combined donation helped fund the $3.5 million Performing Arts Center at the new Zeeland High School. The family's donation provided the cornerstone for $1.9 million in private funds raised for the 973-seat center, which was subsequently named the DeWitt Auditorium. The privately donated funds were used for a state-of-the-art sound system, acoustic enhancements, and a balcony that enlarged the original center by 350 seats. The remainder of the Center project cost, $1.6 million, was supported by taxpayers in the school district. The center is one of the largest high school auditoriums in West Michigan. Marvin's seven children and all of his grandchildren have been schooled in the district.

Reflecting on his charitable donations, Marvin thinks wealthy people make a mistake when they wait to donate until after their death.

"I don't believe in having much left when I die. I feel the time to give is when you're living," he said. "It means so much more when you can see what your money goes for. You can also challenge others to give. The main thing is to give from your heart to something you really believe in. Never give something for the sole purpose of expecting a thank-you or compliment."

Marvin's charitable acts aren't tied just to big-ticket donations for institutions. His Christian beliefs dictate that he try to lend a helping hand to people in need.

One of those was an eccentric neighbor known as the Goat Lady. The elderly woman, Margaret Daleiden, lived with several goats in a run-down shack without electricity. Marvin would check on her to see if she had enough food and medical treatment. When she went into a nursing home for a short stay, he arranged to have a mobile home set up on her property. It was outfitted with electricity and an oil stove. She died in a nursing home in 1982, and Marvin bought a headstone for her grave site.

Another example of his generosity occurred at a National Turkey Federation Convention in Kansas City, where a business associate was supposed to meet him at his hotel room. When Marvin didn't show up, the associate scoured the hotel looking for him. He found him in the lobby making arrangements for a member of a singing group to catch up with her missed bus.

Marvin has also lent money and advice to small-business owners who encountered financial problems – if he determined their hard times weren't caused by foolishness or laziness. Remembering the one time he was turned down for a bank loan, he has also lent money to small businesses that wanted to expand. A good judge of character, all of his investments have paid off.

His charitable acts are grounded in his religious beliefs.

"I learned a lot about the right way of living from my religious faith. It gave me a good value system. I learned to treat my neighbor the way I wanted to be treated. That means you deal honestly and with respect. That means you keep the commitments you make, and that includes your marriage," he said. "I am not saying you have to belong to a religion to have values. There are a lot of people who call themselves Christians and attend church, but they don't act like a Christian in their daily lives. It is not always easy to follow your faith, and I would be the first to admit I am not perfect in that regard. Life is a constant struggle for perfection. Each day, you get as close as you can to that ideal."

If Marvin's generosity is legendary, so is the frugal attitude he embraces from his childhood days during the Depression. Despite his millionaire status, he still buys some low-cost, unbranded products – much to the bewilderment of his wife and daughters, who take issue with him about the extreme thrift. He refuses to put the more-expensive premium gas in his vehicles. The bike he rides for exercise at his property in Florida was purchased at a garage sale. Only after he was chided by business associates did he begin to leave tips for restaurant service. Bil Mar employees and family members alike have been chastised by Marvin for leaving a light on in an unoccupied room.

Business associates have always been amazed at how well he cleans his plate at a restaurant, thinking he must have really enjoyed the meal. Marvin would have eaten everything on his plate even if the meal wasn't delicious because he was brought up to detest wastefulness.

At a Gordon Food Service trade show, a Bil Mar sales associate was about to throw out some cod almondine he had been offering as samples during the event. Marvin showed up as the salesman was taking down the booth. When Marvin heard the fish was destined to become garbage, he said: "You can't throw that out. It is going to be my lunch tomorrow."

Even while golfing, he doesn't forget his frugal roots. He had just teed off with a group of friends who then headed down the fairway. After walking awhile, they noticed he wasn't with them. They looked back and saw him partially hidden behind a tree near the tee they had just left. They called his name but received no response. They called again when another group of golfers approached the tee. Marvin said he would catch up with his party in a few minutes. Finally, one of Marvin's group went back to see what was wrong. He found him fiddling around with a Dixie cup dispenser tacked on a tree. Marvin, wanting a drink of water out of a keg, had mistakenly pulled out two cups and was taking apart the dispenser to return the unused one.

"For those who don't know him, Marvin can be a puzzle when it comes to spending money," said the Rev. Mike VanBuren, former pastor at Ottawa Reformed Church. "He can spend a million dollars at the drop of a hat on something he believes in. Yet he is a conservative at heart and absolutely hates waste. Despite his wealth, he still longs for simplicity."

In between pondering personal money matters, Marvin was still involved in setting Bil Mar's direction.

As the company neared the mid-1980s, he settled a long-simmering dispute about the amount of time and money being invested in the company's retail division. The quarrel came to a head when the decision was made to let the retail division, instead of the food-service division, take charge of sales to grocery delis.

Grocery delicatessen products.

CHAPTER FIFTEEN

THE DELI DISPUTE

The rift between Marvin and Mickey Manaster, the master broker for food-service sales at Bil Mar, only grew wider as the retail division's role in the company became more prominent.

Eight years after retail's inception, Manaster was still protesting about the time and money spent to expand the program featuring Mr. Turkey products. He was always questioning the worth of retail's high-overhead, low-profit supermarket approach versus food service's low-overhead, higher-profit wholesale approach, which involved distribution to restaurants, hotels, prisons, schools, hospitals, in-plant cafeterias, and airline companies.

And Warren Waters' operation of the retail division made an easy target for Manaster. Waters, whose background was with larger corporations, worked according to a budget. Manaster, an independent broker and owner of Chicago-based Mickey Manaster & Co., estimated his Bil Mar sales for a year within a range. When Waters didn't hit his optimistic sales projections, Manaster squawked to Jack DeWitt, who was a strong supporter of food service and executive vice president of operations. Jack, in turn, complained to Gary DeWitt, an original proponent of the retail division and company president. In his position, Gary supported both divisions but he trusted Waters' ability to deliver bottom-line results and believed retail had an important role to play in the company's sales strategy.

Manaster, feeling his influence slipping at Bil Mar, was quick to pounce on any misstep by Waters. In the early days of retail, Waters didn't hire enough qualified people to accomplish his vision. He also was not a very detailed individual, especially when it came to managing people and their sales activities.

Gary preferred to concentrate on Waters' overall performance, which was successful when costs for marketing and new production equipment were taken into account. In retail's defense, Gary argued the big picture.

"In food service, the return on investment was more immediate. In retail, you don't get a quick return on your initial investment. To ensure future pay backs, you have to keep investing through advertising, marketing, and discounts," Gary said. "There are rules of thumb for making money in the retail business. The first year, you are heavily subsidizing your new products. The second year, you hope to break even on your investment. Hopefully by the third year, you have established your product in the consumer market and then start to see some profit. As a whole, with the exception of Jack and Mickey, the management staff could see Warren's vision."

The ongoing tug-of-war between food service and retail only added fuel to a natural rivalry between Gary, the oldest son who was in charge of sales, administration and finance, and his younger brother Jack, who was responsible for the plant operation.

The brothers shared their father's character traits of hard work, persistence and integrity. They also shared a commitment to expand the business. They didn't always agree on the best way to achieve that purpose. Of the two, Gary was more tactful and sensitive, and had a desire to be liked by most everyone. Jack was less patient and more goal-oriented. Feeling the need to be productive, Jack doesn't waste any time getting to the heart of an issue. One of his favorite sayings after asking a question and being met with a long-winded response is "don't build me a clock; just tell me the time."

"There always seemed to be a power struggle between Gary and Jack, even when they were younger. They were strong-willed, like all of us kids. Jack seemed to have more to prove. He was always in the shadow of Gary and dad," said their brother Keith. "The personalities of Gary and Jack clashed. Each of them had his own idea of how the business should be operated. Sometimes that struggle would erupt in them criticizing each other's performance. Gary would complain that Jack wasn't making the product good enough or cheap enough. And Jack said Gary wasn't getting enough money for the product. Everyone in management was well aware of the personality conflict and, as a result, approached Jack and Gary in different ways, sometimes playing one off against the other. The dispute between Mickey Manaster and Warren Waters only intensified the friction between Gary and Jack. On a couple occasions, dad stepped in, as a referee, to bring about a consensus."

Marvin put up with the dispute between the food-service and retail divisions, in admiration for Manaster's sales ability, integrity, and work ethic. After a 20-year business and personal relationship, he treated Manaster as a member of his family. So despite their differences, Marvin had no intention of casting a family member adrift.

He was forced to reconsider that position in the early 1980s when Bil Mar began looking at supermarket delis as a third profit center, along with food-service and retail sales. The delis were the fastest-growing segment in the food business, driven by a consumer demand for more ready-to-eat food products. Meat accounted for about 40 percent of deli sales, with turkey, boiled ham and roast beef the top sellers. Bil Mar had a ready-made advantage in the deli department, where it could offer its wide range of specialty products already being sold to food-service businesses.

However, marketing to delis presented a dilemma for Bil Mar. Should the food-service products be marketed by the food-service sales division, personified by Manaster? Or should the food-service products be marketed by Waters' retail sales division, which by then accounted for about 30 percent of the company's revenues?

Waters convinced Gary DeWitt that retail, already entrenched in supermarkets, should lead the deli charge. And like retail, deli sales would depend on advertising and marketing geared to the consumer. After careful thought, Marvin sided with Gary and Waters.

Manaster objected, arguing that his division was best suited to sell a food-service product because of its familiarity with that line. He also noted that the division was already serving some grocery delis, so was no stranger to the market's operation. As expected, Jack DeWitt lined up behind Manaster. The final decision, made in 1982, favored Waters and the retail division. From that point on, the food-service division would no longer handle deli sales except for existing supermarket accounts.

Manaster would not accept the deli decision and his dissent showed up in a variety of ways. He was reluctant to expand his customer base by moving into new markets where it was harder to make a sale initially. He resisted pursuing smaller food-service distributors. And, along with an investor from Chicago, he even approached the DeWitts in 1983 about buying Bil Mar.

Larry Baker, a former Bil Mar sales representative who once worked in the food-service division, said Manaster's unwillingness to give in on the deli decision was based, in large part, on his desire to exert more control on the company's operations.

"Mickey always wanted more control and more say in the operation of that company. He looked in Michigan and knew he didn't have any claim to the brick and mortar that was Bil Mar. I think he always felt like an outsider and that bothered him," Baker said. "He was responsible for a lot of the company's growth and he saw the potential for even more growth with deli sales. He was especially frustrated by how retail entered the picture. He was upset about all the money spent to get retail up and running. He fought retail every step of the way. Though these types of jealousies and rivalries occur in any type of business, especially one that is growing."

For the sake of Bil Mar, Marvin decided to part company with Manaster in January, 1984. It was one of the hardest decisions he would ever have to make, given his personal relationship with Manaster. Marvin could also not ignore that Bil Mar had grown from $5 million in the mid-1960s, when Manaster signed on, to $170 million by 1984. Manaster, a born salesman and shrewd businessman, could be credited for much of that growth. But Marvin also realized Bil Mar's success wasn't the result of one super salesman. Quality products, superior service, and a lot of other talented people figured in the equation.

"I still feel bad about the break in my relationship with Mickey. The problems started when food service and retail began competing for attention, assets, and management time. Mickey felt like he was losing control of the company. Until that happened, we were good for each other. We made each other successful. It is too bad that such a strong friendship can be lost with some changes and the exchange of a few wrong words," Marvin said. "The way Mickey saw it, the retail side of the business was spending too much and not making enough money. We didn't expect a quick return on our investment with retail. That is not the way retail works. He also thought that Warren Waters had too much say in the operation of the company. Retail was like having a new baby come into the family, and the other kids get jealous when you are paying too much attention to the new arrival. The deli dispute just caused more friction between food service and retail. There seemed to be no better way to resolve the problem than to end our relationship."

Bil Mar agreed to pay Manaster a $2 million settlement to avoid any future legal entanglements about his stake in the business. The agreement included a non-competition clause to prevent Manaster from bumping heads with Bil Mar in the company's market area. In essence, Bil Mar purchased the sales arm of Mickey Manaster & Co. and broke it down into regional offices instead of keeping it centralized in Chicago.

The settlement was set up to pay Manaster in annual increments of $200,000 for 10 years, unless Bil Mar sold the business. In that case, Bil Mar was required to pay the remaining amount in a lump sum as an assurance that Manaster would not be shortchanged by the new owner.

That part of the settlement would prove to be a legal sticking point when Sara Lee acquired Bil Mar in 1987. Sara Lee attorneys interpreted the agreement between Sara Lee and Bil Mar as a merger, not a sale, because the DeWitts were still allowed to operate the business. As a result, they said, the company did not have to pay off Manaster in advance of the 10-year time period. Still upset about Manaster's hostile reaction to the deli decision, Marvin adhered to the strict legal interpretation given by Sara Lee attorneys. Endorsing the interpretation went against the grain of his conscience, which leaned toward honoring the spirit of the original agreement.

"I am a human being, not a saint. I won't say there wasn't some spite on our part about not paying off Mickey after the merger with Sara Lee," Marvin said. "He was nasty to us and we were nasty to him after the decision to combine retail and deli sales. I didn't want him to run roughshod over us anymore."

Manaster was incensed that Marvin would legally sidestep the intent of the settlement. He accused Marvin and Gary of hiding behind the word "merger" and giving into sheer greed. Marvin finally put the issue to rest by reducing the number of payment years so Manaster could receive the full settlement ahead of the original 10-year schedule.

Marvin had no sooner snuffed out the smoldering dispute between Manaster and Bil Mar, when he faced a real test by fire – the $25 million destruction of the headquarters plant in Borculo on Tuesday, Sept. 25, 1984.

Firefighters battle flames on roof of Bil Mar.

CHAPTER SIXTEEN

TESTED BY FIRE

Marvin had just drifted off to sleep about 2 a.m. when a knock on the back door of his home startled him awake.

Exhausted after arriving home late from a Republican fund-raising meeting with Gov. William Milliken in Lansing, he groggily moved toward the sound of a frantic voice hollering "Mr. DeWitt, there's a fire in the plant."

A breathless clean-up worker said a fryer used to brown breaded chicken breasts had burst into flames, prompting Marvin to alert the Blendon-Olive Township Fire Department.

He headed toward the plant thinking the situation could be brought under control before firemen arrived. Thick, black smoke pouring out of the building convinced him otherwise.

Marvin and his wife started calling their children before firefighters arrived. They had a feeling the fire might have major consequences.

One of the first to get a call was Jack. When his dad said there was a fire in the plant, Jack didn't believe him at first. Once before, Marvin had called Jack at home to complain about something at the business that upset him.

That time, Marvin got Jack's attention by saying "there is a fire in the plant." When Jack asked in what area of the plant, his father said "In me, Jack. The fire is in me."

Jack quickly realized the latest call from his father wasn't meant to criticize. This time the fire was for real.

Neither Jack nor Marvin's other sons – Gary, Don, Merle and Keith – thought the worst when they heard there was a fire. Growing up, they had been conditioned to accept fire damage as part of the turkey business. Each of them had watched turkey barns catch on fire over the years. They figured that a fire in the plant would be contained quickly because of the building's concrete and steel construction.

As each of them drove to the plant in the early-morning darkness, they could see the flicker of bright orange flames in the sky from miles away – a sure sign this was not going to be a minor fire.

Their suspicions were confirmed upon their arrival.

Fate of Bil-Mar Workers Up in Air

By Ben Beversluis

While firefighters continued to battle stubborn hot spots through the day and into the night Tuesday, the fate of about 1,100 employees put out of work by an early-morning fire at Bil-Mar Foods Inc. remained in doubt.

"We have no idea how long (until the plant reopens)," said Frederick Hjort, corporate director of human resources, after an afternoon meeting of company executives. "The fire's not even out yet."

While thick smoke still filled the air, Hjort promised Bil-Mar will bring back as many employees as early as possible for clean-up work. Others may be used in temporary production facilities.

"I don't want to say 1,100 people are laid off. Functionally they're out of work" and can begin applying for unemployment compensation, he said.

"A selective process of recalling" will be used, he added. About 90 percent of the production facilities, located north of Borculo on 96th Avenue in Ottawa County, were destroyed.

The turkey frankfurter production area was saved but might not be usable if support facilities such as the butchering and wrapping areas were destroyed, Hjort said.

Bil-Mar is working with the Michigan Employment Security Commission to set up a temporary office to handle unemployment applications, Hjort said.

While firefighters continued hosing down hot spots late Tuesday, Bil-Mar Chairman Marvin DeWitt, who founded the company with his brother William, picked his way through the rubble.

"It's a lot worse than what I thought it would be," he said. "But we started this in 1938 and don't plan on quitting. We're planning on coming back."

Hjort said final loss figures are likely to be "much greater" than the $5 million estimate made early Tuesday. An independent professional adjuster who studied the scene but declined to be identified by name pegged the loss at $8 to $10 million.

Marvin works with firefighters to quell fire.

"Even though I was told there might be a major fire, I didn't really think too much about it at first. We had turkey barns burn nearly every year. We were used to fires on the farm," Keith said. "When I got on the scene, the fire was coming through the roof. But I was still hoping they could get in there and knock it down, confining damage to that one area of the plant."

Marvin's daughter Nancy Haveman arrived to find her father

running in and out of the burning building. She feared for his safety, yet also felt a sense of pride at the way he took control in the face of chaos – the ravaging flames, the choking smoke, the roaring noise from generators and fire pumpers, the bright flickering lights of emergency vehicles, the shouting, the tears, and the disbelieving looks.

"Dad was all over that burning plant. He was the one who entered the electrical room to cut power to the rest of the plant. He helped groups of firemen find their way around the darkened building. He had built that plant from scratch and knew the layout like the back of his hand," she said. "Even in all of that smoke and fire, he never showed a trace of fear. That was his nature. He had to be where the action was. He had to feel like he was doing something. He could never have stood there and just watched it burn."

At the height of the inferno, more than 200 firefighters from 12 departments in Ottawa and Kent counties were on the scene with more than 50 pieces of equipment. Besides Blendon/Olive, the departments included Robinson Township, Zeeland Township, Allendale Township, Crockery Township, Georgetown Township, Holland Township, Port Sheldon Township, Marne, Zeeland City, Holland City, and Coopersville/Polkton.

Aerial trucks from three departments poured water down on the cauldron of fire after the flames shot through the roof. Other firefighters, with hand-held hoses, battled the flames from intact sections of the rooftop until they began to heave from the heat below. Water from the fire hoses boiled in puddles on the roof before sections caved in. Some of the water that fell into the plant flowed back out, like a swift stream, through loading dock doors. Blendon/Olive, the supervising fire department, was on the scene for 36 hours until all

Firefighters attack flames in office area.

of the hot spots were snuffed out. Remarkably, only a maintenance worker and two firefighters sustained minor injuries.

Firefighters were hampered by a number of factors, including the location of the fire in the center of the plant. The blaze originated in a new electrical fryer used to brown breaded chicken. The fryer had been shut off to allow for a cool down before a third-shift night crew cleaned the piece of equipment. But the heat control malfunctioned, leaving the fryer coated in hot oil. When the clean-up crew sprayed water into the fryer there was a flash fire. A hood that drew exhaust from the fryer sucked flames to the building's roof.

Firefighters direct efforts toward burning roof.

The burning roof, consisting of asphalt and tar paper layers from years of additions, caused another obstacle for firemen – intense heat and dense smoke that prevented them from getting at the source of the fire.

Firemen didn't receive any help from the plant's sprinkling system, which was confined to offices and warehouses where the DeWitts believed a fire would likely cause the most damage.

Another hurdle for firefighters came courtesy of Mother Nature. Shifting winds, whipped around by a passing thunderstorm, fanned the flames into a frenzy.

Gary DeWitt first believed a major portion of the plant could be saved because a southeast wind was blowing the flames to the back of the plant. About two hours after the fire started, his optimism was tempered when a 180-degree shift in wind, from southeast to northwest, blew the flames toward the front of the plant.

"When that wind switched, we knew the front of the plant was also going to go up in flames. That is when we started cleaning out the offices. As we finished that task, the flames leapt higher and we knew the fate of the plant was sealed," Gary said. "You emotionally got to the point where you couldn't talk about it. The loss was similar to a death in a family. For me, the fire really hit close to home when flames came shooting out my office window."

As the fire dragged on, radio stations let Bil Mar employees know they didn't have to report for work, though most of them came to the scene to offer assistance. As the fire roared toward them, the employees helped Marvin's children and oldest grandchildren move company records, computer files, office equipment and personal effects out of the building and to the nearby Country Store. To haul as much as they could in one load, some of them used grocery carts from the store. They also salvaged Marvin's extensive collection of stuffed animals killed on his big-game hunting trips. Jack DeWitt's son Steve said the process of relocating the trophies reminded him of a live zoo, with the heads of the animals bobbing and weaving to the movement of the carrier.

Others pulled finished products out of the freezers and put them in the 60 refrigerated semi-trailers parked at the site – some owned by Bil Mar and some lent to the company by area businesses in a show of support.

"It was amazing to watch so many people come to the aid of the DeWitts. They really cared about the DeWitt family, especially Marvin," said the Rev. Mike Van Buren, former pastor at Ottawa Reformed Church. "I watched people risk their lives that day, carrying out computer terminals and files. They had no direct stake in that business, other than being employed there."

The extent of the damage was evident as dawn's light began to shine on the scene. The oldest section of the plant, about 70 percent of the 261,360-square-foot building, was in ruins including areas for slaughter, production, frozen-food processing, and offices. Only one of the plant's three freezers survived. More than 75 percent of the freezer contents, about $7 million worth of processed food, was destroyed by smoke. The damage was estimated at more than $25 million, making it one of the costliest fires in Ottawa County's history.

Only the newest portions of the complex, equipped with fire walls, had been spared. They included part of the maintenance building on the west side; two warehouses, personnel offices, cafeteria, and beef-processing room on the north and east sides; and a warehouse, cooler, freezer, and frank-processing plant on the south side. The 30,000-square-foot hot dog plant had been built in 1982, six years after Bil Mar had started contracting other processors to

Bil Mar plant prior to 1984 fire (above). Fire destroys center of plant (below).

make Mr. Turkey hot dogs. The plant also fabricated hot dogs made with all chicken and all beef, and combinations of beef-pork-chicken, beef-pork-turkey, chicken-pork, and turkey-pork.

Also untouched by the blaze was a $2 million, 45,000-square-foot office complex under construction at the front of the plant. The floor was in, the steel was up, and the roof deck was on. There were no sidewalls or windows installed yet. Instead of working on the new building that day, a crew from Dan Vos Construction, of Ada, assisted in the fire-fighting efforts until it was clear the plant couldn't be saved.

At that point, those on the scene began to wonder aloud if the business could be salvaged. There were a lot of long faces and some tears being shed among the company's 1,200 employees.

"I was shocked. It felt like something of mine had burned and was gone," said Bertha Geertman, a production employee. "I cried really hard out of fear. I didn't know what I was going to do. I had worked there for 19 years and I was in my late 50s. "

Even some DeWitt family members who worked at the plant wondered if they were watching the final chapter close on Bil Mar's history.

Firefighters snuff out last of hot spots.

"It was not easy to stand there watching the place burn. I felt as if I was watching a lifetime's worth of work being destroyed," Jack DeWitt said. "At that point, I had worked at the business for 24 years. It was hard to take when you think of all the hours and effort everyone had put into building the business. That was a tough time for the company. Mickey Manaster had left, and his right-hand man, Don Gardner, followed him out about three months later. And then there was the fire. I couldn't help but think about why this was all happening at once."

Merle DeWitt said a feeling of helplessness overcame him as the morning wore on.

"I went into the plant to see how bad it was. But I got lost in the thick smoke. I was forced back outside and had to watch it burn," he said. "I thought that 'this is all I know; where do I go from here. What am I going to do with the rest of my life.' There was my career going up in smoke."

For one DeWitt, Keith's wife, Mary, there was a double sense of sadness. Her father, Junior Huyser, chief of the Blendon-Olive Twp. Fire Department, led the fire fighting efforts that day.

"I felt sadness for the DeWitts and my dad. They lost the family business, and he couldn't save it. He took it as a personal loss," she said.

Although saddened by the loss, Gary DeWitt never entertained thoughts of Bil Mar's demise. The business, then hiring 100 employees annually, had just posted a record $170 million in sales. The company owned two plants in Iowa and Ohio, farms and a feed mill in the Borculo area, and the partially built office complex. The newest portions of the plant had been saved, giving the DeWitts a foundation to base a new start. More than 11,000 turkeys were still scheduled for daily delivery to the Borculo plant. And the second generation of DeWitts was too young to retire. Besides Gary, who was then the company's president, the second generation included his four brothers: Jack, executive vice president of operations; Don, manager of Michigan farms; Merle, director of turkey manufacturing; and Keith, in charge of buying and selling commodities. Bill Sr.'s son Ray was responsible for refrigeration. Bill Jr. had left Bil Mar earlier that year to operate his own business. Marvin was chairman of the board, while Bill Sr. was vice chairman.

"We had too many assets, too many customers, and a growing business," Gary said. "We couldn't give up."

Gary's confidence was also buoyed by a financial advantage unknown to other family members – $11 million worth of business-interruption insurance. The insurance, on top of a standard fire loss policy held by the company, covered the cost of doing business until a new plant was built, such as making products at temporary locations. Marvin had spoken against paying for extra insurance, never believing a fire at the plant could be devastating. Gary went ahead and purchased the policy anyway, much to the relief of his father.

Even without the extra coverage, Marvin also had no doubt about Bil Mar's survival. While some of the fire departments began to clear the scene late in the morning, Marvin circulated among groups of employees to give them pep talks. Ever the company's cheerleader, Marvin let them know he intended to turn the adversity into an opportunity.

Employees await news of the fire's aftermath.

"Not for one second did I ever think about not continuing the business. It was too successful a business not to carry on. We also had employees and customers who were counting on us," he said. "I have never looked at experiences in life as being all good or all bad, just an opportunity to learn something. If you learn something from a problem, then it is only half bad. That is the way I looked at the fire. It was not a time to give up; it was a time to start over in a bigger and better way."

Marvin expressed the same upbeat message at a noon meeting of salaried employees in the downstairs banquet room at The Old Schoolhouse Restaurant in Borculo. The intent of the meeting was to discuss Bil Mar's future. And Marvin was not in the mood for any negative discussion.

An industrial psychologist, hired as a consultant by Bil Mar before the fire, asked the group of supervisory employees to express their feelings about the loss. Marvin said the last thing Bil Mar employees needed to do at that moment was to wallow in their sorrows when there was so much work ahead of them. He also squelched talk about whether to rebuild the business or take the insurance money and call it quits. One of those who would have cashed in and not rebuilt was Bill Sr., who, at 71, was semi-retired and had little involvement in the business.

Kevin McKenna, working in product development at the time, recalled how Marvin turned the restaurant meeting into a pep rally.

"Marvin started assigning tasks to each person in the restaurant. Before you knew it, 60 guys had six months of work in front of them. Within a half hour, you went from feeling like you lost your job to feeling like you were part of a team that would make something happen. You knew what your part was in keeping that company going," McKenna said. "In so many words, Marvin told the group they should trust in the Lord and do whatever was needed to get the job done – from taking care of the incoming turkeys to finding temporary production sites to talking with a contractor about rebuilding. He finished the meeting by saying, 'OK boys, we have a lot of work to do. Let's get to it.'"

Burned-out office area of plant.

Later that afternoon, as Marvin picked his way through the smoldering rubble, he reiterated his optimism to the community by talking to newspaper reporters.

"It's a lot worse than what I thought it would be. But we started this in 1938 and we don't plan on quitting. We're planning on coming back."

Using the still-standing cafeteria building as a command post, salaried employees began the process of putting Bil Mar back together. Each decision was directed at restoring the facility, returning employees to work, and shipping a steady flow of products to customers.

More than 12,000 live turkeys were diverted for daily slaughter from Borculo to Bil Mar's plants in Iowa and Ohio. Contacts were made with other food processors about using part of their facilities to manufacture Bil Mar products, including beef and chicken. Warehouse space was secured. Office operations were set up in leased facilities in Holland and Zeeland.

Within 24 hours, enough progress had been made so that Gary DeWitt could send this message to customers:

"We are getting our business together and the pipelines will soon be filled with your favorite products once again. We are stepping up production in our Ohio and Iowa plants. We are utilizing some co-packers under our strict supervision, and we are using our tested, tasteful recipes and proven methods. That way you can be sure of not only getting the products but, more importantly, the products with the same high quality and taste. Finally, tragedy brings good friends closer. And we feel that our customers are good friends and, as they have demonstrated, part of the Bil Mar family. We are confident of our ability to continue servicing you through this period of trial, and to serve you better still with our new and improved facilities that are, even now, taking shape."

As the week wore on, Bil Mar found work for more than half of its 1,200-member work force. The company offered production workers jobs cleaning up of the fire-scarred site. Some Bil Mar supervisors were scheduled to work at one of 17 sites in nine states where they would assist in the manufacture of the company's products. Others were kept busy with sales, marketing, distribution and administration.

Despite the turmoil, Bil Mar did not miss a payroll. That week's

Employees survey extent of damage.

paychecks were handed out in the company parking lot. Bil Mar continued health coverage for all employees. For those not able to find immediate work, the company paid their wages during the six weeks before they were eligible for unemployment compensation through the state of Michigan. Bil Mar's personnel department also interceded for employees being squeezed by lenders.

One of the hardest things required of the DeWitts that week was the destruction of nearly two million pounds of raw and processed inventory, which had been tainted by the fire. The USDA required the company to drive over the damaged products with a bulldozer to deter anyone attempting to salvage them from their trip to a landfill.

During the first few days after the fire, the DeWitts realized just how solid Bil Mar's reputation was in the food industry. A number of companies, including some competitors, offered assistance.

Plant fire causes $25 million worth of damage.

"I think the help we received from competitors after the fire said a lot about the respect others in the industry had for us and Bil Mar. We were never the type to crucify someone else just to get an order. Our goal was to put out a better product and provide good service," Marvin said. "With our customers, they truly got what they paid for. We concentrated on our business instead of our competitors."

Among the companies extending a helping hand were Murco Inc., a beef processor in Plainwell; Superior Seafoods Co. in Grand Rapids; and Longacre, a turkey processor in Pennsylvania.

The letter from Murco said: "Just a short note to offer our support in any way we are able during this difficult period. We do have extra freezer space that you may use. We also have corrugated boxes and plastic vac bags as well. Your company has an excellent reputation, built on a solid foundation, which I am convinced will continue to grow even more."

Support for the ailing Bil Mar came in many forms. The president of Longmont Foods, one of Bil Mar's competitors in Longmont, Colo., sent its food brokers, sales representatives, and office personnel a letter admonishing them not to take advantage of the tragedy.

"The situation that confronts Bil Mar Foods is truly unfortunate and tragic. Because of their many contributions to the turkey industry, and their honesty and integrity, we wish to express our sadness and concern, and will do nothing to create any more problems for them. I want each of you to know that we do not wish to take advantage of this situation. Our first responsibility is to service our existing Longmont customers. I do not want you to actively solicit any business from customers currently being supplied by Bil Mar. We look forward to Bil Mar returning to the market as an active and healthy competitor."

Bill Stout, former head of Bil Mar's microbiology lab, was not surprised at the outpouring of assistance from competitors.

"There was a reason for that. Marvin and his family had known so many people in that industry and had kept good contact with them," Stout said. "The DeWitts were well respected and had a good reputation. So, when the chips were down and there were people with no jobs, those contacts paid off."

Even those not in the food business reached out in support. The Good Samaritan Center in Holland offered to assist Bil Mar employees unable to find a job. Holland Youth for Christ extended the use of its conference room for company meetings. And the Rev. Arnold Punt, of Faith Reformed Church, prayed over the fire-damaged site.

Offers of personal assistance also poured in. There were phone calls and cards from friends, neighbors, and fellow church members. Immediately after the fire, meals were brought to the DeWitt home by well-wishers.

The fire brought the DeWitt clan even closer together. Long before the disaster, the family had made plans to celebrate the 45th anniversary of Marvin and Jerene. They made reservations at the Grand Traverse Resort in Traverse City on what turned out to be the weekend after the fire. There was hesitation on the part of some family members, especially those related by marriage, to go ahead with the celebration plans. Most of them agreed to push forward, however.

"At first, I thought that going ahead with a family get-together was strange under those circumstances. I thought 'How can this family go away when this just happened. How can they just get up and leave,'" said Keith's wife Mary. "That says something about the family moving forward and not dwelling on the negative. Surprisingly, we did have a good time playing tennis and golf, and lounging in the hot tubs. We left the problem behind. In hindsight, it was a good thing to get away from it."

Don's wife Minnie was also amazed by the family's refusal to be overwhelmed by the disaster.

"There wasn't much talk about the fire that weekend. In fact, there wasn't any talk about the business, and I found that most unusual. When they got together, they always talked business – even when they said they weren't going to, like during the Christmas gathering."

While the DeWitts were in Traverse City, the Rev. Mike VanBuren chose to use the fire as the centerpiece of his sermon that Sunday at Ottawa Reformed Church. The sermon, titled "Tested by Fire," stressed that life's trials – like the Bil Mar fire – are necessary to not only test but strengthen one's faith in God.

In reading from the Bible's New Testament (I Peter 1:3-9), Van Buren said: "These trials are only to test your faith, to see whether or not it is strong and pure. It is being tested as fire tests gold and purifies it – and your faith is far more precious to God than mere gold; so if your faith remains strong after being tried in the test tube of fiery trials, it will bring you much praise and glory and honor on the day of His return. You love Him, even though you have never seen Him; though not seeing Him, you trust Him, and even now you are happy with the inexpressible joy that comes from heaven itself. And your further reward for trusting Him will be the salvation of your souls."

Even though Van Buren knew the DeWitts would not be in church, he decided to deliver a sermon with the fire topic because the blaze touched so many lives in the congregation. Most members either worked at Bil Mar or knew someone who did.

"The hurt reaches, in one way or another, to so many of you here. That hurt, that confusion, that struggle, that fear is part of the test. Let me name a couple of the things that have been and will continue to be tested along with your faith.

"Things like this disaster test our friendship. It is at times like these that we truly find out who are our friends... a person who will stand by you at any and all times but especially in the most trying and difficult of times... I saw it first-hand at the scene itself. It was especially evident when the wind suddenly switched from the southeast to the west. The wind that was blowing the fire away from the offices suddenly blew it at them. Everyone knew that the plant could be rebuilt. Yet if all the records were lost, where do you start then? No one had to be asked. From older men, who you prayed would not have a heart attack, to employees, to wives and husbands of employees to just plain friends of the company. All of us were going into smoke-filled offices with no light, no electricity, no protective helmets, or boots or coats and carrying out everything we could... I even witnessed firemen... go far beyond what firemen usually do or have to do.

"Trials also test our families... I had call after call, telling me that some of the husbands from Bil Mar might be transferred temporarily to Iowa, Ohio, or Minnesota. These people do this to provide for their families. The wives, out of understanding love, stand beside them and pledge them their devotion, no matter what. Suddenly, when for so many families things seemed to be going so smoothly, it appeared as if it all was falling apart. But was it? Was it falling apart or was it making many of you pull together? As couple upon couple stood watching a job go up in smoke, they were in each other's arms. Couple after couple expressed how they might have to do with much less for awhile, though they still had each other. It so often takes a tragedy to remind us how much our families mean.

"Trials also test our church family. There are people sitting here this morning who may need our help very much – to pray for them and with them that the Lord may open doors of new employment or temporary employment. It makes us suddenly look at our plenty when someone down the pew now has much less, and I pray to the

Lord that we are reminded of how to give, how to share, how to support. We are our Brother's keeper. We have been given so we can give. I had one person walk into my office Friday morning who isn't really physically affected by the fire. When she heard of it, she cried. She was hurting for members of this Christian church family.

" ...Our faith, our friendships, our families and our church family are tested by fires – the real ones, like the one that devastated Bil Mar, and those without smoke that burn our lives nonetheless... If we can look past present fires to the fact of our salvation, then we will know our faith is true."

The faith of Marvin and his family had been tested by the fire and it had not been shaken. After returning home from the anniversary weekend with his family, Marvin looked forward to the challenge of rebuilding Bil Mar.

Construction begins on new Bil Mar plant.

CHAPTER SEVENTEEN

RISING FROM THE ASHES

The Monday after the fire, Marvin returned to work with the same resolve he had exhibited 46 years earlier when the business was started.

Along with his boys and the Bil Mar management team, the 65-year-old began the coordination of manufacturing at 17 temporary locations. He personally supervised the clean up of rubble at the fire-damaged site. And he was involved in the design and construction of a new processing plant.

"The fire turned out to be a blessing in disguise. Bil Mar was going to get a new building that was larger, more efficient, and ultra-fireproof," Marvin said. "And by having to start over, we were given the option of investing in state-of-the-art processing equipment."

The construction of the new plant was put into motion the day of the fire. With one of his characteristic hand-shake deals, he hired

Dan Vos Construction to put up the new plant in tandem with the partially completed administrative office complex. Vos – whose credentials include work for corporations like Amway, Perrigo, Wolverine World Wide and Haworth – was also contracted to help with the clean up.

The most immediate concern was to keep the product flowing to more than 1,000 customers across the country. About 65 Bil Mar employees fanned out to manufacturing sites in nine states, including Michigan, to monitor product quality. Some of the employees were away from their families during the week for more than a year, until full production resumed at Borculo.

Five of the temporary manufacturing locations were in Michigan, including Holland, Plainwell, Grand Rapids, Chesaning, and Detroit. The rest were in St. Charles, Minn.; St. Louis Park, Minn.; St. James, Minn.; Albert Lee, Minn.; Nebraska City, Neb.; Wichita, Kansas; Oak Park, Ill.; Chicago, Ill.; Hammond, Ind.; Massillon, Ohio; Blue Surf, N.J.; and Franconia, Pa.

Production was also stepped up at Bil Mar's other two plants in Ohio and Iowa, where turkeys raised in Michigan were shipped for slaughter, deboning, and processing. Some of the Borculo employees transferred there to help with the increased production.

The duplication of Bil Mar's operation at off-site locations was staggering. Yet Bil Mar employees, expressing loyalty to Marvin and his family, were up to the challenge of manufacturing 540 products, using 600 raw materials from 400 suppliers. Among the raw materials were vegetables, dairy products, vegetable oils, spices, flavorings, red meats, chicken, and seafood.

"We were going in 100 different directions, and the company plane was going back and forth all over the place. First we had to find production space and then lease it, some in existing food plants and some in vacant buildings. Then we had to schedule Bil Mar employees to work at those sites, and make sure they were provided with all the equipment and ingredients they needed," said Kevin McKenna, a former Bil Mar supervisor. "At one site, we had to install a noodle cooker that was critical to a recipe. The cooker would not fit through the door of the building, so we paid $1,000 to knock a hole in a wall to make it fit. Nothing stood in the way of the incredible attitude of Bil Mar employees. There was always a team spirit at Bil Mar but that became more evident after the fire."

Bil Mar production didn't only occur at long-distance sites. Turkey dogs and smoked polish sausage were manufactured in the hot dog plant after it underwent a three-week clean up for smoke damage. Three months after the fire, roasted turkey breasts were coming off a line in a fire-damaged oven room that had been renovated below the second-floor cafeteria. A make-shift microbiology lab was set up in the frank plant, where product samples from off-site locations were inspected. One of the remaining warehouses was turned into a plant to process some of Bil Mar's frozen foods. Before the fire, the company was processing about two million pounds of food a week. Within four to five weeks of the fire, Bil Mar was up to half production at 1 million pounds a week.

Plant rebuilding begins (foreground).

During the rebuilding period, even the long-strained relations between Bil Mar and the USDA eased a bit. The watchdog agency didn't waive any regulations involving public safety. The USDA, recognizing Bil Mar's unique situation, did allow the company to cut some regulatory corners involving labeling and product transfer.

While production lines began to hum again, Dan Vos Construction, led by the founder's son Gary, was busy finishing the administrative complex and building the new plant. Vos did not have to start from scratch on the project's design. Months before the fire struck, Bil Mar executives had been working on preliminary drawings for the plant's eventual expansion and reconfiguration. Those plans laid the footing for the new plant, which was to be more than twice the size of the former 261,000-square-foot facility.

Construction of the new plant began Nov. 4, about five weeks after the fire. More than 150 construction workers were assigned to the project, west of the fire-damaged structure. They worked 12 hours a day but only six days a week in observance of Sunday as the Sabbath, which was respected by Vos Construction and Bil Mar as a day of rest and worship. Vos and the DeWitts were determined to get the processing plant up and running as quickly as possible – yet not at the expense of their religious beliefs.

Bil Mar's insurance company, wanting to limit the amount of business-interruption insurance paid out, protested the seventh-day qualification. The company gave in when it became clear Vos and the DeWitts were not going to budge.

Bil Mar's reception area after the fire.

At the first construction meeting, insurance company executives from New York City told Bil Mar that Sunday work was necessary for a full return on the damage settlement. Vos told them his company didn't work on Sundays. And Jack DeWitt, with a nod from his father, backed Vos up.

"You aren't in New York City. You are in West Michigan and we have a different culture here. No one at Bil Mar or Vos Construction will be working on Sundays," Jack said.

Even without working on Sundays, Vos Construction rebuilt the plant in record time for a building that size. Six months from the day of the fire, on March 25, the first phase of construction was completed, allowing slaughtering and deboning operations to be reintroduced at the Borculo site. At that point, construction of the plant was at the half-way mark and Bil Mar had returned to a prefire production level of two million pounds per week. The office complex was completed a month earlier, well ahead of schedule. The three-story building provided offices for top executives and salaried staff.

Marvin kept track of each construction stage.

"He is a hard driver on himself and others," Gary Vos said. "He kept an eye on most everything. He was there every step of the way. Marvin would come into a construction meeting and look over everyone's shoulder to see what was being done. When he was satisfied that everything was on the right track, he would leave."

Magazine features new Bil Mar plant.

Dr. Phil Weiner, Bil Mar's former research and development chief, made a similar observation about the importance of Marvin's presence during the rebuilding process.

"He had the ability to stand in the background and still know what was going on. He knew when to step in and keep things moving, and when to stand back and let things happen," Weiner said. "The supervisors would meet at 5 a.m. two or three times a week to discuss the layout of the new plant. We would talk for a couple of hours and sometimes get hung up on a point. Marvin had the uncanny ability to be there on the days when we ran into problems. He would just show up out of no where. That was one thing that really impressed me about him."

By the summer of 1985, the second phase of the construction project – involving the retail division – was nearly complete. The first retail product introduced after the fire strayed from Bil Mar's turkey roots – DeWitt Table Ready Meats, a line of fully-cooked, prepackaged beef entrees targeting working couples wanting a quick, but high-quality, alternative for dinner.

The third and last phase of construction – allowing resumption of food-service production – was finished in the fall of 1985, just 13 months after the fire struck. When the entire project was completed in the spring of 1986, the complex included 46,500 square feet of new office space, 400,000 square feet of new production space, and 186,000 square feet of renovated production space. The total square footage, 632,500, was equal in size to about three football fields.

The rebuilding program cost more than $40 million, including the construction of an on-site waste-water treatment plant to enhance the outdated lagoon system. The new system, which can process up to 1.5 million gallons of waste water per day, is equipped with a more complex aeration system that separates waste into water and sludge. The water is pumped into lagoons and thc sludge ends up in two holding tanks prior to removal by waste haulers. Water in the lagoons is used for field irrigation or eventual dispersal into Pigeon Creek.

Turkeys are processed in new plant.

Also built into the reconstruction cost was the purchase of more than $20 million worth of state-of-the-art processing equipment, such as steamers, ovens, freezers, hot-dog makers, conveyer belts, deboning machines, computerized slicers, packagers, and a smoke house. The DeWitts, who collected about $35 million in fire insurance, could have minimized their losses and installed the same processing equipment.

With Marvin's blessing, the decision was made to build the latest, most-expensive technology into the new plant. The preference upheld Bil Mar's reputation in the food industry as an innovative manufacturer of top-quality products.

Weiner was the chief proponent of the new equipment, capable of tripling production capacity.

"I told the DeWitts that if we just replaced the equipment we had, it would be obsolete by the time the new plant was in operation. On one sheet of paper, I put down all the equipment and the processes we had at the time of the fire. On another piece of paper, I put down all the opportunities we had to update ourselves," he said. "In going down the more-expensive list, I noted that some of the equipment was already being used by some of our competitors and some of it would be brand new. I told them we would have the most-sophisticated turkey processing facility in the United States, if they went for the newer list. Marvin and the other DeWitts were so supportive during this time. Whatever I said I needed, they said to go get it."

Weiner considered a number of different processes and many types of equipment, choosing those best suited to Bil Mar's operation. Most of his energy was spent on the design of a water-based system of continuous cooking and cooling. Weiner's continuous conveyor system uses water to cook and chill the product, making it ready for boxing and shipping when it comes out of the oven. Warm water is dripped over the product, sealed in an airtight bag, to accomplish cooking. Then cold water is dripped over the product for three hours to cool it down. Previously, Bil Mar had cooked one load of meat at a time and then moved it to a blast cooler for eight hours. The sophisticated conveyor system shaves about five hours off the cooler time. The system also reduces handling and storage time. Another benefit is a lower cooking temperature, which improves yield by minimizing shrinkage.

Plant's evisceration line.

Once the state-of-the-art plant was up and running, the DeWitts could assess the full impact of the fire. And the appraisal was mostly positive.

Bil Mar owned a larger plant, far more efficient and technologically advanced than any turkey processor in the United States. Despite the massive disruption, the company's sales had only fallen $8.5 million from the previous fiscal year total of $169.8 million. Within two years of the fire, the company was again experiencing a 25 percent rate of annual sales growth that pushed the total to nearly $200 million.

And Bil Mar was able to keep most of its food-service customers. The biggest exception was Gordon Food Service, Bil Mar's largest food-service customer. The DeWitts were disappointed when GFS switched to another supplier out of fear that Bil Mar could not keep up with order demands. In hindsight, now that Bil Mar is again servicing GFS, the DeWitts realize the decision to temporarily drop Bil Mar as a supplier was yet another blessing. Bil Mar was under less pressure to meet production requirements after the fire without GFS as a customer.

On the fire's downside, Bil Mar had to share some trade secrets with competitors who were contracted to manufacture Bil Mar products. One of those processes, the cook-in-bag roasting technology for turkey breasts, was perfected by Bil Mar in the early 1980s. With the air-tight bag technology, Bil Mar was able to increase yields and shelf life by retaining more natural juices and moisture that had been injected into the meat. Prior to the cook-in-bag method, a breast was cooked in foil filled with holes to keep the meat from drying. The juices drained out, which meant 100 pounds of meat could weigh 82 pounds by the end of the manufacturing process. Cooking in a bag also eliminated product repackaging.

But even the disclosure of the cook-in-bag technology was not viewed as a major negative.

Employee prepares sausage line for smoking process.

"We weren't hurt much by letting our competitors know some of our production processes. It was nothing they wouldn't have learned eventually from equipment manufacturers. All we did was speed up their learning curve on some of those techniques," Gary DeWitt said.

Bil Mar's retail division took the hardest hit from the fire. Those products could not be manufactured as quickly and easily as food-service items. The company had to pull out of some new markets, like Florida, Seattle, and Texas. When Bil Mar left those markets, some of its competitors jumped in to fill the vacuum. As a result, the company's retail program is weaker today than if the fire hadn't struck.

Overall, the DeWitts had a lot for which to be thankful. And

Marvin, not prone to giving casual thank-yous, made that clear in an appreciation letter to employees three months after the fire.

"You can well imagine the sick feeling that came over me that fateful day in September – the culmination of my life's work all gone. I never imagined in my wildest thoughts that the whole thing could go. Now when I reflect on what existed then versus what has taken place – the cleanup, the continuation of operations, the reconstruction – I want you all to know I am really touched by your dedication and effort to have made all this happen. I am more convinced than ever that, over a period of time, we will be a better organization as a result of it. Not only will we have modern, more-efficient facilities – but, more importantly, we will have had the benefit of working together and supporting each other through this difficult period of rebuilding. You know me well enough to understand that on a day-to-day basis I have a hard time saying thank you. I guess I am too easily distracted by things I would like to see done differently. You also know this does not mean I am not proud of you and grateful for your participation in bringing about this transformation. It is amazing what has already been accomplished, and I now want to say thank you because you are clearly playing a big part in Bil Mar's development and future. The future is happening now. What is taking place each day is the building of your future, too. We are happy to make the investment of our resources. We trust you will also be pleased to contribute the resources of your time and effort."

Bil Mar's resurrection from the ashes was the topic of stories in a number of trade magazines serving the food industry. The stories reiterated what other food-processing companies already knew – Bil Mar had a history of stability and superior quality. And those traits made it an attractive target for acquisition in the 1980s when consumers were clamoring for low-fat, low-calorie sources of protein, like turkey.

Even before the fire, Marvin had turned away potential suitors because he was not yet ready to give up the family business. His attitude toward selling shifted after the fire when the construction of the new high-tech production plant drew the attention of some big names in the food industry.

Bill and Marvin DeWitt after the merger with Sara Lee.

CHAPTER EIGHTEEN

SARA LEE MERGER

Nearly 50 years after Bil Mar's inception, Marvin seriously began to consider selling the business.

Always resistant to the notion, he had a change of heart in 1986 after the company's first long-range planning session. The meeting was conducted by Braxton Associates, a division of Touche Ross & Co., Bil Mar's accounting firm.

The meeting made Marvin realize the company had reached a major cross road in its history. To achieve the next competitive level, Bil Mar would need significant investment to expand the operation.

That left the company with three clear choices. The DeWitts could raise the capital by taking the company public and selling shares. The family could foot the bill for capital expenditures. Or they could sell the business to a company with significant investment ability.

After careful analysis, selling the business seemed to make the most sense – and not just for financial reasons. Selling would also solve the thorny question of ownership succession.

Marvin, the company's driving force, was 67 and ready to back even further away from the business. His older brother Bill, 73, had been semi-retired since the late 1970s, spending his time planting corn and working on the turkey farms when someone called in sick. Bill Jr. had left the company in the summer of 1984 to operate a business that manufactured fruit-picking equipment.

Marvin's two oldest sons, Gary, as president, and Jack, as executive vice president of operations, were the obvious successors. But the tension between the two brothers, over how the business should be operated, only intensified after the fire.

One instance personified the conflict. When the new plant was being built, Warren Waters, the company's retail division manager, proposed the introduction of some new products, like turkey nuggets, patties and sticks. Gary supported Waters. Jack was dead set against manufacturing new products at temporary off-site locations set up after the fire. The disagreement was settled by Marvin, who sided with Gary and Waters after questioning Jack's judgment.

Jack, who felt slighted, didn't talk to his father for more than six months, even leaving a trade convention early to avoid conversing with him.

While Marvin took the rivalry between the two brothers in stride, he also recognized the potential for future conflict.

"There was a lot of talk about a rivalry between Gary and Jack. I think it was blown out of proportion. I would characterize it more as friction than a full-blown rivalry. The conflict never got to the point where they weren't speaking with each other or that the business was in any danger of being hurt," Marvin said. "There is always bound to be some disagreement in any business, especially a family business. There was always some friction among the growers, the office, and the plant about how to reach common goals. Gary and Jack had their share of disagreements over how the business should be run and each of them thought they were right. Jack would sometimes say the salesmen weren't selling enough and we weren't getting enough money for the product. Gary would sometimes say production wasn't getting the product out fast enough and that quality wasn't always consistent. Those types of squabbles were bound to continue."

There was also the question of how the third generation of DeWitts, the grandchildren, might fit into the business picture. At that point, Marvin and Bill had 36 grandchildren between them, and the next generation of heirs was too young to be formally involved in the business. Besides, family businesses don't have a stellar record of succession. Only a third of companies is likely to survive to the second generation, and far less, about 10 percent, make it to the third generation.

In addition to solving the succession question, selling the business to a larger company seemed the most sensible option from the financial standpoint. In the 1980s, mergers and acquisitions were the norm, not the exception in the fast-changing food industry, and that included turkey processors. Bil Mar had to grow even larger or become lost in the shuffle. Selling to a larger company would certainly provide Bil Mar with the resources necessary to compete in a wider marketing arena.

The acquisitions and mergers were being driven by major international companies purchasing smaller regional brands rather than taking the risk of developing new brands on their own. Family-owned turkey processors, like Bil Mar, were especially hot properties in the 1980s when consumers began to shy away from red meat due to the perceived health and nutrition benefits of poultry. Turkey products, many of them mimicking their red-beef counterparts, contain less fat and cholesterol, and fewer calories than beef and pork.

As a result, consumers were gobbling up more turkey than ever – from 8.5 pounds per person in 1971 to 12.1 pounds in 1985. The increase was shown in turkey-industry sales, which jumped from $1.27 billion in 1980 to $1.82 billion in 1985, the year of Bil Mar's reconstruction. Another indication of changing tastes could be found in turkey sales during the Thanksgiving and Christmas holidays, a traditional time of the year for the bird's consumption. In the early 1970s, 90 percent of turkey sales occurred during the last 60 days of the year. By 1985, that percentage had dropped to 35 percent when only about a quarter of all turkeys grown were sold as whole birds. The remainder were deboned and processed in other forms.

With all the consumer interest in turkey, food companies that didn't have a poultry operation wanted one. Louis Rich became a part of Oscar Mayer. Swift/Butterball and Longmont joined ConAgra. Jennie-O was acquired by Hormel. Perdue Farms bought Shenandoah Valley Poultry and Shenandoah Farms. And two smaller operations, Wampler Foods Inc. and Longacre Inc., merged to remain a market contender.

"To succeed, it was obvious we would have to keep growing in an industry that was in the process of mergers and buy outs," Marvin said. "Selling to a larger company would ensure our continued growth and solve the succession problem."

Selling would provide other tangible benefits. For the first time in Bil Mar's history, the business assets would be liquid for the DeWitt family. Marvin and Bill had made tax- and estate-planning provisions at the time of incorporation in 1966. The two brothers assigned stock to members of their respective families, including the grandchildren. With Bil Mar's standing as a privately held firm, however, the stock was not negotiable as income or dividends. That meant only those family members who worked for Bil Mar benefited immediately from the company's success through their wages.

Marvin in front of Bil Mar headquarters.

"Before the merger, the company was like a piggy bank that just kept growing," said Chuck Stehouwer, Bil Mar's former accountant. "After the merger, the family members could put their hands in the piggy bank for the first time."

For Marvin, selling the company would be the easy part. Bil Mar had been getting such inquires since the mid-1970s when the company entered the retail market with Mr. Turkey products. The difficulty would be finding a buyer who shared his business values.

One of the first food giants to come knocking on Bil Mar's door was Tyson Foods Inc., the world's largest chicken processor. Marvin wasn't impressed, however. Tyson had a reputation for buying companies and then quickly stripping them of their corporate identities.

After the fire reconstruction, during 1986, Bil Mar received about one acquisition inquiry a month. The only one that really interested Marvin was proposed by Chicago-based Sara Lee Corp.

Sara Lee, one of the largest publicly held corporations in the world, had a similar history to Bil Mar's. Both had been nurtured by an entrepreneur who had little formal schooling but who was guided by integrity and perseverance. In Sara Lee's case it was Nathan Cummings, who laid the foundation for the corporate giant in 1939 when he purchased C.D. Kenny Co., an ailing coffee and tea distributor in Baltimore. Cummings – with a background in retail, wholesale and manufacturing – spent the next five decades acquiring established businesses with a reputation for quality, like the Kitchens of Sara Lee, which makes frozen baked goods. The result was the formation of Consolidated Foods Corp., a leading brand-name food company.

The acquisition of non-food companies by Consolidated Foods began in 1966, and it was in that division the company first faltered. In 1974, Consolidated Foods posted record sales, yet reported its first decline in corporate earnings in 19 years. The next year was a financial rerun – disappointing results from some non-food companies and another decline in earnings. The company turned things around by naming John H. Bryan Jr., head of its Mississippi-based Bryan Foods subsidiary, to become chief executive officer.

Under his leadership, corporate senior management instituted tighter financial and operational controls. The composition of the board of directors was changed to include a majority of outside directors. Bryan still wanted a diversified company with a decentralized operating philosophy. But he said the corporate office would provide stronger leadership in the areas of financial control, strategic planning and management development. He also emphasized a policy of growth from within, building on a group of "core" companies with established market positions and above-average earnings potential. Implementing the core business philosophy meant divesting nearly four dozen companies but also acquiring others like Chef Pierre pies; the Hanes Corp., a leading national manufacturer of hosiery, intimate apparel, and underwear; and the Australian Nicholas Kiwi Ltd., operating in more than 40 countries with shoe care, household products, personal-care products and over-the-counter medicines.

In 1985, Consolidated Foods changed its name to Sara Lee as a reflection of the company's evolution to a branded-products company. Sara Lee was chosen for the title because it is universally known and reflects the high quality and consumer marketing orientation of the corporation.

Late in 1986, eager to acquire a poultry company, Sara Lee came knocking on Bil Mar's door. That wasn't the first time the food giant had come calling. In the late 1970s, Consolidated Foods – the forerunner of Sara Lee – approached Marvin with a merger offer, which he turned down.

By the mid-1980s, no longer able to ignore consumer demand for more white meat, Sara Lee decided to pitch a second offer to Bil Mar. At that point, Sara Lee operated only red-meat companies like Bryan Foods, Hillshire Farm, and Jimmy Dean. Sara Lee – with more than $7 billion in 1986 sales – wanted a company like Bil Mar to maintain its standing as one of the largest processed-meat companies, along with competitors Hormel Co. and Oscar Mayer.

"Bil Mar has a significant presence in the poultry industry, which has experienced a strong growth recently. Its high-quality, premium-branded products are strategically complementary to our processed, value-added, branded-meat products," said John H. Bryan Jr., of Sara

Lee, at the time of Bil Mar's acquisition.

Bil Mar – recognized in the food industry for its innovation, quality, and ability to be competitive – had a lot to offer Sara Lee. Bil Mar was one of the top three turkey producers in the United States, processing about 170 million pounds of turkey in 1986.

Bil Mar had gross sales that year of $199.1 million and was shipping products to all 50 states, Canada, Europe, and the Middle East. The company, with a growing work force of 2,400, operated three plants – the new state-of-the-art facility in Borculo, and two sites in Iowa and Ohio.

Always interested in a brand name, Sara Lee was especially attracted to Bil Mar's successful Mr. Turkey retail program. Bil Mar also stood out for its advanced computer system and a professional executive staff – two changes Gary DeWitt promoted and Marvin supported. Bil Mar was a more informal organization when compared to a corporate giant like Sara Lee, though the company was obviously not being managed by a bunch of country bumpkins.

Bil Mar test kitchen monitors products.

"The DeWitts were smart enough to make the changes that had to be made during the heavy growth years between 1978 and 1986. Besides bringing in more professionals, they restructured their information system and sales efforts, rather than continuing to run things by the seat of their pants based on what they did the year before," said Phil Vanden Berge, Bil Mar's former senior vice president of finance, who was instrumental in negotiating the merger with Sara Lee. "By the time of the acquisition, Bil Mar had made the changes necessary to build an organization that was the finest in Sara Lee's whole meat group. It was just one of the things that impressed Sara Lee about Bil Mar."

The feeling of admiration was mutual. Marvin was impressed by Sara Lee's history, especially the role of Nathan Cummings, who died in 1985. Cummings shared a multitude of character traits with

Marvin. For Cummings, there was no limit to a working day. He was obsessed with excellence in performance. He was highly disciplined in his personal and professional life. He believed in community service, and passed on the concept of privilege and corresponding responsibility not only to his family but also the corporation. Sara Lee has a Public Responsibility Committee, which dispenses a percentage of pretax net income to various health, education, welfare and arts organizations.

Marvin was also impressed with John Bryan and his Christian-family background. Bryan's father and uncle had started their Mississippi meat-packing company in 1936, two years before Bil Mar took off. Bryan Foods, with a reputation for honesty and fairness, joined Consolidated Foods in 1968.

Sara Lee's corporate philosophy was also attractive to Marvin, who wanted his sons to keep their management positions for awhile after the acquisition. Sara Lee left existing management structures intact at its subsidiaries and let them run as stand-alone operations. In checking with other Sara Lee meat companies, the DeWitts learned there was a long transitional phase before Sara Lee personnel took over management duties from a founding family. The DeWitts were also confident that Sara Lee would treat Bil Mar's customers, suppliers, and employees equitably.

Marvin's belief that the two corporate cultures shared similar values was confirmed twice during merger negotiations. Sara Lee received the 1986 Lawrence A. Wien Prize in Corporate Social Responsibility. Administered by the Graduate School for Business and the School of Law at Columbia University, the prize honors those corporations that make contributions of outstanding social significance and value on the national or local level.

In January, 1987, Fortune magazine ranked Sara Lee as the most-admired company in the food industry. The ranking was the result of a survey among 8,200 senior executives, outside directors, and financial analysts who rated companies on eight attributes: quality of management; quality of products or services; innovativeness; long-term investment value; financial soundness; ability to attract, develop and keep talented people; community and environmental responsibility; and use of corporate assets.

Despite Marvin's admiration of Sara Lee, he was not about to give the company away. Sara Lee's first offer was far below the $199 million in annual sales posted by Bil Mar in fiscal 1986, and Marvin wasted no time turning thumbs down. He was thinking in the range of $175 to $200 million. A second offer was considered more acceptable. Before the deal was inked, Marvin led a family meeting in the board room at Bil Mar. All family members were invited to attend, including the oldest grandchildren, to discuss the ramifications of merging with Sara Lee.

Not everyone was enthusiastic about the merger. In the end, there was a consensus that the positives outweighed the negatives and the merger should proceed, ending the DeWitt family's dominance of Bil Mar for the first time in 49 years.

"I had mixed feelings about the merger," said Don DeWitt. "One part of me wanted to see it stay in the family. That is what you had known all of your life. We had just built a new plant; none of us was that old, and things seemed to be going pretty good. On the other side, you knew that if a Sara Lee didn't acquire it someone else would someday. That is the way things were going in the turkey industry."

His brother Merle expressed similar feelings.

"The merger with Sara Lee came at the right time, when turkey was a hot commodity because of its low-fat quality. There were also competitive factors that pushed the merger. We would have had to keep growing to stay in the business," he said. "That does not mean it wasn't tough for some of us to let go. There was a sense of pride and ownership in what the family had built. I had always figured that Bil Mar is where I would spend my whole working life."

The grandchildren, the oldest in their teens at the time of the merger, harbor no misgivings about the family giving up the business.

"I have no regrets about Bil Mar being merged with Sara Lee," said Jim DeWitt, one of Jack's sons. "When I was younger, I thought about the possibility of owning it someday. But I really want to do something on my own rather than step into something that someone else has worked hard to build up. I want to prove to people that I can do something on my own and that I don't have to be handed everything in life."

Once agreement on the merger was reached within the family, it fell to Gary DeWitt to inform employees of the decision. In an employee letter dated March 30, 1987, he said: "If agreement is reached, it is Sara Lee's intention that the character of Bil Mar will be maintained and the company names of Bil Mar Foods and Mr. Turkey brand will remain the same. We have made this decision for various reasons. The most important reason being that our product category is growing at such a significant rate that Bil Mar will be stretched to maintain its position in the industry. Sara Lee has demonstrated a management system that has enabled small companies, such as Bil Mar, to maximize their potential under the umbrella of an exceptionally well-managed international organization. We are confident that, if an agreement is reached, Bil Mar employees and its representatives will prosper greatly from this new and exciting relationship."

Bil Mar became a wholly-owned subsidiary of Sara Lee on May 27, 1987. The DeWitts avoided a 28 percent capital gains tax by merging with Sara Lee and exchanging common stock instead of selling for cash. The DeWitt family – 14 adults and 36 grandchildren – shared in 4 million shares of Sara Lee stock. At $40 a share, for a total of $160 million, the family became one of Sara Lee's largest shareholders.

Sara Lee also assumed Bil Mar's debt of $25 million. In addition, Sara Lee agreed to pay Bil Mar employees $5 million over a three-year period, based on salary level and years of service.

Amway co-founder Rich DeVos, in his book "Compassionate Capitalism," called the $5 million gift to employees a "gesture of goodwill and generosity unheard of in corporate America."

"We felt it was right to give a bonus to employees after the merger. They were people who had given their lives to the company," said Gary DeWitt, who originated the gift suggestion. "We were a bonus-paying company to begin with, so this was seen as a natural extension of that. The philosophy of the family is that when you make money, you share that with those who have helped you make it."

With the merger, Marvin and Bill became paid consultants to Sara Lee until their 80th birthday. They had a similar agreement with Bil Mar, crafted by a company attorney as a safeguard to prevent their premature removal from the company by their sons. The agreement – including regular pay, bonuses, raises, and a new company car every two years – was assumed by Sara Lee as part of the merger. Marvin continued to offer advice to Sara Lee until his 80th birthday in June of 1999. Bill officially retired after the merger.

Bill and Marvin sign Sara Lee merger agreement.

"If they asked me a question, I gave them my answer and once in a while I gave them a piece of my mind even if they didn't ask," Marvin said. "I snooped around to find out what our competition was doing and then I talked with the people at Bil Mar who could do something about it. That doesn't mean they always listened to me."

Twelve years after the merger, Marvin doesn't spend much time thinking about Bil Mar. He prefers to focus on other interests – hunting, personal business ventures, and his family, especially the grandchildren and great-grandchildren.

Marvin waits for a leopard in
hunting blind on African safari.

CHAPTER NINETEEN

LIFE AFTER SARA LEE

Marvin may have retired from active involvement in the food industry. But he has no intention of retiring from life.

Even at 80, he shows few signs of slowing down. He brings to his personal life the same enthusiasm that drove his professional life at Bil Mar.

Neither arthritis, a knee replacement, heart pacemaker placement, prostate surgery, breast cancer treatment, nor a hip replacement have stopped him from pursuing his pastimes for very long.

His son-in-law Tom Norman said an incident at Marvin's hunting camp in Reed City proved to him that the family patriarch is not yet ready to slack off.

Marvin had invited Norman and his brother Jim to hitch a ride on the back of his tractor for a tour of the property. The two brothers stood on the tow bar and hung on to the tractor seat while Marvin went flying along a road rutted from rain. When Marvin wouldn't heed their pleas to slow down, they jumped off. Shortly after, the tractor hit a bump, careened off the road and tore down a bunch of saplings before coming to a stop. Unhurt, Marvin thought the incident was hilarious.

"Even at his age, he is full of adventure and mischief," Norman said. "The moral of the story is that once he gets going, there is nothing going to stop him until he crashes. He has been that way his whole life."

Norman's son Michael had a similar "adventure" with Marvin, when his grandfather asked him for help in moving an aging road grader three miles from Bil Mar property to his father's barn. They couldn't get the vehicle started because the fuel pump wasn't working properly. They poured gas down the carburetor numerous time, yet the tired grader's engine just wouldn't turn over. Marvin, never one to give up and always resourceful, siphoned gas out of the vehicle's tank with a hose. After the gas started flowing, he put the other end of the hose into the carburetor. The continuous flow of gas acted like a pump to get the unmuffled engine roaring. Marvin jumped into the cab and headed down the Bil Mar driveway toward 96th Avenue, with Norman pursuing in another vehicle.

"He drove that old grader out onto 96th with sparks flying out the exhaust. He then went down Polk to 88th and down to my father's barn. He rolled down that gravel road at 60 mph without lights and very little braking power," Norman said. "By the time he got to the barn, there was a ball of flames coming out from underneath the hood. I had to pour a bucket of water on the engine to put the fire out. He could have killed himself. Unfazed, he jumped off that grader

Family hunting camp

with a big grin. He was just like a kid with a toy. He had a ball driving that thing to the barn."

Marvin spends much of his spare time at the family hunting camp in the northern Lower Peninsula – raising crops for deer feed, hunting, and reflecting on old times with his good friend Lou Taylor, of Allendale.

The two men have much in common. Only a year apart in age, they both grew up on farms near Borculo. As teenagers, they played softball and attended Ottawa Reformed Church. Taylor later worked full-time at Keeler Brass in Grand Rapids, and earned extra money by hauling Bil Mar turkeys to a freezer plant in Muskegon.

Lou Taylor and Marvin process a deer.

Their biggest mutual interest is hunting. Taylor has been a regular at the hunting camp ever since Marvin bought the 650-acre site in the early 1990s. Taylor treasures the time alone with his friend.

"At the hunting lodge, it's so relaxing. I would count my time with Marvin as one of my most enjoyable experiences. It's a chance to get away with someone I can relate to," he said. "I am not in his class as far as wealth. Yet that doesn't make any difference in the way he treats me. He never brags about his wealth. He seems to be attracted to the guys he grew up with or those who have similar tough backgrounds. He is not one of these people who attempt to make you believe they are somebody than who they actually are. He has never forgotten his humble roots."

Given his adventuresome nature, Marvin doesn't confine his elderly hunting activity to Michigan. In the summer of 1997, still recuperating from hip surgery, he led a DeWitt family safari to Bulawayo, Zimbabwe, Africa. The 21 participants included his sons, sons-in-law, grandsons, and grandsons-in-law. Marvin, at 78, was the oldest member of the group, while his grandson Alex, 13, was the youngest.

At a family gathering, Marvin mentioned he was planning a fourth safari to Africa and some of his grandsons brought up the idea of a family hunt. Up until then, the only family member to join him on an African safari was his son Merle. The large family group drew a lot of attention in Zimbabwe. No one in the region could remember such a large group of family members on safari. If Marvin's health holds up, he plans to return for one last African safari.

Steve DeWitt, Marvin, and Jack DeWitt on safari in Africa.

When Marvin isn't hunting, he keeps active by overseeing several business ventures. His most ambitious since leaving Bil Mar is the development of an 800-unit mobile home park known as West Olive Estates between Holland and Grand Haven.

His partner in the project is Leonard Maas, owner of Gillisse Construction Co. near Grand Rapids. The company specializes in projects involving roads, water mains, and sewers.

When Marvin conceived the idea of the mobile home park, he contacted the development office at Hope College to inquire whether there were any Christian businessmen in the area who had experience in that type of enterprise. He was given the name of Maas, whose background also includes the development of mobile homes parks in Muskegon, Ottawa, and Kent counties.

"One day, Marvin called me up out of the clear blue sky and asked me if I would be interested in becoming a partner with him in a mobile-home development on 320 acres," Maas said. "He said he needed $150,000 and I gave it to him with no questions asked, even though I had never met him. I knew about his business success, and his connections to the Reformed Church through Hope College. That was enough for me."

The partners also plan to develop another 120 acres near the park for a single-family housing subdivision. When completed, the two projects will be worth $20 million.

Like his cultivation of Bil Mar, Marvin has given full attention to the housing development. The partners visit the park at least once a week checking on the progress. Maas usually shows up in a business suit, while Marvin arrives – from another chore – in dirty work clothes. The partners have spared no expense at making the mobile home park one of the nicest in the region. They installed underground sprinkling, free cable TV, $30,000 worth of playground and recreational equipment, and a $50,000 garbage compactor that eliminates refuse containers and reduces the number of weekly trash pick ups .

No longer tied down to Bil Mar, Marvin also has more time to dote on his 23 grandchildren and 24 great-grandchildren. Family members noticed him beginning to mellow after the merger with Sara Lee when he seemed to shed the pressure inherent with business ownership.

"My father-in-law has mellowed over the years as he became less driven by the business," said Merle's wife Sheri. "He is quicker to smile. His attitude toward life is more light-hearted, and you can kid him a lot more than before. He will now spend time with the younger grandchildren and great-grandchildren, even putting them on his lap. It is so nice to see him fuss over the younger ones and hold the babies. He seems genuinely interested when he asks how the grandchildren and great-grandchildren are doing. He didn't do that with the older grandchildren. Back then, he just didn't have the time. He was too involved in the business."

The oldest grandchildren, now in their late 20s and early 30s, didn't see him much unless it was related to work at Bil Mar or the hunting camp. Most of the older grandchildren had the opportunity to work part-time at Bil Mar – on the farms, in the plant and office, or at the Country Store. The younger ones have worked for him at the camp, the mobile home development, and the property surrounding his Stanton Street home, which is north of the Bil Mar plant.

Younger or older, they have all come under the influence of Marvin's waste-not-want-not gospel, even when it comes to incidental things. If one of the grandkids leaves their car running, he asks them if they are not shutting it off because something is wrong with the starter. If they don't clean their plates, he says "well, it looks like your parents didn't teach you about cleaning up your plate, so I'll have to." They have all been scolded for not turning a light off after leaving a room. Their grandfather has also instructed them to never leave the water running continuously while washing dishes or during teeth brushing. He also frowns on showers lasting more than five minutes.

"Anywhere I went with grandpa, he would give you the rules," said Jack's son Steve. "You knew them and you obeyed them with no questions asked. You never want to be standing around when working with grandpa. You kept moving and you kept working. When you were around grandpa, there was always something to do."

Grandchildren celebrate Christmas at family party.

Despite Marvin's insistence on law and order, the grandchildren express a deep respect for what he stands for and what he has accomplished. They speak in awe of his super-human work habits, rigid moral stance, and unflinching generosity. They describe him as their role model and mentor.

"When you are an adolescent, it is hard to be told what to do," said Michael Norman, the oldest grandson and Marilyn's son. "Yet you still respected what he said. I look back and realize the major impact he has had on my life. He had big expectations for us – to work hard and live a good life. You would not want to disappoint a person of his stature."

Following in his grandfather's entrepreneurial footsteps, Michael is one of two grandsons to operate a business. With a partner, he owns MD Automotive Repair and Advantage Marine Repair in Zeeland.

The other grandson with a business is Jack's son Jim. He is partnering on Hogquest Farms, a hog-growing operation in Fillmore Township, south of Holland.

Jim's interest in farming developed while cleaning barns and driving tractor alongside his grandfather at Bil Mar. He was also given a taste of the DeWitt work ethic by doing chores with Marvin at the hunting camp – stringing barbed wire, picking up rocks in the fields, clearing brush, and planting and harvesting crops such as squash, carrots and corn. He credits his work habits, in large part, to his grandfather.

"He was tough on his grandkids when it came to working. Some of them thought he was a mean guy. I would tell my younger cousins to just do what he says, and not to take any criticism personally – let it go in one ear and out of the other. No matter what, do it his way. And do it right the first time," Jim said. "Up until about five years ago, he could still outwork me. I would say 'grandpa, you are going to kill yourself with all this work.' He would say 'I can't think of a better way to go.' He is very intelligent, has an excellent memory, and nothing escapes his attention. He learns from every experience and every person he encounters. I have learned so much from him –

Marvin stands in front of a building that was designed to showcase his big-game hunting trophies.

from everyday repairs to how to get by with what you have. I admire him for his work ethic, his self-acquired knowledge, his generosity, his frugality, his trustworthiness, and the way he lives his faith. He has had a great influence on me – directly and indirectly through my father."

The same influence is rubbing off on Marvin's younger grandsons who work with him at the hunting camp and around his Stanton Street home.

"I have never seen the rough and tough side of him. He is more relaxed than when he ran the business," said Merle's son Aaron. "But he has made it clear to us that you strive to do your best. And once you start a job, you finish it no matter what it takes."

Marvin at his Stanton Street home.

His cousin, Keith's son Eric, has learned the importance of starting the job on time. One summer, he was landscaping around Marvin's home and usually started work at 8 a.m. One day, he didn't show up until 8:15. Marvin's disappointment was evident in his greeting: "I hope you don't plan on me paying you for that 15 minutes." From then on, Eric arrived by 8.

Marvin's belief in hard work's ability to build character was not only shared with his grandsons. Even some of Marvin's granddaughters were indoctrinated. Jack's daughter Laurie Wierda made a trip to the hunting camp with her grandfather and grandmother while on break from college. She thought the day would mainly consist of good food and conversation. She should have known better when her grandfather complained about a late departure after leaving his house at 6 a. m. Unknown to her, Marvin had planned a day's worth of manual labor, including the installation of fence poles.

"I should have known my grandpa could never go to the hunting camp and just sit. He was always doing odd jobs and creating things to be done – a true workaholic," Wierda said. "By the end of the day,

I was exhausted and could hardly believe what we had accomplished. He would always say something to make you feel good after completing a job. But you had better finish the job and do a good job."

Those grandchildren who didn't have the opportunity to work with him were still touched by the power of his personality.

"My grandfather has always been a good role model," said Lisa Van Der Kolk, the oldest granddaughter and Gary's daughter. "He has a good work ethic and, despite his wealth, remains humble. He is extremely generous with his time, talent and money – traits that have been passed on to the generations. We were always taught to be the best we can be, and not to settle for less. We were taught to persevere, no matter what hurdles are thrown in front of you. All the DeWitt's are very goal-oriented and competitive as a result of that attitude. "

Carrying on a long-standing tradition, the youngest grandchildren and the older great-grandchildren occasionally stay overnight with their grandparents. Like it was for the older grandkids, the DeWitts keep a snack cupboard stocked with cookies and candy. Missing is a sign-up sheet on which the older grandchildren had to take turns scheduling their visits because there were so many of them.

Marvin visits South Pole penguins.

The younger offspring stay at the DeWitt home on Stanton Street, instead of the homestead property on 96th Avenue in the shadow of the plant. The ranch house, built by Marvin in 1949, is now used for storage space by Bil Mar. Like the 96th Street location, the Stanton Street property features a swimming pool.

The grandchildren who share memories of staying overnight voice a common theme – a comfortable, nurturing experience created by a doting grandmother who turned a house into a home. Jack's daughter Jackie Curtiss remembers her quiet spirit and patient

Marvin and his wife in Chile.

personality. Don's daughter Deb Koop said her grandmother was always thinking about everyone else and seemed to derive satisfaction from taking care of others. All of the older grandchildren remember her as the peacemaker, the calm in the midst of turmoil surrounding the business, and the sounding board who took care of things at home.

"Grandpa wasn't there too often," said Nancy's daughter Amy DeKruyter. "When he was, the kids would quiet down, watch what they were doing, and behave a little bit more. Grandma would let us do whatever we wanted. She was so gentle and caring, always willing to sit down and listen to you."

Jack's son Steve recounted a similar memory.

"No matter what she was doing, grandma would find time to play with you or read you a book. She made you feel very special. From her, I learned to be humble and quiet, and to listen carefully when someone is speaking to you."

Marvin and Jerene divide their time between the house on Stanton and their condominium in Florida, which they purchased in 1971. They spend about nine months of the year at the Stanton property, which is appropriately adorned with reminders from Marvin's days as a turkey farmer. A copper weather vane, in the shape of a turkey, points to the wind direction from the home's roof. A life-size plaster turkey greets visitors on the front step. A stained-glass turkey – created by Zeeland artist John Vanderburgh – decorates the front door.

The DeWitts spend about three months each winter in Florida, where Marvin takes the opportunity to wind down a bit. He rides a bike, and plays golf and shuffleboard. They also spend a lot of time visiting friends and entertaining their children, grandchildren, and great-grandchildren.

Even on hiatus in Florida, Marvin has lessons to teach his offspring.

Jack's daughter Linda Berghorst learned about giving people a second chance. She accompanied her grandparents to a new restaurant where everything went wrong. The service was slow and the food arrived cold at their table. Linda was disgusted and vowed never to go back. Her grandfather responded in a more understanding fashion: "We'll give it one more try. Maybe they are having a bad day. Wouldn't you like a second chance?"

For Marvin and Jerene, the times down South have been mostly uneventful – except for 1993, when they were mugged.

The episode occurred while they were visiting some friends in another Florida town. Instead of driving back to their condo, the DeWitts decided to stay overnight in a motel. Marvin was hauling the luggage to the room when his wife was attacked outside the car. A thief jumped out of the shadows of the motel and grabbed her shoulder purse. She lost the struggle to hold on when the culprit knocked her to the ground. Marvin gave chase through the parking lot, shouting at the man to drop the purse. Marvin would have caught him had he not tripped over a curb. As the armed thief prepared to jump a fence, he wildly fired a round from a pistol at Marvin. The shot missed its mark.

"He is lucky I didn't catch him. He scared us, broke my wife's rib, and took her purse. That didn't make me very happy," he said. "He got away with a couple of hundred dollars and our extra set of car keys. We were awake most of the night wondering if he would come back for the car. He didn't and we never recovered anything."

On a steamy summer afternoon, back at his Stanton Street home, Marvin was recounting his Bil Mar experiences. The pool outside, which he calls a "community pool," was a beehive of activity with splashing children. Built for the younger DeWitt grandchildren and the great-grandchildren, the pool is also open to neighbors and members of Ottawa Reformed Church who don't run afoul of Marvin's latest pet peeve – males wearing earrings. He is still not real fond of men with long hair or beards but those grooming styles no longer rile him like males adorned with jewelry.

He recalled a day when a youngster with an earring came walking up the driveway headed toward the pool. He cut the boy off and told him to come back when he wasn't wearing the jewelry. However, Marvin hasn't reserved his comments about the latest fashion fad to the DeWitt property.

At a hardware store in Zeeland, he refused to give an earring-wearing clerk his money for a purchase, saying he didn't do business with men who wore jewelry. Another clerk, without an earring, had to step in to complete the transaction. And then there was the time at Bil Mar's Country Store when Marvin pointed to the earring of a young clerk and asked whether he was planning to have a sex change. Marvin also told the clerk, in no uncertain terms, that he would not be wearing an earring if the DeWitts still owned Bil Mar.

Watching the children swimming in his pool, Marvin abruptly switched the discussion from male earrings toward his growing family. With great pride, he noted that the large family is still tight-knit, lives within a 20-mile radius of each other, and – as a result of their religious underpinnings – has yet to record a divorce. Family members come together for the birthdays and wedding anniversary of Marvin and Jerene, and for Mother's Day, the 4th of July, Thanksgiving and Christmas. In 1991, the entire DeWitt clan celebrated the 52nd wedding anniversary of Marvin and Jerene by taking an Alaskan boat cruise and bus trip.

DeWitt family explores Alaska.

In the earlier years of the family, the highlight of the Christmas gathering was for everyone to weigh in and then record who had gained and lost the most number of pounds since the last holiday. Marvin was the official record keeper at the get-togethers held at the plant. Nancy's daughter Jody Machiela also remembers other holiday highlights: ducking the turkey hooks while roller skating in the plant, raiding the candy room in the cafeteria, and waiting in line with other grandchildren to crank the ice cream machine. The DeWitts now convene for the Christmas gathering at Request Foods, a frozen-foods plant owned by Jack.

"Overall, the family is still close-knit," said Gary's wife Joyce. "We have drifted apart somewhat because of our own expanding families and social lives. But we are always there for each other if someone needs help and we still get together on a number of occasions during the year."

Despite the family camaraderie, Marvin and Jerene wondered aloud on that summer afternoon whether the family's values of hard work, honest dealing, and community service can survive through future DeWitt generations. The second generation, the couple's sons and daughters, are well aware of the sacrifices made to build a successful business. The older members of the third generation, the grandchildren, are appreciative of those hardships. They are familiar, to some extent, with the operation of Bil Mar. The second and third generations have learned from Marvin and Jerene that money doesn't guarantee happiness. Happiness comes from your attitude toward life and your relationships with people.

"I am proud of my family and how they all turned out to be good citizens and good Christians. I give my wife most of the credit for that. I will put them up against any family around here," he said. "Yet you can't help but wonder if the fourth generation will be spoiled by wealth they haven't earned. Hopefully each generation can pass on the basic values of the family."

His discourse was interrupted by his granddaughter Ashley, who is Keith's daughter. In her hands, she was cradling a dead bird that had slammed into a window of the DeWitt home. She asked him about the identity of the bird and he pulled out a bird book. He suggested that she attempt to determine the bird's name by going out on the porch to study the book for awhile.

As she turned away, Marvin winked to a visitor at his home, indicating he already knew the bird's identity.

The young girl studied the book for a short while before coming back into the house all excited. Ashley told her grandfather she was sure about the identity and pointed to a bird in the book. Marvin said she was most likely right.

The girl walked away smiling, delighted that she was able to discover the answer on her own. In his role as the family's mentor, that was exactly the way Marvin wanted her to learn – with a sense of pride and accomplishment.

Bil Mar continues to thrive after the merger with Sara Lee in 1987. And so do members of the DeWitt family who once worked in management positions.

The company, with annual sales of more than $600 million, ranks as one of the top manufacturers of turkey products in the nation. Sales today are more than triple what Bil Mar was reporting just before the acquisition.

Employing nearly 2,000 workers, the company is among the largest manufacturers in Ottawa County. That list also includes Johnson Controls [formerly Prince Corp.], Haworth Inc., Herman Miller Inc., Donnelly Corp., Gentex Corp., and LifeSavers Co.

Marvin's son Gary was the last family member to work at Bil Mar, retiring in July of 1996 after serving as a consultant for a year. He had been president and CEO, a position now held by George Chivari since 1994.

Sara Lee, a world-wide company with 139,000 employees and $20 billion in sales in fiscal 1997-98, has made some changes in Bil Mar's operation. Sara Lee has formalized strategic planning and financial reporting, put more emphasis on safety, and organized participative-management work teams. However, the corporation also allows its affiliate companies a great deal of independence in their day-to-day operations. Sara Lee adheres to a decentralized management philosophy in which executives are given the authority to lead individual companies and are then held accountable for the performance of those businesses.

One former Bil Mar manager said she didn't perceive any real negatives arising from the merger, just a difference in operating style.

"With Sara Lee, things are done from a formal perspective rather than an informal basis like with the DeWitts. You have a more-tightly run, fiscally responsible operation," said Marge Boersen, who retired as Bil Mar's computer operations manager. "It was not as comfortable working for Sara Lee as it was for the DeWitts. It is the difference between a new and older pair of shoes. They both fit, yet one is more comfortable than the other. That is the trade-off you get by going from a private family-owned company to a publicly held company."

Since the merger, Bil Mar has added a few chapters to its corporate history:

- 1988, went national with Mr. Turkey retail brand. To give the products an image of higher quality, the Mr. Turkey logo was changed in 1993 from a fancy-dressed turkey to a chef. Since then, the chef logo has been eliminated from the packaging in favor of just the Mr. Turkey name.
- 1989, introduced turkey bacon for consumers who can't eat pork or those looking for a low-fat alternative.
- 1990, sold its frozen-foods division to Marvin's son Jack and a group of investors. At its peak, the division accounted for 10 percent of Bil Mar's business. Bil Mar had also been among the top three suppliers to the airline industry, producing more than 12 million airborne meals a year.
- 1992, closed the Ohio satellite plant after deciding the operations could be handled more efficiently and profitably at the main plant. Bil Mar employed 300 workers in Ohio. The property was sold for $1.5 million to a speculator.
- 1993, introduced Sara Lee line of Premium Deli Meats. Bil Mar has the distinction of making the first food products, other than baked goods, to be sold under the Sara Lee brand. Bil Mar's selection for the honor acknowledges the company's reputation for quality, according to Gary DeWitt who promoted the idea.
- 1998, forced to recall 15 million pounds of meat tainted with rare strain of listeria bacteria. More than 20 deaths and nearly 100 illnesses nationwide were linked to the contamination. To ensure product safety, the company reconfigured the plant, introduced new germ-killing technology, and increased envi-

ronmental and laboratory testing. The outbreak may have been caused by dust kicked up during a maintenance project on a refrigeration unit.

- 1999, shifted turkey growing, slaughtering and boning from Borculo – where the focus will be on processing and packaging – to the satellite operation in Storm Lake, Iowa. The decision affected 330 workers at the main plant, 60 company farm employees, and 25 independent and contract growers in Michigan who supplied turkeys to Bil Mar. The company's feed mill on U.S. 31, north of Holland, was subsequently sold to Hamilton Farm Bureau.

  Turkeys for the Iowa plant are being purchased from Bil Mar farms and contractors in Iowa, and independents in that state, Minnesota, and North and South Dakota, a region where land, labor and grain prices are cheaper. The shift in Bil Mar operations followed the leveling off of year-round turkey consumption in the 1990s, producing a glut on the market. In the 1980s, when consumers started to become more health conscious, sales growth in the turkey industry shot up to 15 percent a year. The growth leveled off at 3 to 5 percent – partly due to market saturation, and after red-meat companies began to trim more fat off their products and add the lower-fat poultry to some of the items, like pork sausage and hot dogs.

- 1999, a partnership consisting of Gary DeWitt and area turkey growers affected by Bil Mar's relocation decision plans to open a slaughtering and boning plant in the city of Wyoming near Grand Rapids.

Between the Borculo headquarters facility and Iowa plant, Bil Mar processes more than 12 million turkeys a year for such products as roasted breasts, luncheon meats, smoked sausage, ground meat, and hot dogs.

Bil Mar also makes some beef, pork, and chicken products with meat purchased from packing plants around the country. But of the 290 million pounds of meat processed yearly by Bil Mar, nearly 80 percent – or 225 million pounds – comes from turkey.

Bil Mar products are sold across the country through three divisions – food service, whose customers include restaurants, hotels, hospitals, schools, prisons, and convention centers; retail, under the Mr. Turkey brand; and deli, under the brands of Sara Lee Premium Deli Meats, Bil Mar Deli, and Deli-Perfect.

Food service adds up to 50 percent of Bil Mar sales. The other half is evenly divided between retail and deli.

Bil Mar is one of 17 packaged-meat companies owned by Sara Lee, including such well-known brands as Hygrade, Jimmy Dean and Hillshire Farm. The total makes Sara Lee the world's largest packaged-meat company. Bil Mar plays an integral part in the packaged-meat division. Besides manufacturing all-turkey products, Bil Mar serves as the primary source of raw turkey used by some of Sara Lee's packaged-meat companies to lower the fat content in their red-meat products. Bil Mar also makes some of Hygrade's Ball Park franks.

The meat companies are part of the Sara Lee Foods group, which includes baked goods. Four other business groups include Coffee and Tea, Branded Apparel, Household and Body Care, and Food Service.

After Bil Mar's merger with Sara Lee, Marvin's family members slowly filtered out of the company.

His son-in-law Tom Norman was the first to leave in 1988 to start a construction company. He had been purchasing manager and maintenance engineer at Bil Mar. Today he is also a volunteer project coordinator for HOME (Housing Opportunities Made Equitable).

Jack DeWitt, who had been executive vice president in charge of production/processing/farms, was the next to leave in 1990 when Sara Lee decided to sell off the frozen-foods division of Bil Mar. Jack led a group of investors who bought out the division and turned it into Request Foods, where he remains president.

Marvin's youngest son, Keith, who had been Bil Mar's meat-commodities manager, left in 1991 to start DeWitt Marketing, a free-lance poultry-trading business. The company buys and sells large volumes of poultry to match the needs of suppliers and food processors.

Don DeWitt, who had been Bil Mar's director of farm operations, left in 1993. Semi-retired, he now does hobby farming for himself and work for area farmers. He also owns D & B Motor Sports and is assisted in the venture by his son Brian. The company races a super-stock car at a track in Marne.

Merle DeWitt, who had been Bil Mar's director of operations, left in 1995 to join Request Foods in a similar position.

Ironically, Marvin – one of the first DeWitts on the Bil Mar payroll – was the last family member to draw a company check. The arrangement, in which he served as a consultant to Bil Mar, ended in June, 1999, when he turned 80-years-old.

Marvin's brother Bill, six years his senior, officially retired from Bil Mar after the merger with Sara Lee but also drew a consultant's fee until his 80th birthday. He now spends most of his time at his residence in Sun City, Arizona, following the death of his wife, Martha, in 1997. He also resides part-time at the house he built in 1943 on Polk Street, southwest of the plant.

Bill's oldest son, Bill Jr., once Bil Mar's director of farm operations, owns Blueberry Equipment Inc. and Michigan Orchard Supply. Bill's other son, Ray, formerly in charge of refrigeration at Bil Mar, is involved in a race car business in North Carolina.

1938 Marvin and William DeWitt start Bill and Marve's Turkey Farm with 17 birds.

1941 First brooder house built.

1947 Hatchery opened. Company name changed to Bill and Marve's Turkey Farm & Hatchery.

1950 Small feed mill added to brooder house.

1954 Largest barn in the Midwest built for breeder and brooder operations.

1957 Sale of live and minimally processed turkeys ended in favor of oven-ready fresh and frozen birds.

1958 First processing plant built.

1961 Further processing begun by cutting the bird into boneless parts and cooking the meat to manufacture an assortment of mostly white-meat products, like roasted split breast and roasted whole breast. Most of the products are sold to food-service customers, such as restaurants, hotels, schools, prisons and hospitals.

1962 First outside turkey growers contracted to help meet production demands.

1964 Broad-breasted white turkeys grown to eliminate ink spots on skin caused by colored pin feathers of other breeds.

1965 First addition on processing plant built to include offices and oven room for roasting products. Company offices had been in hatchery building. Had used inefficient rotary bakery ovens before walk-in ovens installed.

1966 Company incorporated as Bil Mar Foods.

On-site feed mill operation, which had been expanded in 1961 with conversion of a storage building, moved to reconverted Harlem feed mill on U.S. 31, north of Holland.

1967 First grow-out barn built.

1971 Addition built for convenience-foods division, which fabricated frozen bulk entrees and dinners for food-service customers.

1973 Country Store, on-site retail shop for Bil Mar products, opened in former hatchery building.

1977 Mr. Turkey line of retail products introduced. Products are made from further-processed dark-meat parts to resemble competing pork and beef items, like hot dogs and luncheon meats.

Satellite processing plant purchased in Storm Lake, Iowa.

16-story computerized feed mill built to replace old Harlem Mill.

1980 Second satellite processing plant purchased in Garrettsville, Ohio.

1981 Production workers at main plant walked out, causing the most violent and prolonged strike in history of Ottawa County. Dispute ended with decertification of Teamsters-backed union.

1984 Fire destroyed 90 percent of production capacity at main plant. Processing temporarily farmed out to 17 sites in nine states.

1985 $40 million, 632,000-square-foot plant completed on fire-ravaged site.

1987 Bil Mar merges with Sara Lee Corp.

GERRIT S. DEWITT

MARY MEIJARD (DEWITT)

Marvin DeWitt's great-grandfather Gerrit S. DeWitt was the first member of the family to settle in America from the Netherlands. He was born April 10, 1830, in Eenrum Province of Groningen. In Gerrit's own words, the following is a brief history of his arrival and first years in this country:

"On the 20th day of March, 1848, at the age of 17, I started for America in the sailship from Zoutkamp to Amsterdam and then to Hellevoetsluis. There we had to wait a few days while the ship was made ready for the journey. Each passenger had to get his own food for the trip. The supply was checked so that there was enough for everyone and then it was all weighed before being placed on the ship. The drinking water was supplied by the captain and was portioned out each day. This did not always work so well. All the passengers had to wait in line and sometimes the wait was almost too long to bear. Two or three persons died on the trip and were buried at sea.

After bobbing around on the ocean for 41 days, we arrived at New York. From there, we went on a steamboat to Albany and then to Buffalo by canal boat where we boarded a steamboat for Chicago. In Chicago, we transferred to a sailboat for Holland, Michigan. When we had crossed the lake and neared Holland, we could not enter the channel because the wind and waves were too strong. So we went on to Grand Haven. The next day we returned to the entrance of Black Lake. The channel was filled with sand so we had to place our belongings on a raft and pull it through the channel to the lake. The lightened boat was able to float through the channel and we again boarded it and sailed on to Holland.

We expected to see a city. Instead we found dense woods that were almost impassable. A passage large enough for an ox team to pass through had been cut along River and Eighth streets. We asked for the city and were told that we were in the middle of it. We turned around and went back to the edge of the lake where we put up a shelter of boards and remained for a day and night. It was then about the 20th of June, the exact date I did not know after a trip of about three months. I then had Peter Naber as my guardian and was 18-years-old at the time.

Model of the Southerner, which transported many Dutch emigrants to America including Holland's founder, Albertus Van Raalte.

The next morning we went with an ox team through the woods to the place now called East Holland. A few families were living there at the time and they kindly welcomed us into their homes. After looking around for a couple of days and sizing up the land, a group of us decided to go to Kalamazoo to seek work. The first day, we walked as far as Allegan, where we stayed with a widow. The next day we got a chance to ride with a farmer as far as Cooper, which was six miles north of Kalamazoo. We worked at several area farms during the summer.

In the fall, I worked on the Michigan Central Railroad for 75 cents a day. I had to pay 25 cents a day for board. When winter came, everything was covered with snow, the railroad work was finished and I did not know what I was going to do next. I was alone and had no relatives here. I then experienced God's care and guidance. I found work on a farm about 15 miles from Kalamazoo, and stayed there until the following fall. On that farm, I saw my first large machine. It was drawn by 15 horses and threshed the wheat and put it in bags. Here I first began to realize that the Lord was watching over me and caring for me.

In the summer, more Hollanders came looking for work at the farm. We met on Sunday in the barn to worship the Lord. The barn also served as our bedroom. My next place to work was a farm a mile farther east of Schoolcraft. The farmer was a good man who kept family worship, and was superintendent of the Sunday School of the Presbyterian church.

Four and a half years had passed since I came to Michigan and I had lived among strangers. I now had a team of horses of my own and started to work for myself on the land of a widow, a sister of the former farmer. I went once a year to the colony, or Holland settlement, to see my friends. The first time I took a team of oxen along for Peter Naber and the following year a pair for John Naber. Another time, I took a horse along which I traded with the Indians for 40 acres of land in Fillmore Township in Allegan County. This later became my homestead.

When I started working for myself, I had to find a new place to board every once in awhile. This became very tiresome and so I started to look around for a suitable girl to become my wife. I went to Kalamazoo that winter to work as a teamster. I boarded at Albert Kaping's. There I met Mary Meijaard and on the 10th day of April, 1853, my 23rd birthday, we were married in the church of Rev. C. Vander Meulen. Mary was 20-years-old.

We went to live 14 miles southeast of Kalamazoo in Climax Township, on the farm of a lawyer from Kalamazoo. There I lost all respect for lawyers. He wanted his share all right, but did not want to do it according to the contract. We lived there two years.

After leaving the farm, I had to find something else to do. I got in touch with a man named Kamfiel, and we decided to buy a breaking team to plow land that never had been plowed. We used five yoke of oxen with my team of horses as leaders. But Kamfiel was a wicked man, or a man without God. If you read the first Psalm, it tells how dangerous it is to associate with such people. After working with him for two years, we decided to go to Holland.

It was the fall of 1856 when we packed our household belongings and set out for the colony to seek our fortunes. Only those who have experienced it know what it means to make a beginning in the thick woods where a tree has not yet been chopped – hard work and poverty. I had however lived for seven years among the Americans and had learned the language fairly well. I had also learned how the work had to be done, which helped us a great deal.

We arrived at Fillmore Township in December and stayed at John VendenBelt's for the night. The next day we found a house that belonged to Isaac Fairbanks and had been built by the Indians. We stayed there for the first winter because cold weather set in before we could complete our log house on the homestead property.

In the spring, we built a shanty and began the hard task of clearing land in the dense forest. We chopped down trees and made them fall as much as possible in heaps. In between these heaps we planted corn and potatoes. The work went fairly well, though it was hard to find soil enough to cover up the plantings. We covered them with leaves and dirt the best we could. The Lord blessed our work with a good crop of potatoes, yet the corn was not so good. To plant the corn, we chopped a hole in the ground between the roots and stumps. There was no way to cultivate it.

The next year was a little better. We had a team of oxen and soon had the land cleared. The third year everything was a failure. We had a couple of acres of wheat that looked fine. However, in the month of June, we had a heavy frost that froze the wheat and we had to mow it down for hay. The potatoes and corn rotted in the ground, and the buckwheat also froze. We ate nothing but turnips, rutabagas and cornmeal throughout the winter. We had to kill the pigs because we had nothing to feed them.

In those days, the Methodist preacher came to the schoolhouse to preach and Mr. Clapper came sometimes to hold revival meetings. As we had not as yet made confession and thought that there were many good Christians among the Methodist, we often went to the meetings in the schoolhouse. Not long after this, Rev. Van Raalte came to visit us and promised to come again in the near future. On his next visit, he was accompanied by two elders. After conversing with them for some time and answering a few questions, they agreed to accept us as members of their church and to baptize our four children. This was done a short time later in the schoolhouse, which was then known as the Brook School District. We were then members of the church in Holland, which was afterwards known as the Ninth Street Church. Later, the church of Ebenezer was built on the Ottawa-Allegan county line and we became members there.

Turning back to life in the country and some of the difficulties, I remember one of the early years when the crops were a failure. Six men – with one woman to cook for us – went to Laketown to cut cordwood for H. Walsh, who had a general store in Holland. We built shanties and stayed there from Monday morning until Saturday. My wife then had to stay alone with the four children and take care of the animals. So we worried through another winter. In the spring, after an exceptionally long winter and before boats came in, the need was sometimes very great. But the Lord always sent deliverance."

Gerrit's granddaughter Mary Farowe wrote in a family history that life for her grandfather and grandmother improved in time. He added more acreage to the farm, and even returned to the Netherlands to buy some Holstein and Frisian cattle. From that herd, his wife made butter, which they sold in Holland. They also sold wheat for a cash crop. Gerrit served as the township drain commissioner and was an elder in the Ebenezer Reformed Church.

Gerrit and his wife had nine children: Mary, Gertrude, Ida, George, Albert, John, Cornelia, William and Anna. George DeWitt was Marvin's grandfather. He married Anna Boeve and they raised four children: Gerrit, Henry, Mary and Wilbur. Gerrit was Marvin's father. He married Susan Van Den Berge and they raised six children: Georgianna, Angeline, William, Marie, Sena, and Marvin.

Marvin married Jerene Bekius and they have seven children, 23 grandchildren, and 24 great-grandchildren.

Their children are Gary, Marilyn, Jack, Don, Nancy, Merle, and Keith. Their offspring are as follows:

Gary and Joyce DeWitt family: Back row, from left, Dirk DeWitt and Gary DeWitt. Middle row, Tyler Van Der Kolk, Jon Van Der Kolk, Tracy DeWitt, Alex Van Der Kolk, Joyce DeWitt, and Christopher Pieters. Front row, Nicole Van Der Kolk, Rita Van Der Kolk, Lucas Van Der Kolk, Bryce Pieters, Rita Pieters, Brynne Pieters, and Brittany Pieters.

GARY

Gary and his wife Joyce have three children, Lisa, Rita, and Dirk.

Lisa received an associate's degree in sales and marketing from Davenport College. Her husband Jon Van Der Kolk, a graduate of Davenport College, is a salesman at West Michigan Interiors. They have four children: Nicole, Tyler, Alex, and Lucas.

Rita received a nursing degree through a Hope College/Calvin College program. Her husband, The Rev. Christopher Pieters, a chaplain at Grand Valley State University, is a graduate of Hope College and Western Theological Seminary. They have three children: Brittany, Bryce, and Brynne.

Dirk, a Hope College graduate, is a Lieutenant junior grade in the United States Navy. A graduate of Officer Candidate School, he is stationed aboard the minesweeper U.S.S. Defender at Corpus Christi, Texas. Dirk is trained in the disposal of underwater explosives. His wife Tracy is a graduate of Oakland University where she received a degree in physical therapy.

Tom and Marilyn Norman family: Back row, from left, Megan Grimes, Dale Grimes, Tom Norman, Marilyn Norman, Michael Norman, and Mackenzie Norman. Front row, Julie Grimes and Laura Norman.

MARILYN

Marilyn and her husband Tom Norman have two children, Michael and Julie.

Michael, who graduated from Hope with a degree in business administration, co-owns MD Automotive Repair and Advantage Marine Repair in Zeeland. His wife Laura works at the family business and in the administrative offices for Holland Christian Schools. They have one child: Mackenzie Lynn.

Julie, who graduated from Hope with a degree in accounting, is an associate CPA at Plante and Moran. Her husband Dale Grimes, also a Hope graduate, is a teacher for Delton/Kellogg Public Schools. They have one child: Megan.

Jack and Mary DeWitt family: Back row, from left, Kyle Curtiss, Coby Curtiss, Jim DeWitt, Blaire DeWitt, Jack DeWitt, Ryan Berghorst, Linda Berghorst, Samuel Wierda, Chris Wierda, and Steve DeWitt. Front row, Casie Curtiss, Jackie Curtiss, Colton Curtiss, Lynae DeWitt, Blake DeWitt, Mary DeWitt, Maxwell Wierda, Laurie Wierda, Zachary DeWitt, and Melissa DeWitt.

JACK

Jack and his wife Mary have five children, Jackie, Laurie, Jim, Steve, and Linda.

Jackie graduated from Calvin with a business administration degree and later received a degree in elementary education at Grand Valley State University. Her husband Kyle Curtiss, who graduated from Central Michigan University with a degree in marketing, is general manager at Holland Wire Products. They have three children: Colton, Casie and Coby.

Laurie graduated from Hope with a degree in elementary education. Her husband Chris Wierda, a graduate of Trinity Christian College with a degree in business administration, owns a Ford dealership in Cedar Springs. They have two children: Maxwell and Samuel.

Jim, a graduate of Central Michigan University with a degree in accounting, co-owns Hogquest Farms. His wife Lynae is a graduate of Chic University of Cosmetology. They have two children: Blake and Blaire.

Steve, who graduated from Hope with a degree in business administration, is participating in the management trainee program at Request Foods. His wife Melissa graduated from Hope with a degree in elementary education. They have one child: Zachary.

Linda, who graduated from Hope with a degree in elementary education, is employed at Zeeland Public Schools. Her husband Ryan Berghorst, who graduated from Hopc with a degree in business administration, is in charge of purchasing at B.J.W. Berghorst & Sons Inc.

Don and Minnie DeWitt family: Back row, from left, J. P. Koop, Don DeWitt, Brian DeWitt, and Chris Muyskens. Middle row, Debra Koop, Mayleah Koop, Minnie DeWitt, Briana DeWitt, Lisa DeWitt, Kathy Muyskens, and Brooklyn Muyskens. Front row, Donald Koop, Jennifer Koop, Danielle DeWitt, and Jessica Muyskens.

DON

Don and his wife Minnie have three children, Debra, Brian, and Kathy.

Debra graduated from Grand Valley State University with a degree in elementary education. Her husband J.P. (John Peter)

Koop, who graduated from Davenport College with a degree in business administration, owns Koleaseco trucking company. They have three children: Mayleah, Jennifer, and Donald.

Brian, a graduate of Zeeland High School, is a salesman at V & S Siding/Riemersma Roofing. A member of the Olive Township Fire Department, he also assists his father with D & B Motor Sports, which races a super-stock car at a track in Marne. Brian and his wife Lisa have two children: Danielle and Briana.

Kathy, a graduate of Zeeland High School and Excel Academy, is a manicurist at Body Perfections salon. Her husband Chris Muyskens, a graduate of Zeeland High School, is fleet sales manager at Nykamp Tire. They have two children: Jessica and Brooklyn.

Bob and Nancy Haveman family: Back row, from left, Tracy Haveman, Bob Haveman, and Dave DeKruyter. Middle row, Ronald Haveman, Nancy Haveman, and Amy DeKruyter. Front row, Beth Haveman, Dan Machiela, and Jody Machiela.

NANCY

Nancy and her husband Bob Haveman have four children, Amy, Jody, Ronald, and Tracy.

Amy, coordinator of volunteer programs for the Reformed

Church in America, received a bachelor's degree in Spanish and psychology/sociology from Hope and a master's degree in social work from Western Michigan University. Her husband David DeKruyter, a graduate of Calvin, teaches at Holland Christian Middle School.

Jody, a graduate of Western with a degree in business administration, is in Israel with her husband Dan Machiela, a graduate of Grand Valley State University with a degree in business administration. He is studying religion at Jerusalem University College.

Ronald, a graduate of Hope with a degree in geology, works in Montana as a geologist. He is pursuing a master's degree in that field. His wife Beth, a graduate of Calvin College, is employed as a nurse.

Merle and Sheri DeWitt family: From left, Aaron DeWitt, Alyse DeWitt, Sheri DeWitt, Merle DeWitt, and Alex DeWitt.

MERLE

Merle and his wife Sheri have three children, Aaron, Alex, and Alyse.

Keith and Mary DeWitt family: Back row, from left, Keith DeWitt and Jason DeWitt. Front row, Mary DeWitt, Jodie Engelsman, Eric DeWitt, and Ashley DeWitt.

KEITH

Keith and his wife Mary have three children, Eric, Jason, and Ashley. Eric is studying architecture at Lawrence Technological University. His fiancée Jodi Engelsman is self-employed at Engelsman Greenhouses.

Of Marvin's grandchildren, only three worked full-time at Bil Mar – Brian, on company farms; Jackie, in the human resources department; and Jody, in payroll/accounts receivable.

The 80-member family of Marvin and Jerene DeWitt.

The Bill DeWitt Sr. family. Back row, Bill with his late wife, Martha. Front row, Shirley DeDoes, Julia Morrison, Bill Sr. and Ray.

BOOKS

Almanac of American History, Arthur M. Schlesinger Jr.,1983.

Collier's Encyclopedia, 1996.

Compassionate Capitalism/People Helping People Help Themselves, Rich DeVos, 1993.

Compton's Encyclopedia and Fact Index, 1992.

Curious Customs/The Stories Behind 296 Popular American Rituals, Tad Tuleja, 1987.

Don't Know Much About History/Everything You Need to Know about American History but Never Learned, Kenneth C. Davis, 1990.

Eighty Acres/Eulogy for a Family Farm, Ronald Jager, 1990.

Legends, Lies, and Cherished Myths of American History, Richard Shenkman, 1989.

Michigan, An Illustrated History of the Great Lakes State, George S. May, 1987.

Michigan Place Names/The History of the Founding and the Naming of More Than Five Thousand Past and Present Michigan Communities, Walter Romig, 1986.

New American Desk Encyclopedia, 1984.

New Illustrated Encyclopedia of Knowledge, 1986.

Panati's Extraordinary Origins of Everyday Things, Charles Panati, 1987.

Poultry and Poultry Keeping, Alice Stern, 1988.

Poultry Farmer's Veterinary Book, Norman Barron and Ray Feltwell, 1959.

Raising Your Own Turkeys, Leonard S. Mercia, 1981.

Tradition of Looking Ahead/The Story of Bryan Foods, Carroll Brinson, 1986.

Webster's Desk Encyclopedia and Almanac, 1983.

When We Were Young/A Baby-Boomer Yearbook, Rita Lang Kleinfelder, 1993.

MAGAZINES

Builder & Contractor, Jan. 1987.

Business Week, (1) The Best Entrepreneurs, Jan. 8, 1996. (2) Review of Real Time/Preparing for the Age of the Never Satisfied Customer, Regis McKenna, Oct. 6, 1997. (3) Review of Corporate Creativity/How Innovation and Improvement Actually Happen, Alan Robinson and Sam Stern, Oct. 20, 1997. (4) Review of The Leadership Engine/How Winning Companies Build Leaders at Every Level, Noel M. Tichy with Eli Cohen, Oct. 27, 1997. (5) Putting Your Company on the Block, Jan. 26, 1998.

Farm and Ranch Living, Oct./Nov. 1978.

Feedstuffs, Jan. 1979.

Food Business, Feb. 1987.

Forbes, May 18, 1987.

Fortune, Oct. 28, 1976.

Frozen Food Age, Nov. 1984.

Meat Industry, March 1980 and Dec. 1985.

Meat Processing, North American edition, March 1984 and June 1996.

Michigan Business, Feb. 1986.

Michigan Farmer, Nov. 1970 and April 1979.

Michigan Travelogue, Nov. 1976.

National Provisioner, Feb. 1983 and Jan. 1995.

Newsweek, A bare-knuckled brawl (James Hoffa Jr. vs. Ron Carey), Dec. 9, 1996.

Poultry & Egg Marketing, Feb. 1980 and Oct. 1985.

Poultry Tribune, Sept. 1995.

Prepared Foods, Feb. 1987, July 1987 and Sept. 1988.

Processed Poultry, Sept./Oct. 1988.

Turkey World, May/June 1971, Nov./Dec. 1976, Nov./Dec. 1978, Nov./Dec. 1979, Jan./Feb. 1983, July/Aug./1985, Jan./Feb. 1987, and Sept./Oct. 1988.

NEWSPAPERS

Advance Newspapers
Chicago Tribune
Detroit News
Detroit Free Press
Grand Haven Tribune
Grand Rapids Business Journal
Grand Rapids Press
Holland Sentinel
Muskegon Chronicle
New York Times
Zeeland Record

INTERVIEWS

Larry Baker, Ron Bakker, Eunice Bareham, Mel Baron, Dale Bekius, Linda Berghorst, Marge Boersen, Jim Bultman, Bill Chaddock, Joe Cotton, Chuck Curtis, Jackie Curtiss, Amy DeKruyter, Mary Delrue, Frank DeWind, Aaron DeWitt, Bill DeWitt Jr., Bill DeWitt Sr., Dick DeWitt, Don DeWitt, Eric DeWitt, Gary DeWitt, Jack DeWitt, Jerene DeWitt, Jim DeWitt, Joyce DeWitt, Keith DeWitt, Marvin DeWitt, Mary (Jack) DeWitt, Mary (Keith) DeWitt, Merle DeWitt, Minnie DeWitt, Sheri DeWitt, Steve DeWitt, Bob DeYoung, Henry Geerlings, Bertha Geertman, Deb Goerbig, Paul Gordon, Harold Haas, Ed Hanenburg, Bob Haveman, Nancy Haveman, Dr. Carl Hoyt, Egbert Kuyers, Preston Kool, Deb Koop, Ed Lamse, Ray Lokers, Arend Lubbers, Leonard Maas, Jody Machiela, Joe Mancilla, Kevin McKenna, Jerold Morren, Marilyn Norman, Michael Norman, Tom Norman, Don Pike, Don Prince, Vee Prins, Dr. David Pyle, Bernie Schipper, Casey Staal, Greg Steinblock, Chuck Stehouwer, Marie Steketee, Bill Stout, Lou Taylor, Sid Teusink, Pastor Mike Van Buren, Phil Vanden Berge, Menser VandenHeuvel, Lisa VanderKolk, Tom Van Hall, Angie Van Hoven, Sen. Bill Van Regenmorter, Gordon Van Wylen, Jacob Voetberg, Gary Vos, Sena Vugteveen, Neil Wagenaar, Gloria Waterman, Warren Waters, Lois Weaver, Dr. Phil Weiner, and Laurie Wierda.

OTHER SOURCES

Bil Mar history wall.

Bil Mar plant tour.

Cryovac ad in 1991 Fortune Magazine.

DeWitt Genealogy, 1830 to 1952.

Film clips from 1984 fire coverage by television channels WWMT (Kalamazoo), WOOD (Grand Rapids), and WZZM (Grand Rapids).

First 100 days of the 1981 strike documented by Ken Meyer, Bil Mar human resources representative.

History of the National Turkey Federation/50 Years of Service, 1939-1988.

Janssen's Hatchery video.

Material from the collections of Gary DeWitt, Jack DeWitt, Keith DeWitt, Marvin DeWitt, Henry Geerlings, Dr. Carl Hoyt, and Marilyn Norman.

National Turkey Federation Answer Book.

Notes from Christian Leadership seminar conducted by Anthony D'Souza, from the Haggai Institute, Atlanta, Ga., on July 21, 1998, at Evergreen Commons in Holland.

Scrapbooks on 1981 strike documented by Deb Goerbig, former Bil Mar employee and Teamsters union member.

Special issue of Interchange/50th anniversary of Sara Lee Corp., 1939 to 1989. Interchange published by Sara Lee's Corporate Affairs Dept.